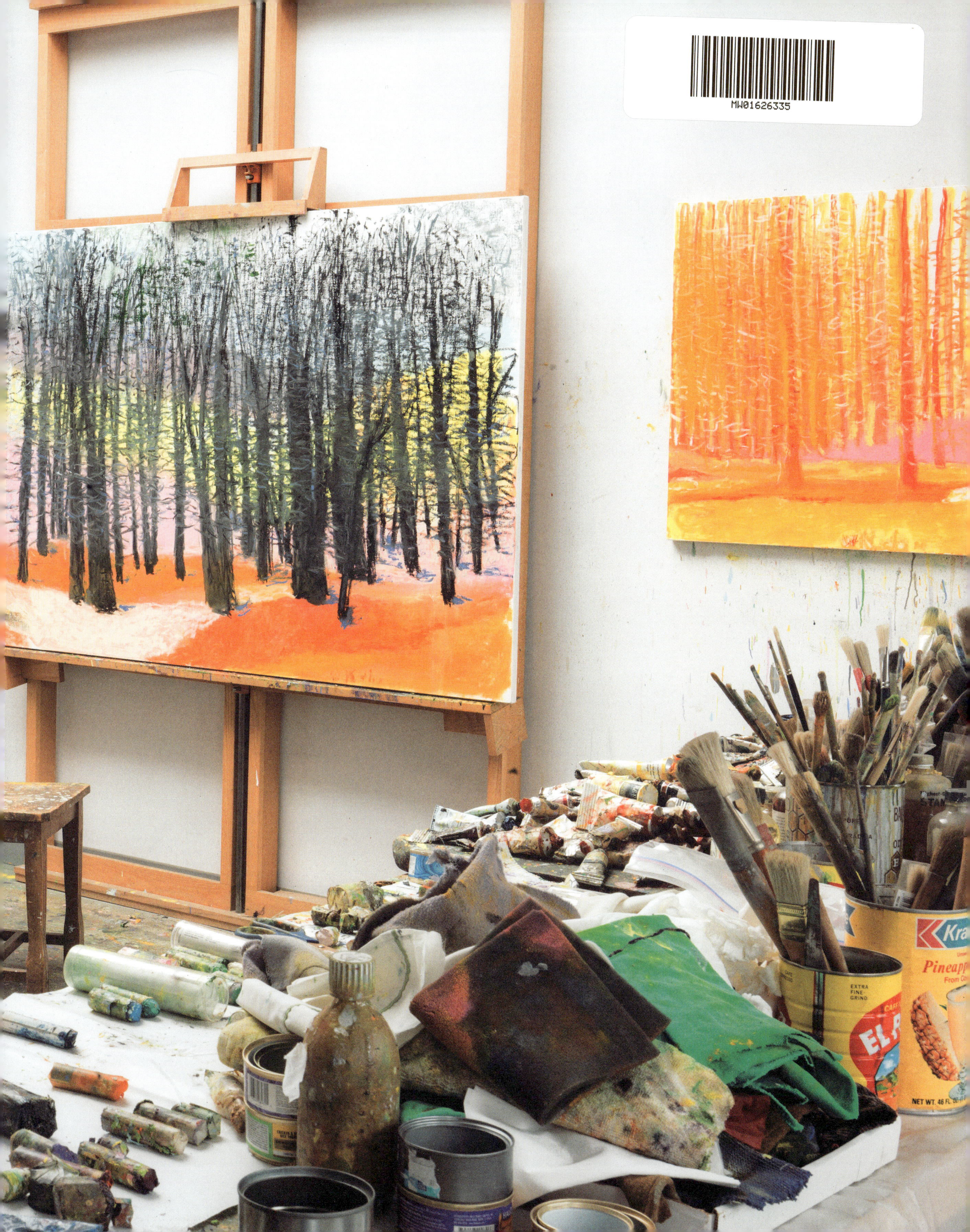
EXTRA
FINE
GRIND

Wolf Kahn

PAINTINGS AND PASTELS 2010-2020

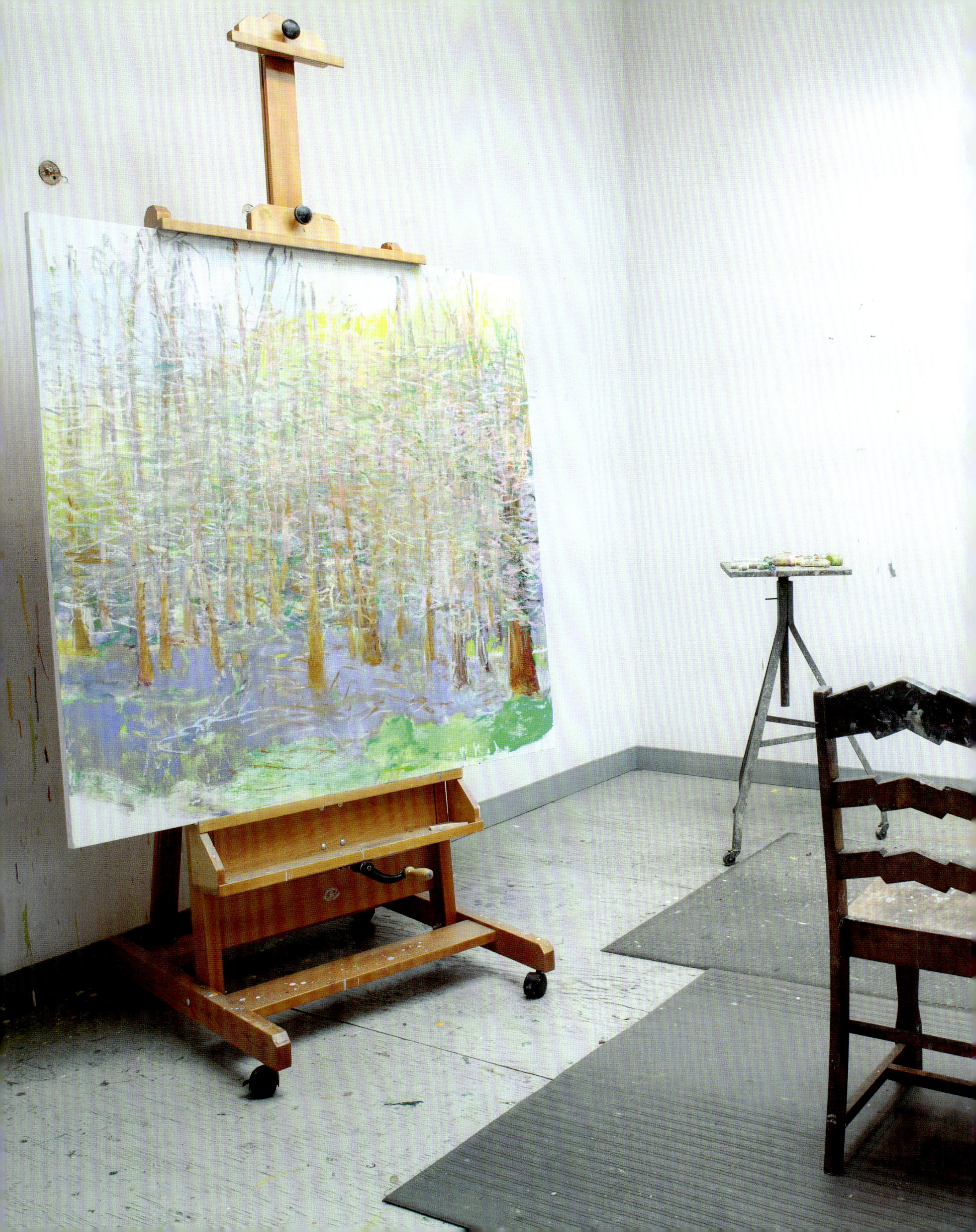

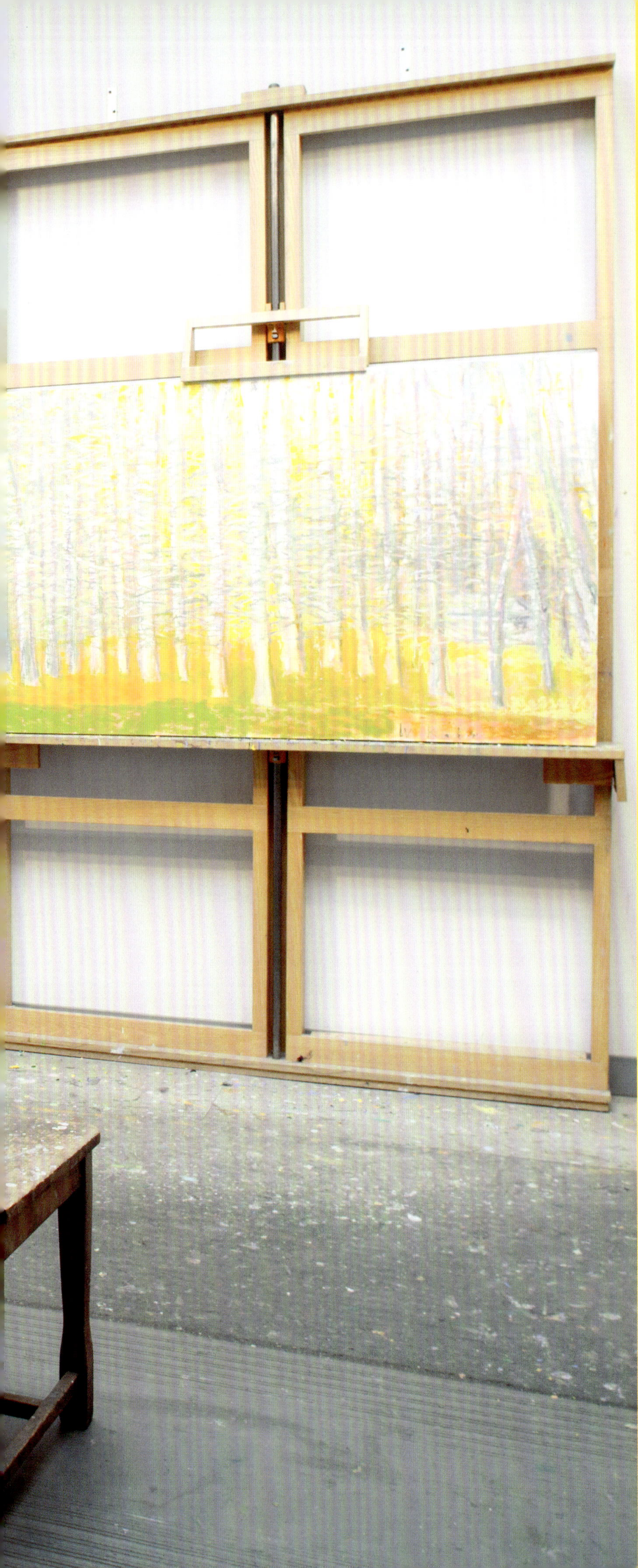

Wolf Kahn

PAINTINGS AND PASTELS 2010–2020

Sasha Nicholas

Interview with William C. Agee and Wolf Kahn

Poem by J. D. McClatchy

RIZZOLI Electa

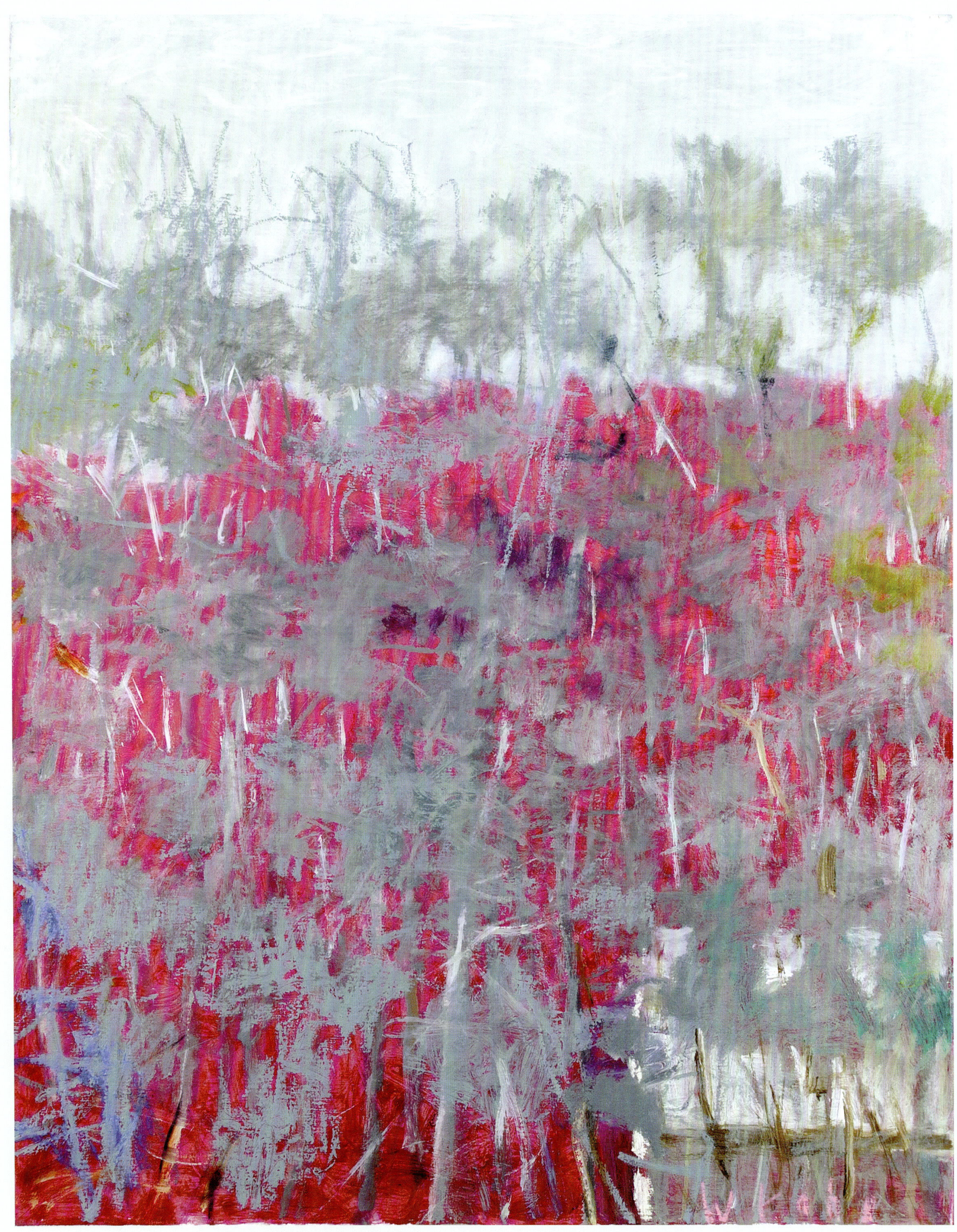

CONTENTS

Low Barn
2010
oil on canvas
40 x 32 inches

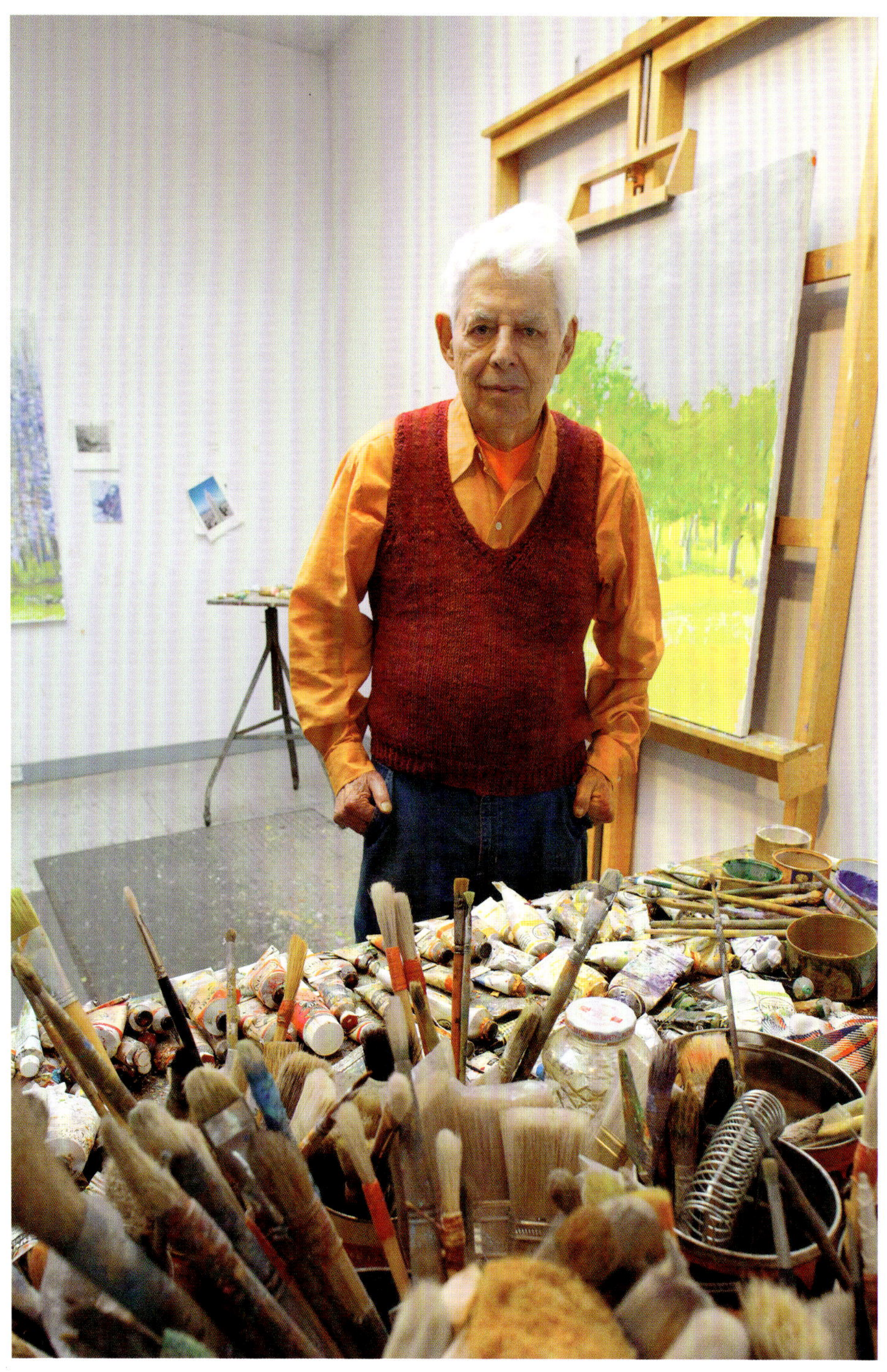

Wolf Kahn in his New York studio, 2015

PREFACE

I've never enjoyed talking about my work, but I must use the occasion of this publication to reflect on what it all means to me. I've always regarded painting as a serious calling worthy of sustained effort, and I'm hoping that my work collected in book form will give evidence to the dedication I've consistently brought to it.

WOLF KAHN

A NOTE TO THE READER: Wolf Kahn died on March 15, 2020, just prior to the printing of this volume. The artist was integrally involved in its preparation and design, and his voice is woven throughout the text. The last study of Kahn's art to be produced during his lifetime, this publication now serves as a tribute to his remarkable talents and legacy.

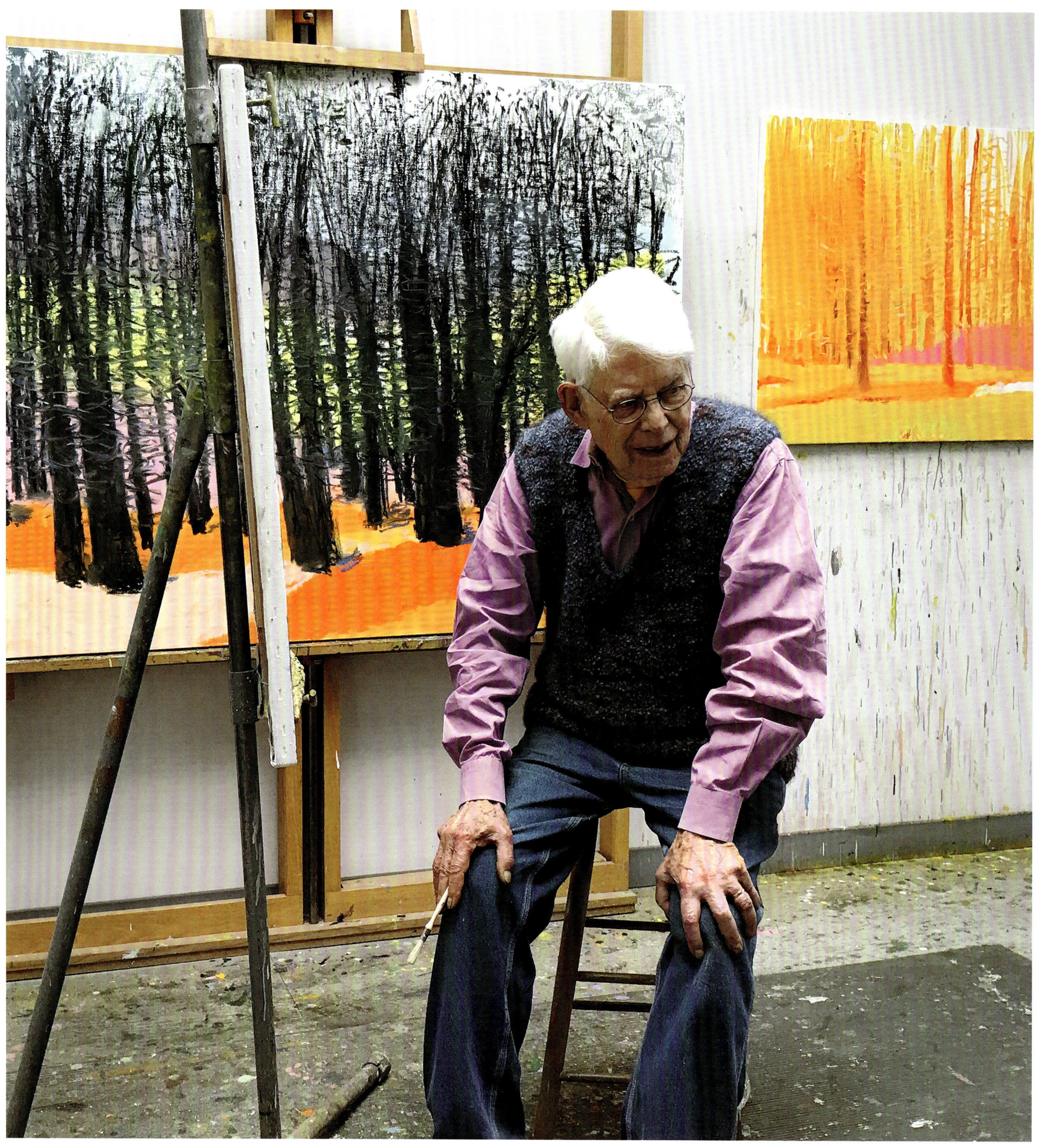

Wolf Kahn in his New York studio, 2017

Born Anew Each Day: Wolf Kahn's Last Decade, 2010–2020

SASHA NICHOLAS

With his characteristic humor, Wolf Kahn inventories his "reasons not to paint a landscape." The nonagenarian artist has evolved this list over the past twenty years, making additions as well as subtractions, and occasionally sharing the results with audiences large and small. On a recent studio visit, he boiled it down to four reasons:

1. It's all been done.
2. It's difficult to make a political statement.
3. It's the preferred method of Sunday painters and amateurs.
4. It's easy to do once you have plenty of green paint.[1]

Hearing Kahn recite this list is a bit startling, however playful the delivery. He is an artist, after all, who has built his distinguished, seven-decade oeuvre on depicting the landscape. His signature subject is the rural outdoors of the American Northeast: dense woodlands, placid seascapes, capacious hillsides, and solitary barns, all devoid of explicit human presence. The last decade has seen Kahn expand the complexity and visual bite of this imagery, now rendered in bespoke hues of acid yellow, hazard orange, and electric violet. But despite his many years of experience, Kahn maintains that he is not entirely comfortable with what he does. This is, perhaps, inherent to his sensibility. He will be the first to tell you that he prizes uncertainty, ambiguity, and surprise and loathes work that feels knowing or calculated. Kahn's insistent self-questioning may also stem from his artistic origins. He came of age as a painter in the dogmatic aesthetic climate of postwar America, in which abstraction reigned supreme. His turn to representational subject matter, in this context, was beyond the pale. Even today, despite his myriad accomplishments, he continues to see himself as an outsider.

Above all, Kahn's appraisal of the pitfalls of landscape painting invokes critical questions we might ask of his art. Namely, is painting nature still relevant in our contemporary world of ever-intensifying mechanization and technocapitalism? And is it possible that Kahn's landscapes, with their abundant visual pleasures, are too accommodating, too traditional, too satisfying to the eye? As the artist himself observes, "It is very hard to be a landscape painter and surprise people . . . You can easily be seen as catering to public taste."[2] Kahn's exceptional feel for the sensuousness of paint and color only heightens such a risk. Like the art of the modernist masters whom he counts among his key influences—Pierre Bonnard, Henri Matisse, and Mark Rothko—Kahn's work is sometimes dogged by the assumption that a lush surface is incompatible with rigorous inquiry. The canonical story of modernism, celebrating heroic avant-garde rebellion against bourgeois excess, has trained us to see beauty as problematic, as a convention to be regarded with suspicion and disdain. This may explain why Kahn, unexpectedly, describes his best paintings as the ones that achieve "austerity."[3] Though his exuberant color seems anything but austere, for him the word signifies that a work possesses nothing extraneous—that he has fulfilled its demands rather than the other way around. Kahn's desire to meet these demands leads him to describe his canvases as peculiarly alive, not unlike the natural subjects he depicts. "The painting has to be able to tell me what it wants," he states. "If I tell the painting constantly what I want, I don't think I'm going to get anything very wonderful."[4]

If Kahn's "reasons not to paint a landscape" offer a tongue-in-cheek critique of his chosen artistic path, then the work he has produced since 2010 forcefully argues for his idiosyncratic vision of contemporary landscape painting. During this period he has not slowed his pace, as one might expect of an artist who turned ninety in 2017, but instead has started working with increased exigency and ambition. This pertains to both his practice and his art itself, which abounds with a new visual energy. Whether in New York City or southern Vermont, where he spends extended summers at the farm he shared with his spouse, the painter Emily Mason (who died in December 2019), Kahn is active in the studio seven days a week. Some paintings come together with relative speed, and he is untroubled by this; at his age, he notes, "Suffering over one's work is no longer so important."[5] Yet he remains fastidiously attuned to details of form and color. Surveying the canvases in progress in his studio, he is skeptical about a ribbon of frothy pink in one ("too assertive") and finds fault with the color adjacencies in another ("the red and green don't really shake hands").[6] Not infrequently, such assessments lead him to return to a completed painting months later, modifying areas that require renewed attention.

Perhaps the most pronounced change in Kahn's work—what some have called his late style, though the artist shuns such hard-and-fast classifications—is the introduction of improvisatory linear marks that buzz horizontally across his compositions, untethered to the representational imagery. Punctuating the landscape, Kahn's marks skitter around the canvas surface and at times coalesce into scrawled layers of fluctuating density. Whether rendered in a pale staccato or a dark, congested weave, as in the respective canvases *Dispersed and Concentrated* (see p. 234) and *Black Tangle* (see p. 113) (both 2014), this line work typically overlies a series of strong vertical forms: a copse of trees at the forest's edge. Kahn's newfound emphasis on drawing is connected to a change of technique. In the last decade, he has shifted almost exclusively to using oil stick, which accommodates his reduced physical mobility by allowing him to work while seated. He sometimes softens and blends the lines of the oil stick with turpentine, but more frequently he takes full advantage of the medium's graphic possibilities. The resulting "scribble-scrabble," as he calls it, gives rise to a lively and often cacophonous sense of motion—a departure from the poetic calm of his earlier landscapes.[7] Like all of his art, the paintings Kahn has produced since 2010 operate in the gray area between abstraction and representation. But their calligraphic dynamism unmoors them from the real world, from the real places that were touchstones of his earlier work. With his cryptic markings, the artist disrupts the illusionism of the painted space, inviting us to see it, in his words, "no longer as a landscape, but as a texture, as something that you don't try to decipher."[8] Suspended between familiarity and mystery, empiricism and fantasy, elegance and agitation, Kahn's recent canvases revel in contradiction. He asserts that "newness" is not his goal, but it is difficult to think of any other paintings that resemble them.[9]

However distinct, Kahn's latest decade of work remains true to his enduring pursuit of the unexpected and the unfashionable. Hans Wolfgang Kahn was born in Stuttgart in 1927, the fourth child of an affluent German Jewish family that immersed him in creative culture from his earliest years. His father, Emil Kahn, was the conductor of the Stuttgart Philharmonic, and

White Roof in a Dark Tangle
2014
oil on canvas
36 x 44 inches

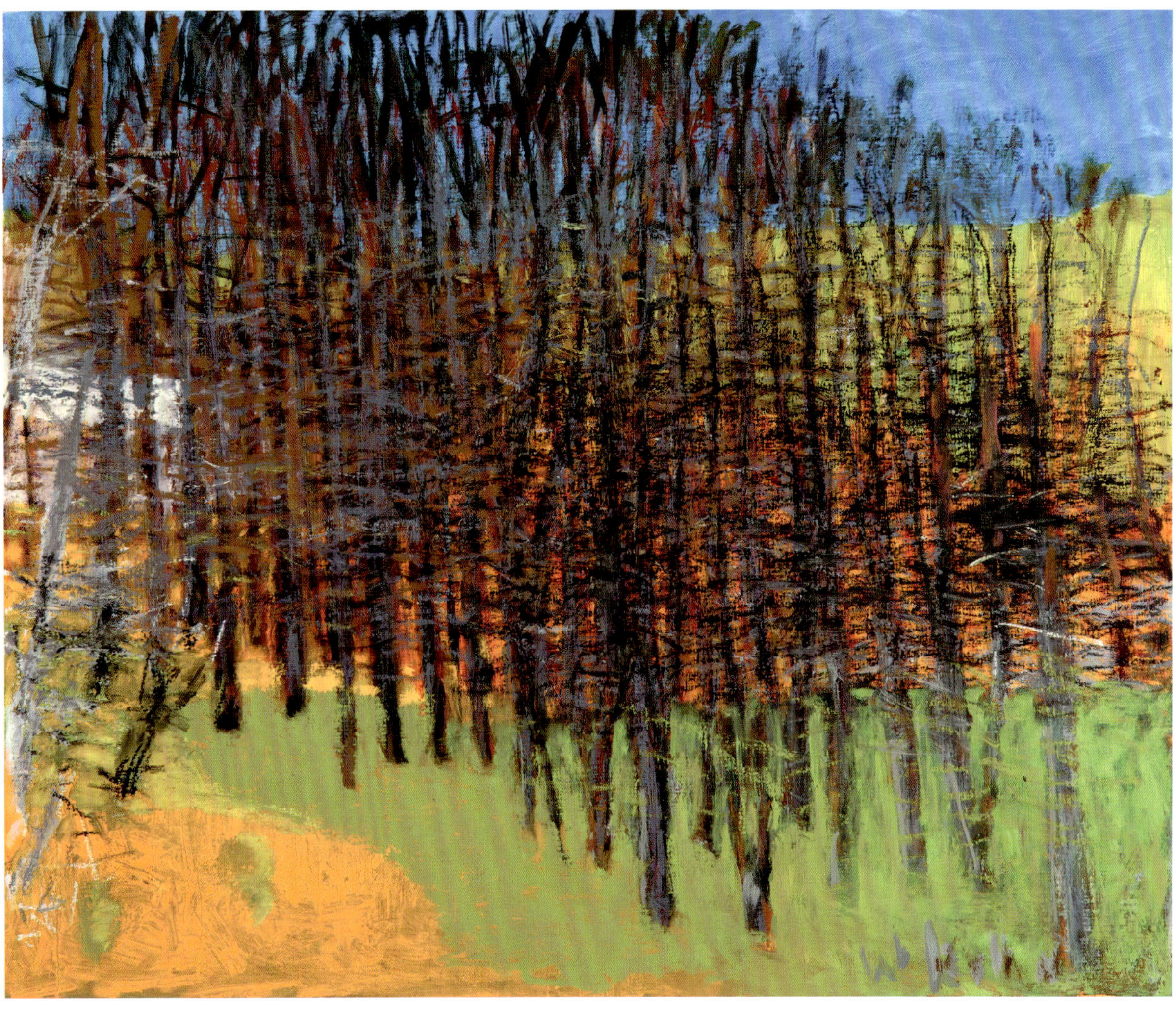

his grandparents on both sides were collectors who filled their homes with art and antiques. Kahn hardly knew his mother, Nellie, who left when he was an infant to follow Rudolf Steiner's anthroposophy movement, a spiritual program that advocated free will based on inner creative experiences; she died several years later in a sanitorium. After his father remarried, Kahn was separated from his siblings and sent to be raised by his paternal grandmother, Anna Kahn, in Frankfurt. As the artist describes it, what might have been a painful rupture was instead a stroke of good fortune; he escaped his harsh, "Grimm's fairy-tale" stepmother for his grandmother's comfortable household, where he was tended to by a maid and governess.[10]

As the Nazi threat intensified in the early 1930s, Kahn's father and siblings left for America, while he remained behind. During this time, he was largely sheltered from the growing perils of his situation by his grandmother and his equally doting maternal grandparents, Siegfried and Ella Budge, all of whom adhered, the artist notes, to the German upper-class tradition of maintaining "rigorously separate child and adult worlds."[11] Playing in the safety of Anna Kahn's apartment and the building's adjacent garden, receiving private art lessons, and drawing caricatures to entertain the household, Kahn was the beloved center of attention. These experiences helped form him into the witty, sensitive, opinionated, and erudite person he remains today; as he has joked, he was "able to keep infantile megalomania going for a lot longer than most people."[12] It was only after the Kristallnacht pogrom of 1938 that the adult world came crashing in, as stormtroopers looted his grandmother's apartment. The following year, on the brink of World War II, eleven-year-old Kahn escaped to England via the Kindertransport rescue program, joining his family in the United States in 1940. His three grandparents, who stayed behind, were sent to the Theresienstadt concentration camp and never heard from again.

Arriving in America after this frightening and unsettled period, Kahn found refuge in art. At New York City's High School of Music and Art, he continued to develop his childhood interest in drawing.[13] Following graduation and a brief stint in the Navy, the nineteen-year-old began studying in 1947 with renowned German-born teacher and painter Hans Hofmann, whom he still counts as his most formative influence.[14] Kahn's fluency in German secured him a job assisting Hofmann at his pioneering Hans Hofmann School of Fine Arts, one of the first American schools to teach modern art.[15] For eighteen months, Kahn steeped himself in the charismatic master's pedagogy, learning to elicit tension between the flat, two-dimensional canvas surface and allusions to three-dimensional space—Hofmann's famous "push and pull" dictum.[16] Treating color as a structural force was a key lesson, as Hofmann would cover and uncover areas of a painting to demonstrate how each chromatic juxtaposition altered the composition and its expressive impact. Above all, Hofmann imparted a commitment to art as a "high calling," teaching Kahn that an artist must struggle to speak deeper truths about experience.[17] "When we imitate," Hofmann exhorted, "we realize only the external connection to nature. When we create we interpret the inner."[18] Kahn's exposure to such ideas was enhanced by the school's Friday night critiques, where he encountered key figures of the emergent Abstract Expressionist movement—among them Willem de Kooning, Arshile Gorky, Jackson Pollock, and critic Clement Greenberg, who curated the first group exhibition to feature Kahn's work.[19]

Kahn, however, did not become an Abstract Expressionist. Bucking the era's orthodox embrace of abstraction, he fused expressionistic painting with real-world subject matter. This placed his work in dialogue with parallel efforts by a number of young contemporaries, including fellow Hofmann students Jane Freilicher and Larry Rivers, as well as his friends Richard Diebenkorn and Fairfield Porter. "I tried to do abstract paintings," Kahn explains, "and it always seemed to me that I was throwing out a baby with the bathwater.."[20] But this independent course was an uneasy one. Upon leaving Hofmann's school, Kahn was "mired for a time in self-doubt and melancholia verging on depression," and he left New York, completing an undergraduate degree at the University of Chicago in 1949.[21] When he returned, he embarked on his first mature works: a series of portraits marked by high-key color and twitchy brushwork that suggest the influence of Vincent van Gogh, one of his early artistic heroes. Among them is a self-portrait in his studio, in which the smock-clad artist stands frontally at the foreground's edge, his face, body, and the surrounding studio animated by slashing strokes of acerbic pigment (fig. 1). Despite his commitment to such brooding imagery, some viewers saw formal concerns as equally vital to these works. Artist and critic Elaine de Kooning, for example, asserted that Kahn was "obviously more interested in the activity of his fierce, separated colors and wild impastos than he is in communicating . . . about the people and scenes he depicts."[22] After Kahn met Emily Mason, his future wife, in 1956, his art gave way to an airy palette and serene domestic imagery redolent of Matisse and Bonnard. Canvases from the couple's idyllic first summer together in Provincetown, Massachusetts, portray Mason at work or quietly reading, as in *On the Deck* (*Provincetown*) (fig. 2).

First exhibited at the Hansa Gallery, an artists' cooperative Kahn cofounded with several other Hofmann students, these early paintings won praise from influential postwar critics, including Dore Ashton, Thomas Hess, Frank O'Hara, and Meyer Schapiro.[23] By the late 1950s, the efforts by Kahn and other members of his generation to move beyond abstraction were gaining traction. His last exhibition before departing in

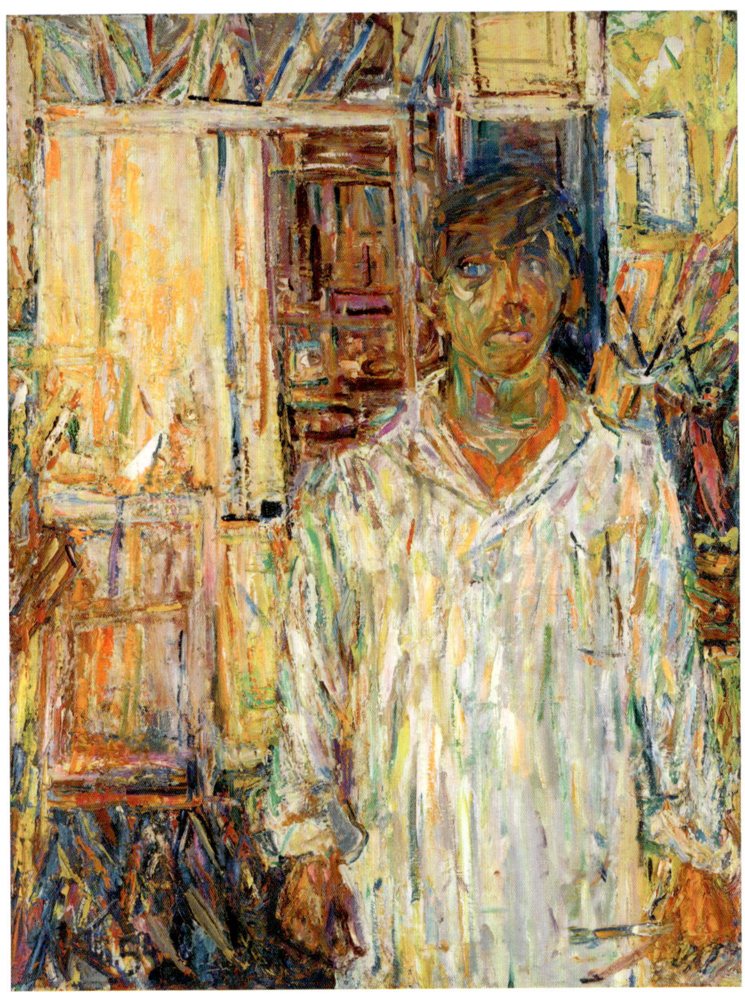

FIG. 1: Portrait of the Artist
1954
oil on canvas
52 x 40 inches

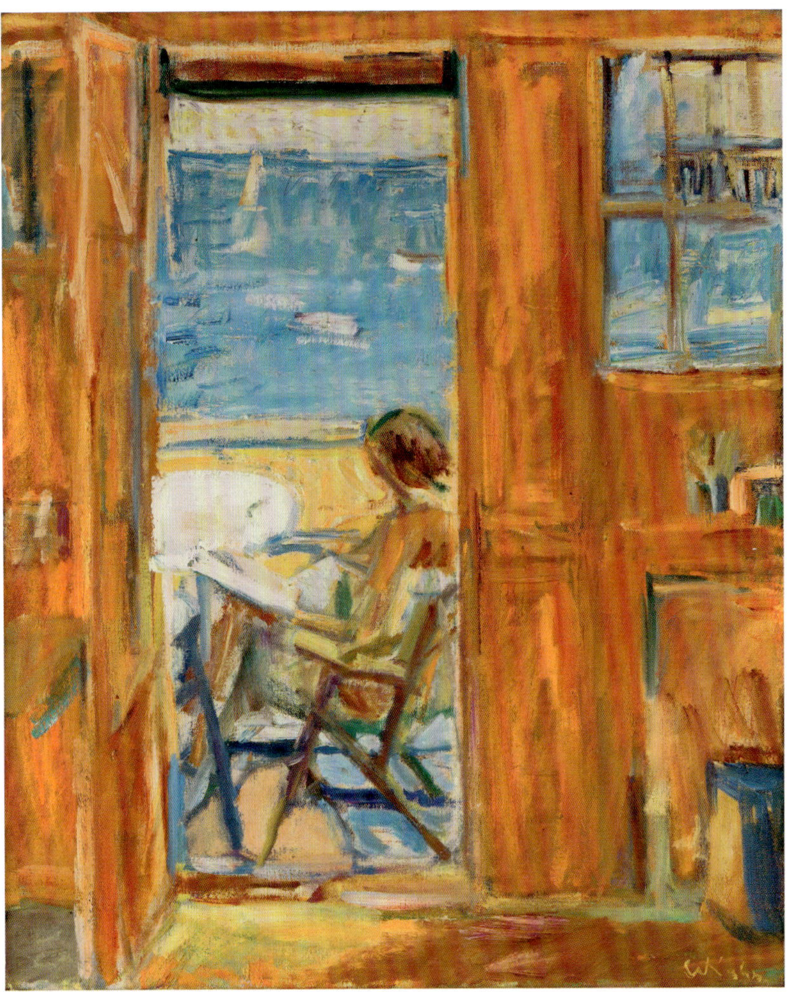

FIG. 2: On the Deck (Provincetown)
1956
oil on canvas
29 x 24 inches

1957 for Italy (to join Emily, who had won a Fulbright grant) sold out prior to its opening, a remarkable feat for a thirty-year-old artist. But success encouraged Kahn, ever the contrarian, to transform his art. While he has always felt comfortable mining art history "with larcenous intent," he became convinced that his efforts to paint the figure too closely resembled those of other artists he admired.[24] In Venice and Spoleto between 1957 and 1959, he transitioned to landscape. This was accompanied by an aesthetic shift. Kahn, who was stunned to return to a New York art world freshly in thrall to Pop Art's slick commercialism, held fast to his gestural approach. However, he abandoned color almost entirely. For the next ten years, he limited himself to muted grays and blues, producing nearly abstract canvases whose subject, more than anything else, is light and atmosphere. Paintings such as *The Further Shore* (*Martha's Vineyard*), 1960 (fig. 3), recall the watery landscapes of the nineteenth-century English painter J. M. W. Turner and the French Impressionists. For Kahn, as for contemporaries such as Philip Guston and Joan Mitchell, the diffuse luminosity and texture of these precedents proposed an alternate direction amid the wane of Abstract Expressionism and the ascendancy of Pop.[25] Reductive but resplendent, Kahn's new paintings did not receive the same approbation as his earlier work had, even though they presaged the engagement with light, process, and materiality that would be central to American art by the late 1960s. His densely

layered pigment at times evoked "scarred battlefields," bespeaking an arduous period of self-examination.[26] It was as though he had to purge his work of all but the essentials to rediscover his own voice.

In the late 1960s, color came back in full force in Kahn's art, and it has played a starring role ever since. According to the artist, this turnaround was prompted by the spectacular sunsets he encountered on a summer Maine sojourn, which made him chafe at the constraints of his spartan palette. With an influx of vivid color combinations came an explicitly representational approach. Kahn began to focus on scenes from Vermont, especially the ragtag barns and precipitous hills of his West Brattleboro farm. After he and Mason purchased the property in 1968, they began spending summers there with their two young daughters, Cecily and Melany; they remained for the rest of the year in New York, where Kahn never felt similarly compelled to paint urban subjects ("my brush just doesn't accommodate itself to all that geometry").[27] Yet if his canvases, then and now, seem unmistakably fixed in his rural Vermont environs, Kahn resists the impulse to see them as literal representations. "Realistic painting, in my mind, means unsuccessful painting," he states. "You've got to take it somewhere else." Kahn has advanced a rather paradoxical term for his paintings: "nondescriptive landscapes," which conveys his ambition to satisfy the competing demands of both nature and art, observation and abstraction.[28]

This tension is fundamental to all of Kahn's landscapes. On the one hand, they draw upon the rich tradition of American landscape painting, from the mystic nineteenth-century pastorals of George Inness and Albert Pinkham Ryder to Edward Hopper's nostalgic, quintessentially modern visions of small-town solitude. Comparing Kahn's *High Summer*, 1972 (fig. 4), to Hopper's iconic *Cape Cod Evening*, 1939 (fig. 5), suggests the two painters' shared sensitivity to the emotive potential of natural light in conversation with the Northeastern landscape and its quirky vernacular architecture. In both, the juxtaposition of verdant greens and inky darks, of a nebulous thicket encroaching against an angular building, introduces not merely formal intrigue, but also an air of enigma, melancholy, and a hint of danger in an ostensibly benign scene. On the other hand, Kahn's vibrant color continually foregrounds the abstract underpinnings of his landscapes. This is true even in his earliest Vermont pictures, which, unlike the later work, utilize mostly naturalistic hues. *The Red Barn* of 1970 (fig. 6), for example, emerges from veils of scrubbed tomato red and tangy chartreuse that focus the eye not on discrete representational objects but on color as form, defined by permutations of tone and transparency. Pulling light into the canvas and pushing it back out, Kahn's diaphanous masses produce a pulsing pictorial dynamism, as in the color field paintings of Mark Rothko (fig. 7). In a play on Paul Cézanne's fabled claim regarding the seventeenth-century landscapes of Nicolas Poussin, Kahn has teasingly remarked on his own his desire to "do Rothko over from nature," an aim achieved by wedding evanescent light to physical structure.[29]

By the 1980s, Kahn began to heighten the abstraction of his landscapes by turning to nonassociative color. Barns now appeared in shades of violet, foliage in

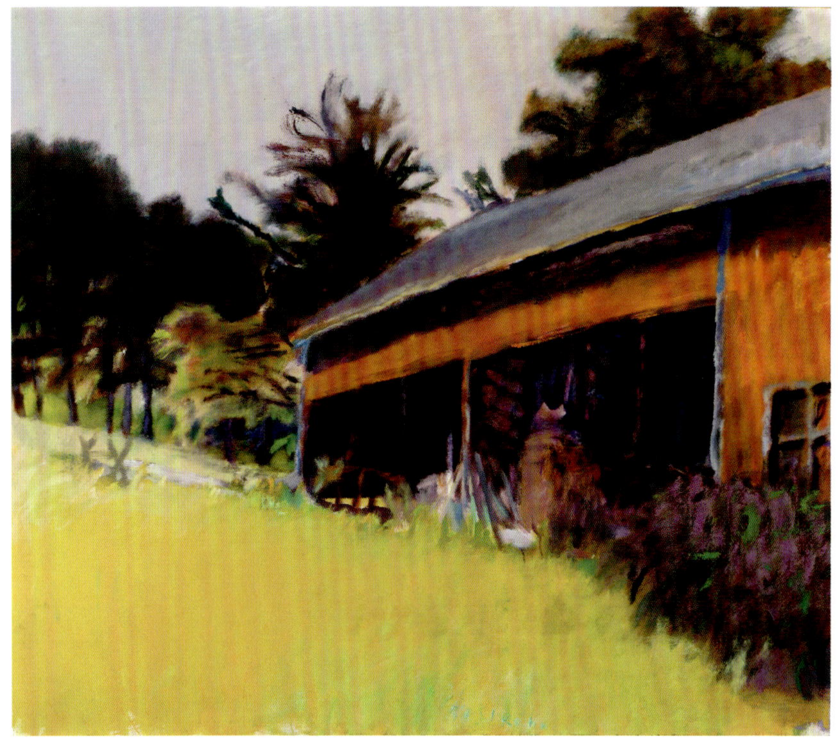

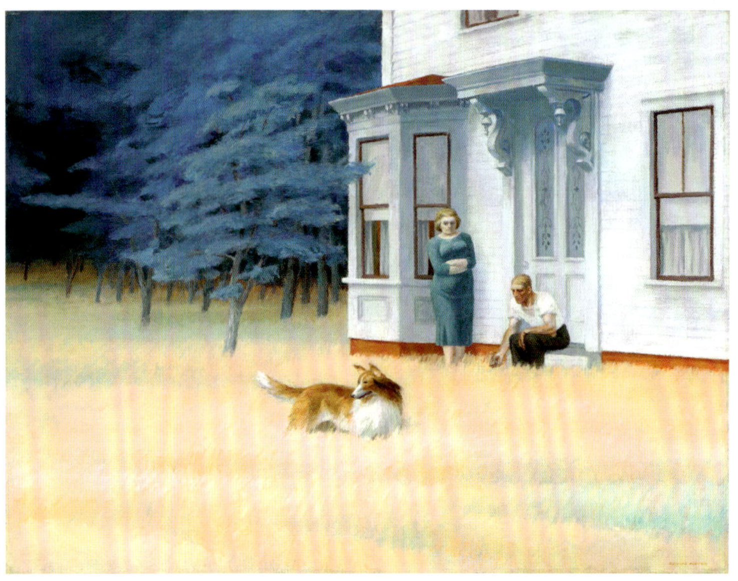

FIG. 3, OPPOSITE
The Further Shore
(Martha's Vineyard)
1960
oil on canvas
40 x 50 inches

FIG 4, TOP
High Summer
1972
oil on canvas
50 x 58⅝ inches
Collection Smithsonian
American Art Museum

FIG 5, ABOVE
Edward Hopper
Cape Cod Evening
1939
oil on canvas
30 x 40 inches
National Gallery of Art,
Washington, D.C.
John Hay Whitney Collection.
1982.76.6

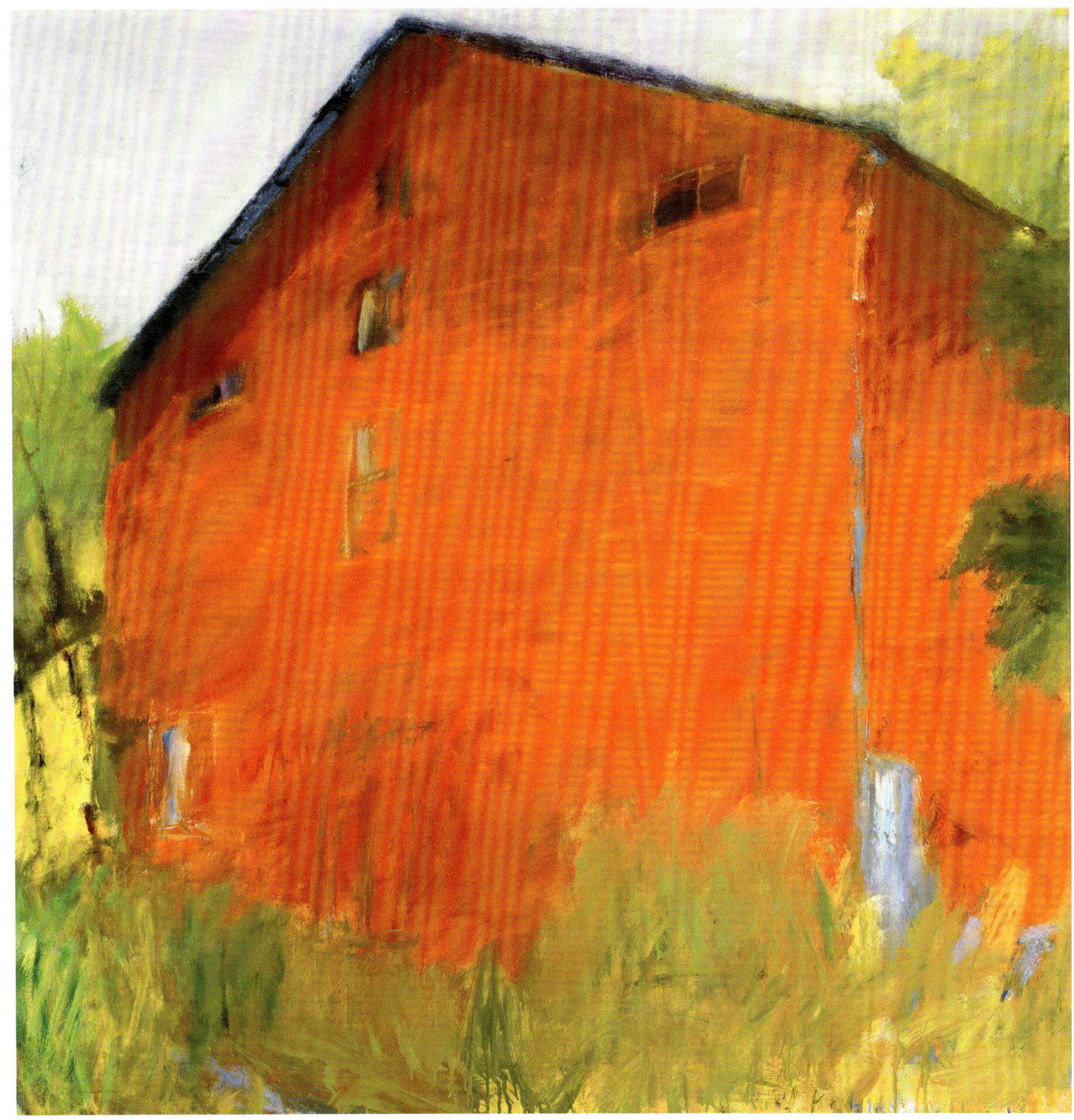

FIG. 6, LEFT
The Red Barn
1970
oil on canvas
51 x 51 inches
Collection Brooklyn Museum of Art

FIG. 7, OPPOSITE, LEFT
Mark Rothko
Untitled
1949
oil on canvas
54 ⅞ x 43 ⅞ inches
Collection Christopher Rothko
© 1998 Kate Rothko Prizel & Christopher Rothko / Artists Rights Society (ARS), New York

FIG. 8, OPPOSITE, RIGHT
Agnes Martin
Untitled #5
1994
Acrylic paint and graphite on canvas
5 feet x 5 feet
© 2020 Agnes Martin / Artists Rights Society (ARS), New York

fuchsia, and oceans in tangerine—and such chromatic leaps of faith felt logical, even natural, in Kahn's deft hands. Reveling in these multifarious possibilities, his art seemed to realize Hofmann's aspiration "to swim with color through all its mysterious regions and to be so familiar with it that I can express everything I want." As Kahn's voluptuous palette drew new attention, he began to teach, lecture, and travel extensively, making images inspired by places from California and Hawaii to Mexico and Egypt. But he wrote that such voyages gave him anxiety, reminding him of his time as a refugee when he "*had* to travel, to avoid terrible troubles." The artist's lyrical paintings of Vermont, meanwhile, spoke to the tranquility that came with putting down roots. His barns, such as *The Yellow Square*, 1981, with its mellifluous lavenders, embracing horizontals, and the glowing beacon of the eponymous yellow square—particularly evoked a vision of home as a self-described bulwark of "comfort and security." In such works, Kahn relinquished the angst of his modernist artistic upbringing for an art that felt, in his words, like "putting on my Sunday clothes." And yet true to his formalist origins, he continued to assert abstract structure within the landscape, keeping the two in vigorous dialogue. This was supported by his practice of developing his paintings in the studio, relying on memory and invention even if a work's initial concept originated *en plein air*. Thus, a crystalline composition like *Calm*

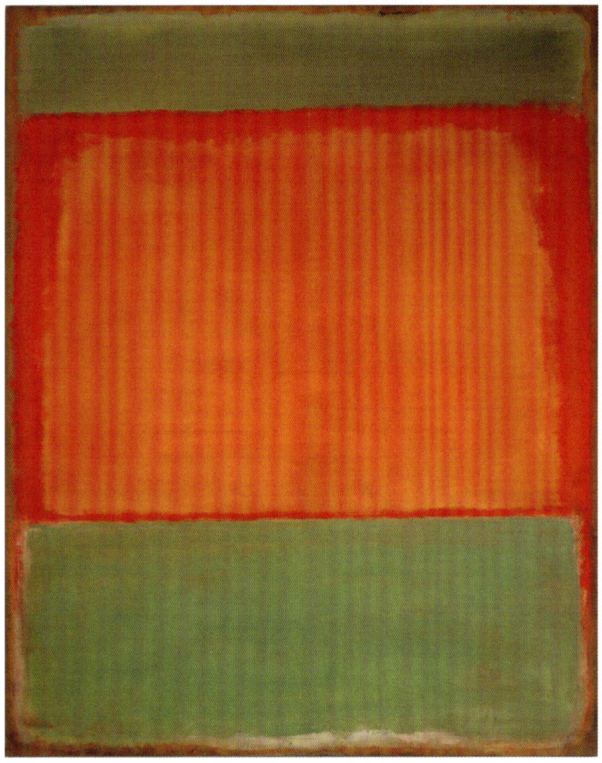

Sea, (fig. 10) 1995, feels as connected to the spare, shimmering geometries of the postwar Canadian-American painter Agnes Martin (fig. 8), whose work Kahn often cites as an influence, as to the Romantic seascapes of ninteenth-century German Caspar David Friedrich. Equally resonant within traditions of abstraction and representation—but not quite at home in either—Kahn's art was, and is, difficult to place.

In his seventh decade as a painter, Kahn is pushing his art into new territory. Aided by a custom range of high-intensity paints, he has suffused the color of his recent canvases with ever-greater brilliance.[34] Some works center on a single hue; these include *Yellow Square* (see p. 191), 2018, in which vivid tonalities, both joyful and jolting, recall the artist's observation that "yellow is the color of buttercups—and of warning signals."[35] Others employ piquant pairings, like the electric oranges and blue-violets of *Blue Stage, Orange Wings* (see p. 202), 2019, to dazzle and challenge the eye. Dancing over and across these radiant hues, Kahn's "scribble-scrabble" sets his canvases into flickering motion. These extemporaneous marks upend the secure, relatively traditional compositions and burnished surfaces of the artist's earlier paintings in favor of overall texture, at times impeding the legibility of the landscape. As critic Karen Wilkin observed, "We feel as if we are seeing *through* a wealth of unstable pictorial incidents, rather than, as in traditional landscapes, seeing *into* the picture."[36] A kind of visual noise, Kahn's "incidents" restlessly confront the gaze and send it pinballing around the image surface, pausing at times to slide in and out of pockets of illusory depth. The varying density and clip of his strokes, meanwhile, produce an array of effects. Often the marks conjure natural phenomena, making the image appear to grow and change before the eyes. In *Horizontal/Silvery* (see p. 103), 2013, for example, an open, lacy filigree evokes trembling leaves, while in *Blue Below and on the Sides* (see p. 177), 2017, cobalt hatchings over a lambent golden field suggest a glimmering cascade of sunlight. Some of Kahn's latest canvases trade the gestural cadences of the "scribble-scrabble" for more aggressive interventions. In the aptly titled *Difficult to Enter (Small Version)* (fig. 9), 2019, his linework fuses into a tightly woven barricade that seems to throttle the trees that peek out from behind. In *Redwoods* (see p. 207), also 2019, it

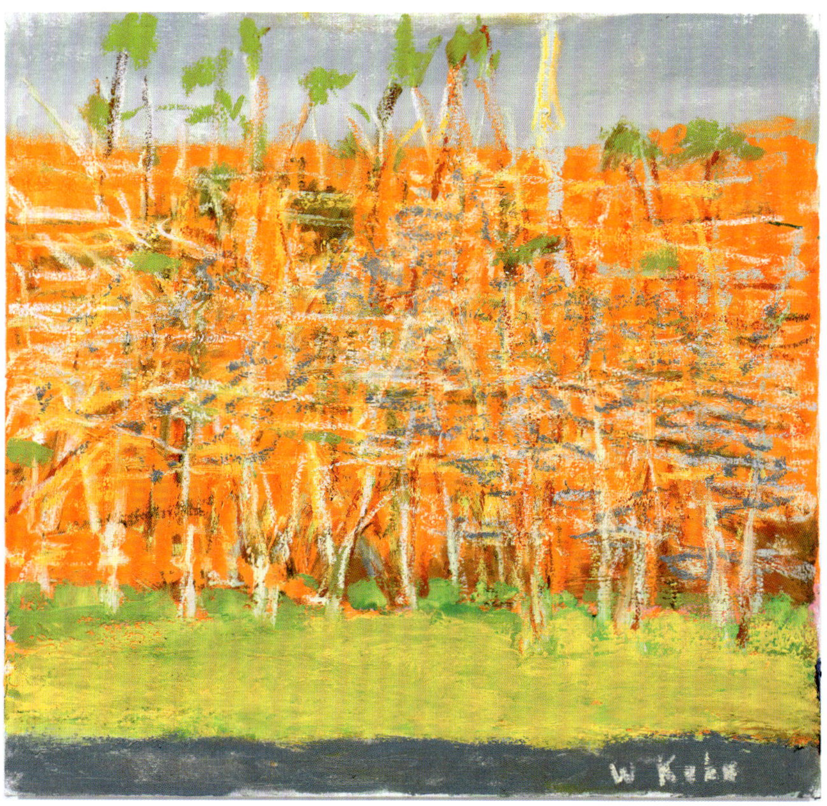

FIG. 9: Difficult to Enter (Small Version)
2019
oil on canvas
24 x 26 inches

metamorphoses into a spidery matrix that ominously portends to overgrow the landscape altogether.

Kahn first introduced his "very fast and uncontrolled calligraphy," as he describes it, in his pastel drawings.[37] He believes that all artists have a single, foundational medium that defines all of their other output; for him, pastel plays this role, offering an essential site of experimentation and, in some cases, direct material for a new painting.[38] In pastels from around the turn of the millennium, Kahn began to manipulate the medium's graphic quality as he would subsequently do with oil stick, adding darting strokes of color. This approach was also inspired by fresh encounters with the work of Jackson Pollock, who famously declared, "I am nature," aligning his improvisatory tactics with the unpredictable forces of the natural world. Kahn tends to chafe at such grandiose claims, but as an artist whose long experience had instilled greater self-assurance, he found new inspiration in Pollock's association of "a certain carelessness with 'the natural.'" In his own work, Kahn began to question the value of order, which, he notes, "is, by definition, predictable, convention-bound, habit-prone."[39] By contrast, being "careless" fostered greater immediacy in the process of painting. "If I start thinking of a branch and I paint it as a branch, it doesn't become nearly as good as if I paint it as a brushstroke," he explains.[40] As Kahn abandoned the modeling of his earlier paintings, he more assertively unified color with form, as in the work of the artists he valorized throughout his career, from Van Gogh and Bonnard to Matisse, Hofmann, and Rothko.

Kahn matched this effort to cast off the order of his previous aesthetic with growing attention to what he calls the "mess" of nature. More often than not, he now eschews the pastoral, cultivated landscape for a natural world that is unruly, mysterious, and at times foreboding. His former architectural subjects, meanwhile, tend to disappear or recede, buried within the snarled overgrowth. Implicit in this shift are questions about how we ascertain value and beauty in the landscape. In a wry reference to the real estate industry's term for undeveloped property, Kahn calls his new imagery "unimproved land." Indeed, the artist's chosen woodland motifs—lacking a clear visual center and regularly spanning the full height of the canvas—forsake the supposed "improvements" of the classical anthropocentric landscape tradition, or what he describes as "the human interference that permits us to see borders, roads, mowed fields, houses, or penetrable forests."[41] Since his earliest Italian landscapes, Kahn has occasionally used trees as principal compositional actors in this way. In some works, he focused on real-life examples, from orderly rows of Italian cypresses to maples in a Vermont woodland, while other canvases such as *Calm Sea*, 1995 (fig. 10) employed near-abstraction. Increasingly, Kahn has pursued the latter direction, treating particularities of place and time as not merely insignificant, but as obstructions to the work. As he states, "You're never going to be able to see whether it's evening or morning or whether it's an oak tree or an ash, because those things keep you from being inventive."[42]

With their recursive compositional framework and lack of specificity, Kahn's trees direct our attention to the boundless possibilities—visual and emotional—yielded by variations of color, form, texture, and density. Some ascend skyward, others congregate in familial clusters, and still others crash to the ground or obstruct the gaze, conjuring potent metaphors of growth, connection, confrontation, and separation. In *Rows* (see p. 155) and *Blue Trees* (see p. 163), both 2016, the trunks form a barbed, incarceratory barrier, while in *Green to Gold* (see p. 51), 2011, they are ethereal and lithesome, like "dancers with their arms raised above their heads."[43] When Kahn occasionally hides a barn or cottage within the woods, the result is tantalizing, if also tinged with menace—a return to a Grimm's fairy-tale world (see *White Roof in a Dark Tangle*, p. 11).[44] The same holds true of the forests themselves. As the artist himself notes, his wild thickets may represent painful or frightening journeys, as well as hopeful outcomes: "Our passage through native brambles and tangles is slow, painful, and harmful to outer garments, and often, skin," he observes, "but in pictures these impediments allow for . . . textural inventiveness, and for breadth of execution."[45]

Taken together, Kahn's vertical arboreal bands and horizontal calligraphy imbue his compositions with a loose, gridlike structure. In certain moments, they recall Piet Mondrian's early canvases, in which the Dutch painter broke down trees into spindly, increasingly abstract linear scaffolds (fig. 11), the precursors to his stark Neo-Plastic grids. For Mondrian this involved a spiritual-scientific mission to find "the foundation of things," a quest stimulated by the anthroposophical theories that captivated Kahn's mother during the same period.[46] Kahn's gridlike armatures do not similarly initiate severe formal distillation. But they do facilitate his stated mission to take his work "somewhere else," to

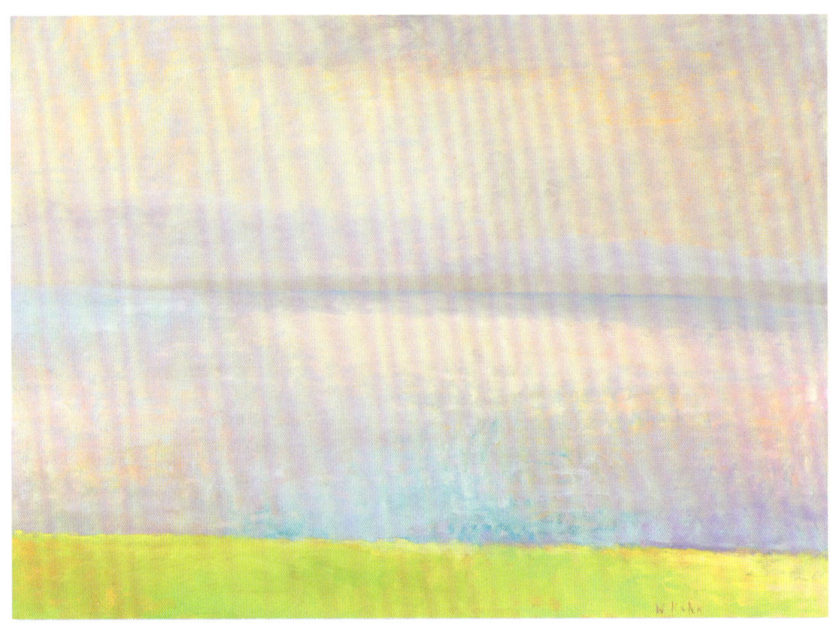

FIG. 10, ABOVE
Calm Sea
1995
oil on canvas
43 x 60 inches

FIG. 11, BELOW
Piet Mondrian
The Tree A
c. 1913
Oil paint on canvas
39½ x 26½ inches

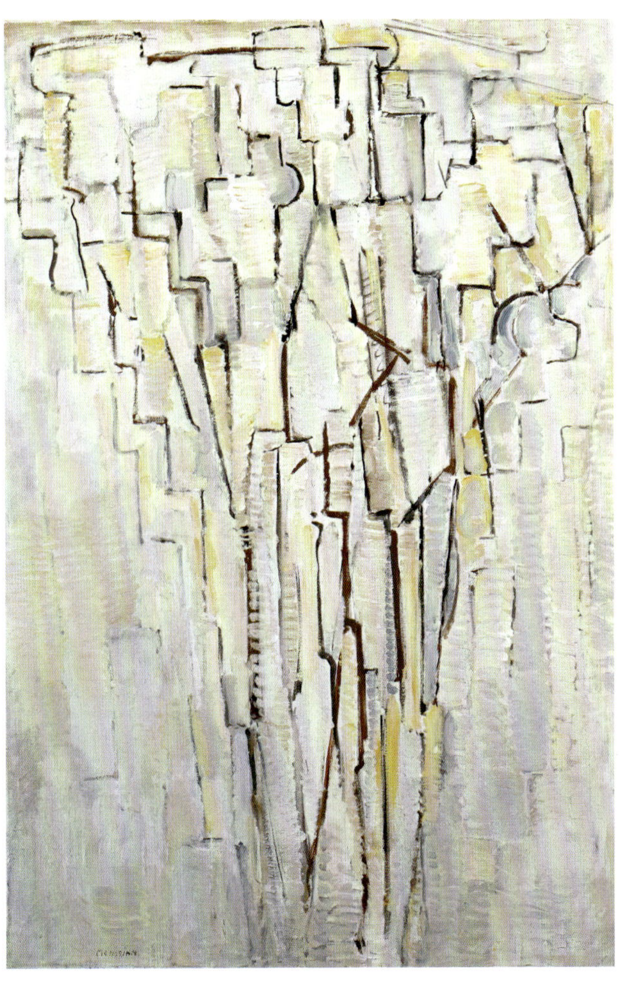

make paintings that are both earthly and transcendent. Instead of imposing order over unkempt reality, the regularity of this organizing principle is, for Kahn, the key to invoking nature's motley proliferations and indefinite, ceaseless flux. Pushing the eye in and out of verticals, across horizontal pathways, into reverberatory motion, his paintings summon an animate world beyond the mimetic. They attain what Hofmann called "breathing depth," a surface that undulates "like the breast moves up and down . . . like the skin, under which we feel this divine movement."[47] This sense of movement, in Kahn's paintings, can conjure delicate biological rhythms, or may be as dissonant as it is divine, suggesting a mysterious and elemental struggle.

What, then, are we to make of these recent landscapes? Far from reassuring domestic idylls, they envision wild nature, in which unknowable forces are at work. And despite their visual delights, they often project urgency and unrest. Kahn quips that there are no politics in landscape painting, and he cautions against mistaking him for an environmentalist. But like generations of American landscape painters before him, he has obliquely raised questions about human engagement with the natural world. On occasion, this has even been overt, as in the early 1990s, when Kahn returned to the site of Hudson River School painter Thomas Cole's famed meditation on wild versus domesticated nature, *View from Mount Holyoke, Northampton, Massachusetts, after a Thunderstorm—The Oxbow*, 1836, to depict its present-day form. Now, as the last decade has made clear that nature is profoundly threatened—that its systems, long held to be impervious to change, are under extreme duress—it is difficult *not* to see some kind of warning in Kahn's pungent chemical palette, in the tension between his landscapes and the turbulent calligraphy that obfuscates them. In the aesthetic world he has created, the organic processes of nature and painting seem indistinguishable: shaped by human entanglements, but propelled by their own imperatives that must be met, or suffer the consequences. The correlation between Kahn's turn to "unimproved land" and his renewed painterliness is a reminder that both, at present, seem ever-more archaic, like remnants of a vanishing age. As he observes, "We never talk about the landscape . . . we never look at the landscape," so the person who relishes painting it must be a "perverse individual."[48]

While contemporary artists often take a definitive stance on such questions, Kahn remains elusive. Ambiguity, he believes, serves an essential purpose of art: "to be allowed to have one's cake and eat it too, to indulge in paradox."[49] And his last decade of work compellingly achieves this, managing at once to be structured and chaotic, alluring and jarring, commonplace and strange, entrenched in visceral nature and more abstract than ever. What is not ambiguous in Kahn's art, however, is its insistence on active viewing. One of the artist's closely held values is "innocence of the eye," which he describes as maintaining childlike wonder and openness, allowing ourselves "to be born anew each day."[50] And when asked whether he could list reasons *to* paint the landscape—as opposed to reasons *not* to—Kahn responds that it epitomizes this quality. Landscape, he asserts, is the freest of constraints, allowing one to invent in ways that are impossible in a figurative mode. It frees him to explore the most basic elements of perception, which we develop in our earliest months and years of life: "the up and the down, the left and the right, the thick and the thin, the hard and the soft . . . all of these things are part of the landscape," he affirms.[51] Kahn's last decade of paintings returns us to these deceptively simple, endlessly complex relational possibilities, rewarding the focused, inquisitive looking that today's frenzied "attention economy" has made so rare. In a time when the traditional narrative of modern art as a progression of "isms" is collapsing, and artists are finding unimagined life in what was presumed outmoded, Kahn's paintings invite rediscovery. In turn, they will let us see the world anew.

I wish to thank Wolf Kahn for graciously spending many hours in conversation and sharing helpful feedback in preparation for this essay. My sincere appreciation also to Diana Urbaska, whose meticulous knowledge of the artist's work and research support were invaluable, and to Ellen Cohen at Rizzoli for inviting me into this project.

1. Wolf Kahn, interviewed by the author and Bill Agee, New York, NY, June 6, 2019. Kahn has also presented variations of his "reasons not to paint a landscape" on television and in public lectures.
2. Kahn, "Six Reasons Not to Paint a Landscape," lecture, Wheaton College, September 2002.
3. Kahn, interviewed by the author and Bill Agee, New York, NY, June 17, 2019.
4. Kahn, "Control and Letting Go," lecture, Brattleboro Museum and Art Center, October 11, 2014.
5. Kahn, interviewed by Bill Agee, New York, NY, May 15, 2019.
6. Kahn, interviewed by the author and Bill Agee, New York, NY, June 6, 2019.
7. Kahn, in *Wolf Kahn: Pastels*, introduction by Barbara Novak (New York: Harry N. Abrams, 2000), 130.
8. Kahn, "Control and Letting Go."
9. Kahn, interviewed by the author and Bill Agee, New York, NY, June 17, 2019.
10. Kahn, "Growing Up Privileged, and Jewish, in Nazi Germany," lecture, Center for Holocaust Studies, Keene State College, Keene, NH, September 18, 2006.
11. Ibid.
12. Kahn, quoted in Justin Spring, *Wolf Kahn*, second edition (New York: Harry N. Abrams, 2011), 12.
13. During this time, Kahn was especially interested in political caricature, admiring the work of late nineteenth-century German-American cartoonist Thomas Nast as well as contemporary *Time* magazine cover portraits by Boris Artzybasheff.
14. Kahn and his brother Peter both studied with Hofmann under the auspices of the G.I. Bill.
15. Hofmann's school opened in 1934. By the 1940s, its main competitor was Black Mountain College, in North Carolina, where the arts curriculum was led by Bauhaus artist and German émigré Josef Albers. Whereas Black Mountain encouraged artists to experiment with a broad range of media, from painting and sculpture to architecture and dance, Hofmann's students focused exclusively on a single medium (typically painting) and were taught only by Hofmann himself, who espoused a more rigid curriculum. For further information, see Tina Dickey, *Color Creates Light: Studies with Hans Hofmann* (Canada: Trillistar Books, 2011).
16. Kahn learned Hofmann's formalist principles not only through classes, but also through preparing formal diagrams for the elder painter's essay compendium, *Search for the Real* (1948).
17. Kahn, "Hofmann's Mixed Messages," *Art in America* 78 (November 1990), 189.
18. Hofmann, quoted in Dickey, *Color Creates Light*, 26.
19. The exhibition, titled *New Provincetown '47*, took place at the Seligmann Gallery in New York, and was composed of students from Hofmann's summer course in Provincetown, Massachusetts.
20. Kahn, "In Conversation: Wolf Kahn with David Kapp and Robert Berlind," *The Brooklyn Rail* (2 May 2007), https://brooklynrail.org/2007/05/art/wolf-kahn-with-david-kapp-and/.
21. Kahn, *Wolf Kahn's America: An Artist's Travels*, introduction by John Updike (New York: Harry N. Abrams, 2003), 15.
22. Elaine de Kooning, quoted in Martica Sawin, *Wolf Kahn: Landscape Painter* (New York: Taplinger Publishing Company, 1981), 12.
23. Hansa was one of the earliest of several important artist cooperatives to open in New York in the 1950s and 1960s; it operated from 1952 to 1959. The gallery was named in honor of its founders' teacher ("Hans") and also referred to the German Hanseatic League, since both Kahn and Jan Müller, another cofounder, had fled Nazi Germany and liked the implication of a cooperative alliance. Other members included Jane Wilson, Allan Kaprow (a high school friend of Kahn's), Richard Stankiewicz, John Chamberlain, and Lucas Samaras. Art historian Melissa Rachleff describes Hansa as "a laboratory for the generation of artists who succeeded the New York School painters and were interested in expanding beyond abstraction to explore the material conditions of everyday life." Rachleff, *Inventing Downtown: Artist-Run Galleries in New York City, 1952–1965* (New York: Grey Art Gallery, 2017), 53. Early press coverage of Kahn's work includes: Dore Ashton, "Wolf Kahn," *Art Digest* 28 (1 November 1953), 22; Thomas Hess, "U.S. Painting: Some Recent Directions," *Art News Annual* 25 (1956), 75–76, 80; Frank O'Hara, "Nature and New Painting," *Folder* no. 3 (New York: The Tiber Press, 1954); Meyer Schapiro, "The Younger American Painters of Today," *The Listener* (26 January 1956), 146–47; and "Art: The Younger Generation," *Time*, 11 March 1957.
24. Kahn, in *Wolf Kahn: Pastels*, 34.
25. The connection to Impressionism was important for many painters in the 1950s who sought to extend the breakthroughs of Abstract Expressionism but divorce their work from Cubism's long and seemingly inexorable influence over modernist abstraction. Indeed, a number of critics used the term "Abstract Impressionism" to describe the work of younger abstractionists, including Mitchell, Guston, Sam Francis, and Helen Frankenthaler. Their work often was compared to Claude Monet's late, semiabstract paintings, a subject that Clement Greenberg discussed in his 1956 essay "The Later Monet."
26. Sawin, *Wolf Kahn: Landscape Painter*, 46.
27. Kahn, "Wolf Kahn: Profile," interview by Fran Stoddard. Public Broadcasting Service, 10 September 2004.
28. Kahn, interviewed by the author and Bill Agee, New York, NY, June 6, 2019.
29. Kahn, quoted in Sawin, *Wolf Kahn: Landscape Painter*, 22. Cézanne stated that he wanted to "do [Nicolas] Poussin all over from Nature."
30. Hofmann, quoted in Dickey, *Color Creates Light*, 243.
31. Kahn, in *Wolf Kahn's America: An Artist's Travels*, 10.
32. Ibid.
33. Kahn, "Growing Up Privileged, and Jewish, in Nazi Germany."
34. This line of "Radiants," as the paints are called, was developed by Robert Gamblin in collaboration with Kahn, and is commercially available.
35. Kahn, quoted in Christina Kee, "Continuing the Conversation: Color, Space, and Variation in Wolf Kahn's Recent Work," in *Color and Consequence*, exh. cat. (New York: Ameringer McEnery Yohe, 2011), 10.
36. Karen Wilkin, "Late Work," in Spring, *Wolf Kahn*, 164.
37. Kahn, in *Wolf Kahn: Pastels*, 130.
38. Kahn explains: "In Turner's case, for example, the artist's oil paintings aspire to the quality of watercolor. Daumier's use of line and tone in every medium recalls the marks that a lithographic crayon makes on a stone. Van Gogh's brush marks and palette-knife slashes are the colored equivalents of the lines a quill pen makes on paper. In my work, the determining medium is pastel." Kahn, in *Wolf Kahn: Pastels*, 15.
39. Kahn, in *Wolf Kahn: Pastels*, 130.
40. Kahn, "In Conversation: Wolf Kahn with David Kapp and Robert Berlind."
41. Kahn, in *Wolf Kahn's America*, 164; Kahn, in *Wolf Kahn: Pastels*, 146.
42. Kahn, "Control and Letting Go," 2014.
43. Kahn, in *Wolf Kahn: Pastels*, 47.
44. Justin Spring similarly notes the Grimm's fairy-tale quality of the 1964 canvas *Edge of the Woods*, which depicts "a dreamlike area, apart from the known world, where elemental conflicts find expression." Spring, *Wolf Kahn*, 55.
45. Kahn, in *Wolf Kahn's America*, 96.
46. Piet Mondrian, in a letter to H. P. Bremmer, 29 January 1914, quoted in Carel Blotkamp, *Mondrian—The Art of Destruction* (London: Reaktion Books, 2001), 81.
47. Hofmann, quoted in Dickey, *Color Creates Light*, 28, 30.
48. Kahn, "Six Reasons Not to Paint a Landscape."
49. Kahn, in *Wolf Kahn: Pastels*, 132.
50. Kahn, in conversation with the author, May 20, 2019; "Wolf Kahn: Profile," interview by Fran Stoddard.
51. Kahn, "Six Reasons Not to Paint a Landscape."

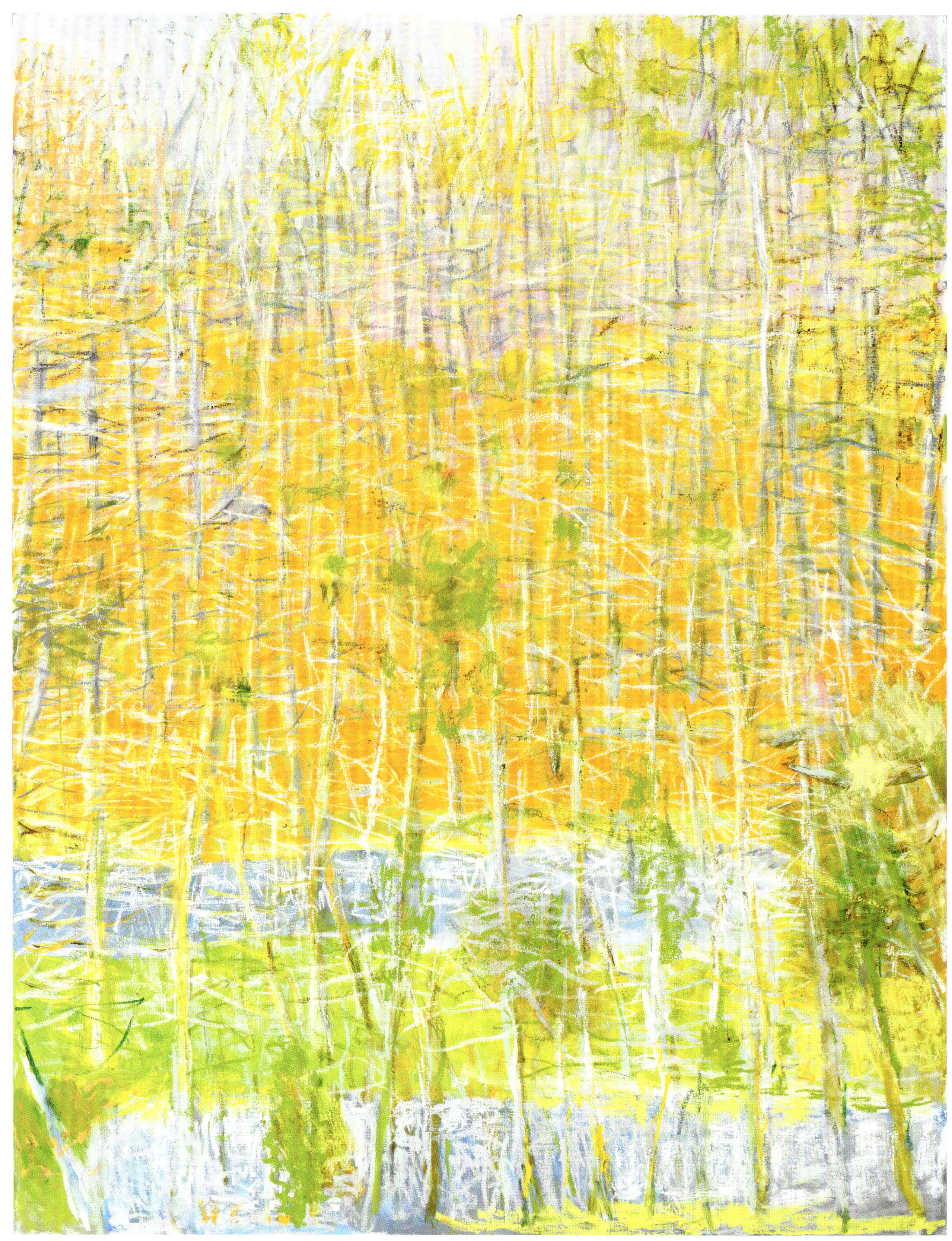

Wolf's Trees

BY J. D. McCLATCHY

If trees fall in a wood and no one hears them,
Do they exist except as a page of lines
That words of rapture or grief are written on?
They are lines too while alive, pointing away
From the primer of damped air and leafmold
That underlie, or would if certain of them
Were not melon or maize, solferino or smoke,
Colors into which a sunset will collapse
On a high branch of broken promises.
Or they nail the late summer's shingles of noon
Back onto the horizon's overlap, reflecting
An emptiness visible on leaves that come and go.

How does a life flash before one's eyes
At the end? How is there time for so much time?
You pick up the book and hold it, knowing
Long since the failed romance, the strained
Marriage, the messenger, the mistake,
Knowing it all at once, as if looking through
A lighted dormer on the dark crest of a barn.
You know who is inside, and who has always been
At the other edge of the wood. She is waiting
For no one in particular. It could be you.
If you can discover which tree she has become,
You will know whether it has all been true.

for Wolf Kahn

Saplings
2011
oil on canvas
66 x 52 inches

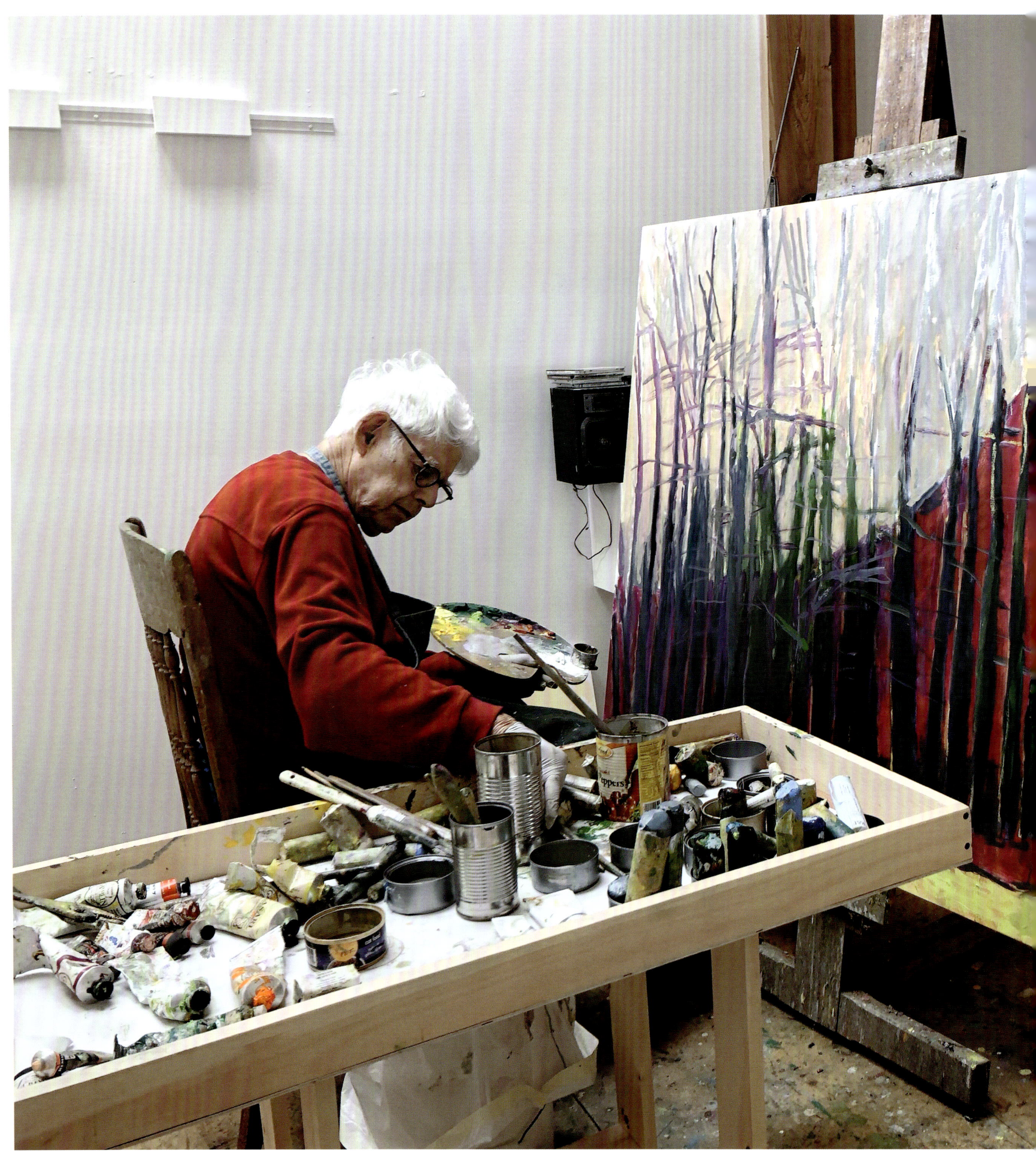
Peppers

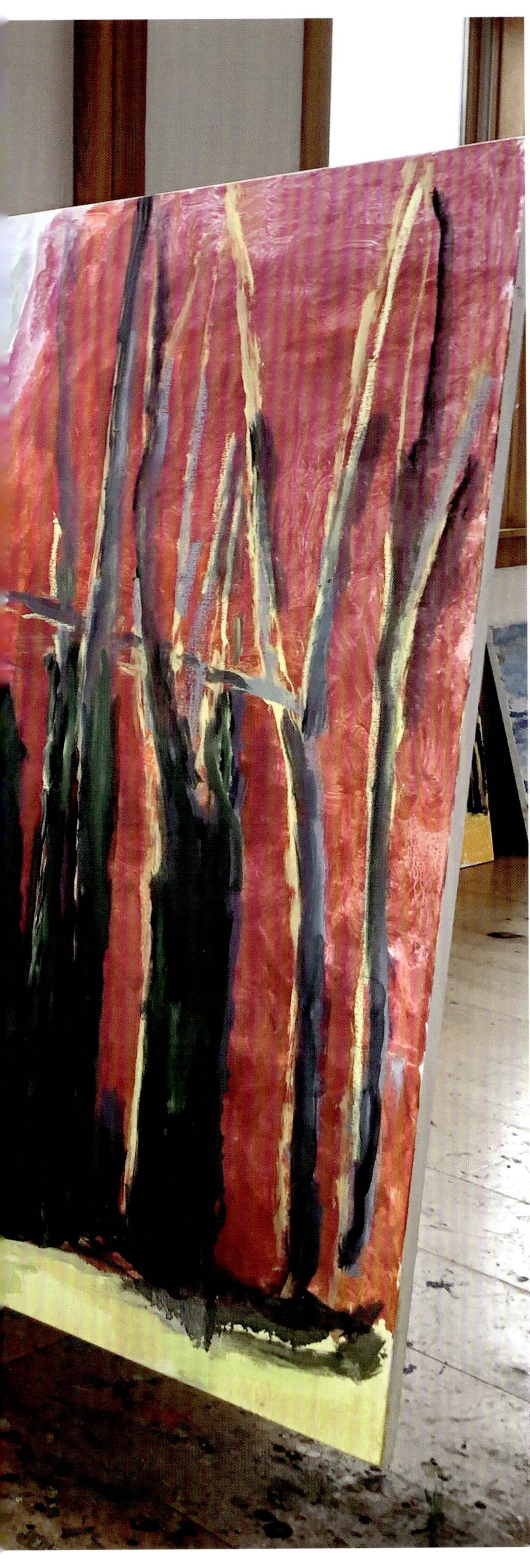

Plates

Wolf Kahn in his Vermont studio, 2018

Orange Fantasia
2010
oil on canvas
44 x 52 inches

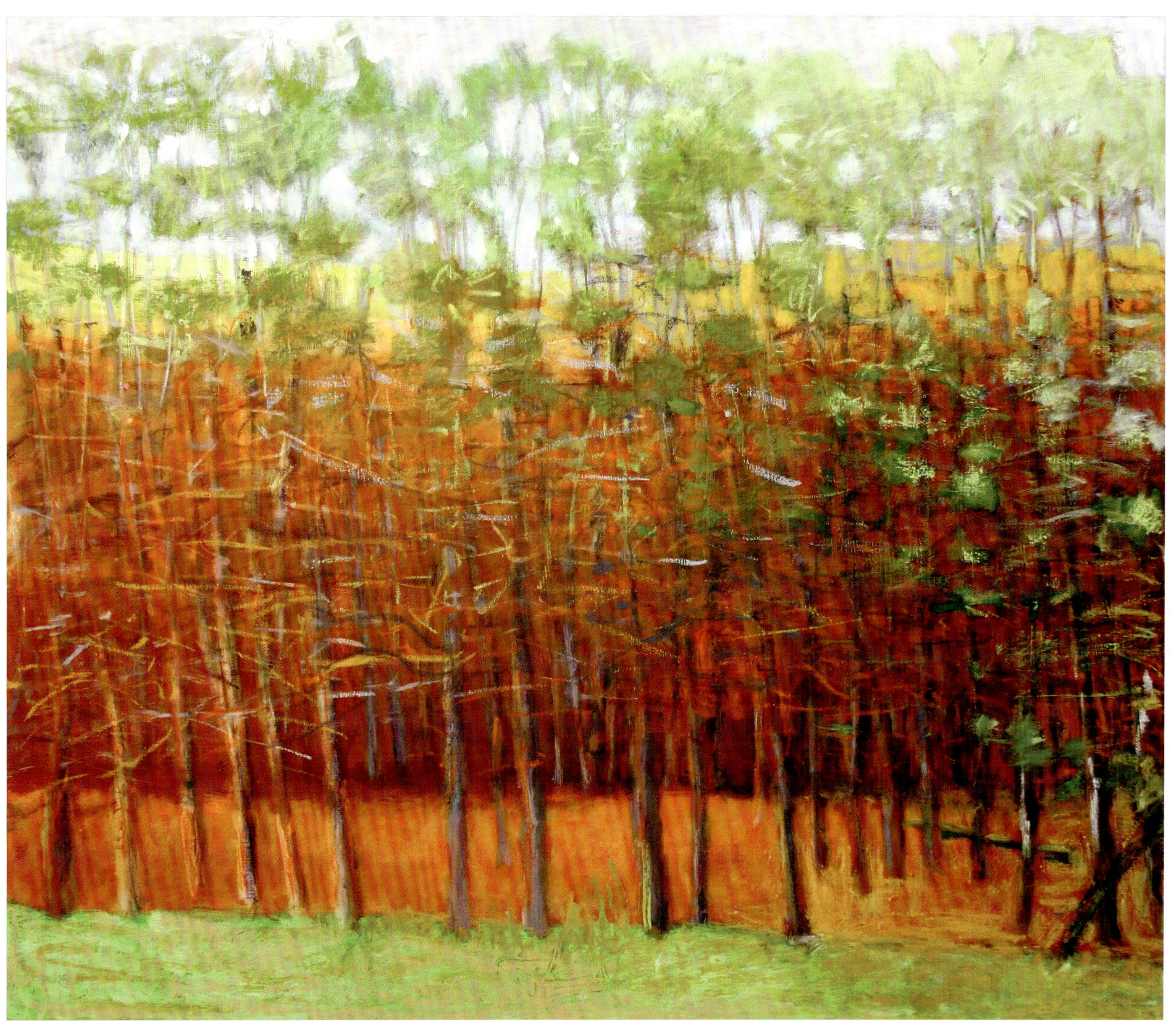

Order in Disorder
2010
oil on canvas
52½ x 66 inches

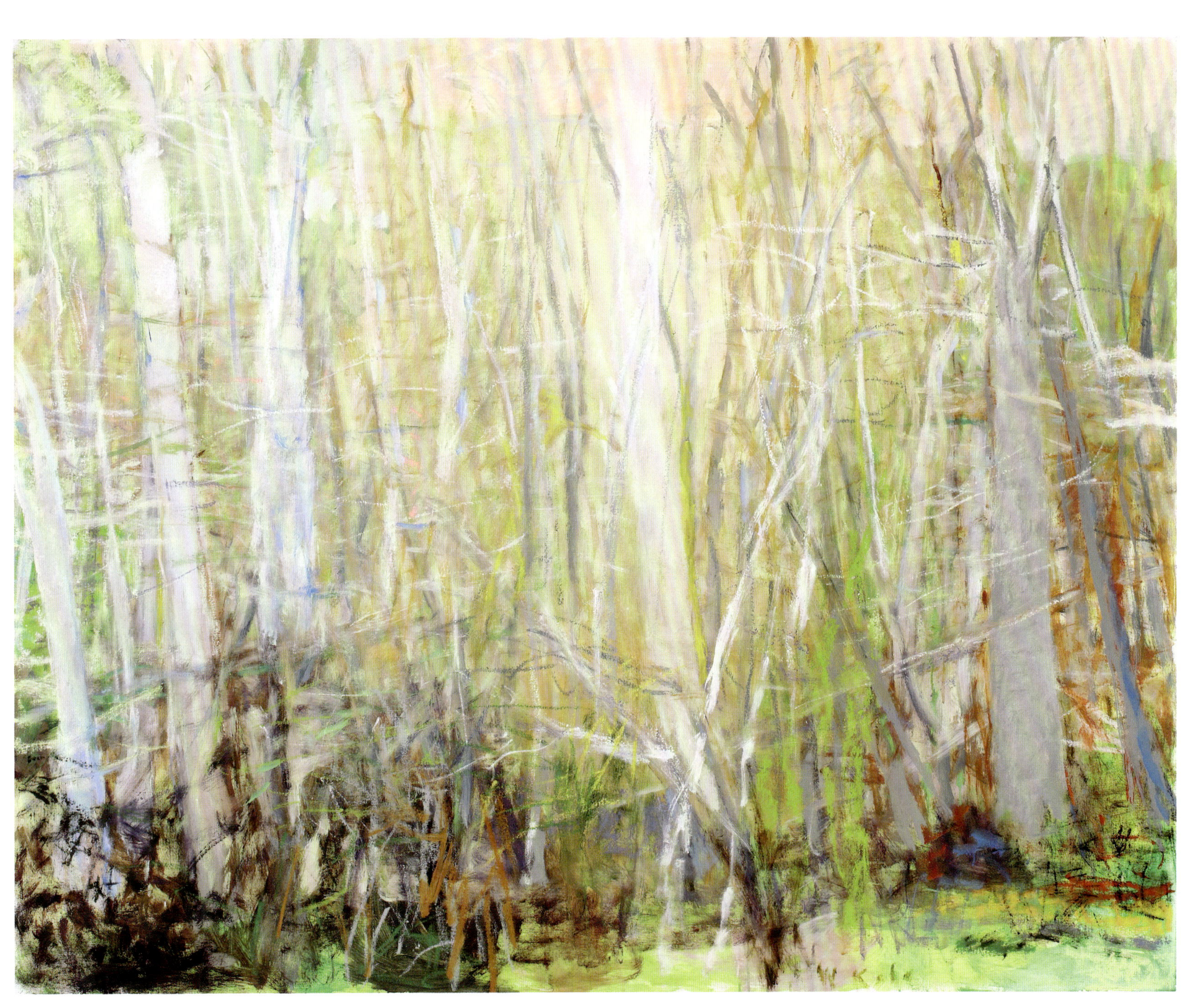

Upper Potomac III
2010
oil on canvas
52 x 60 inches

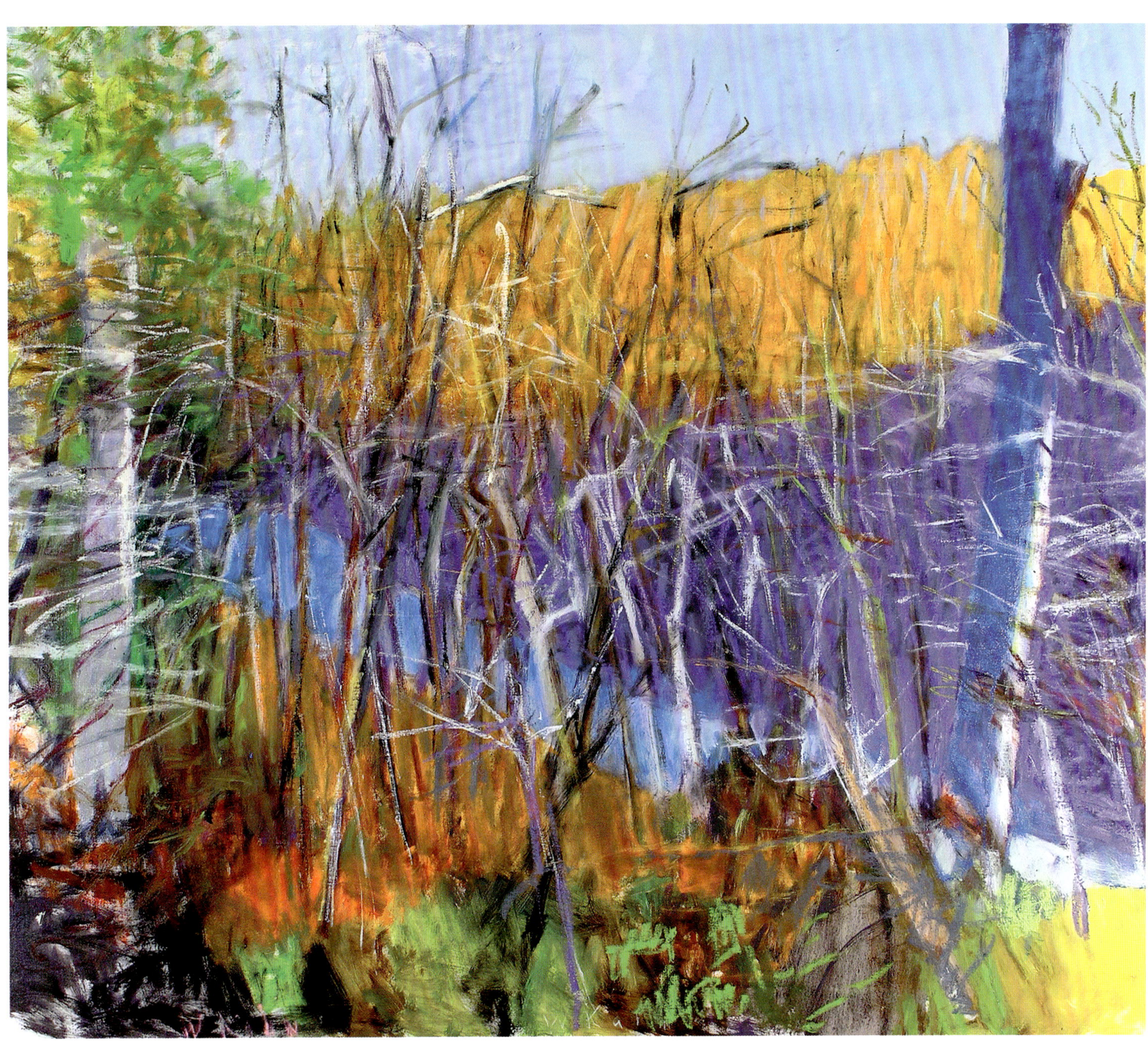

Kiawah Creek
2010
oil on canvas
28 x 44 inches

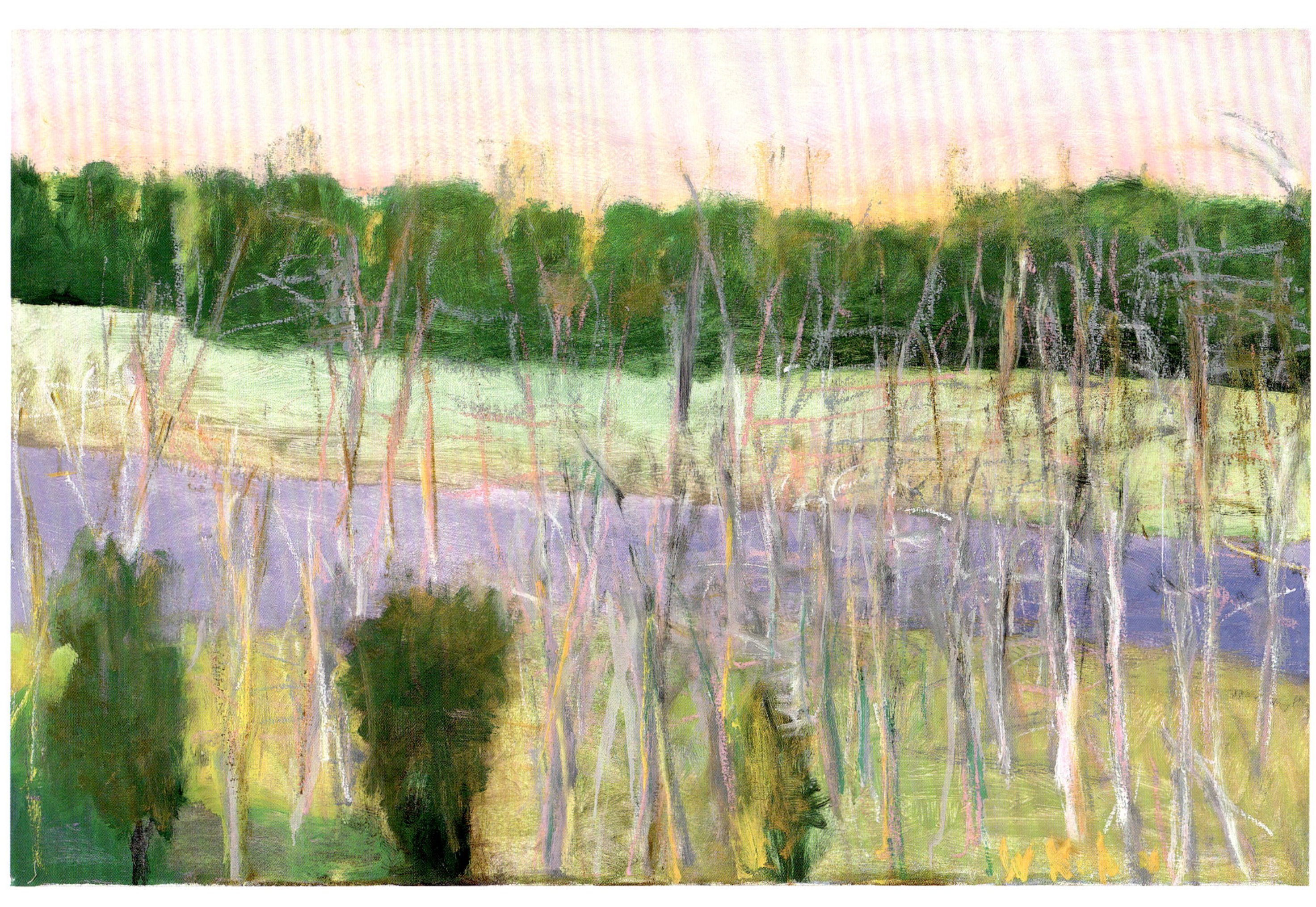

Clearing on the West
2010
oil on canvas
42 x 52 inches

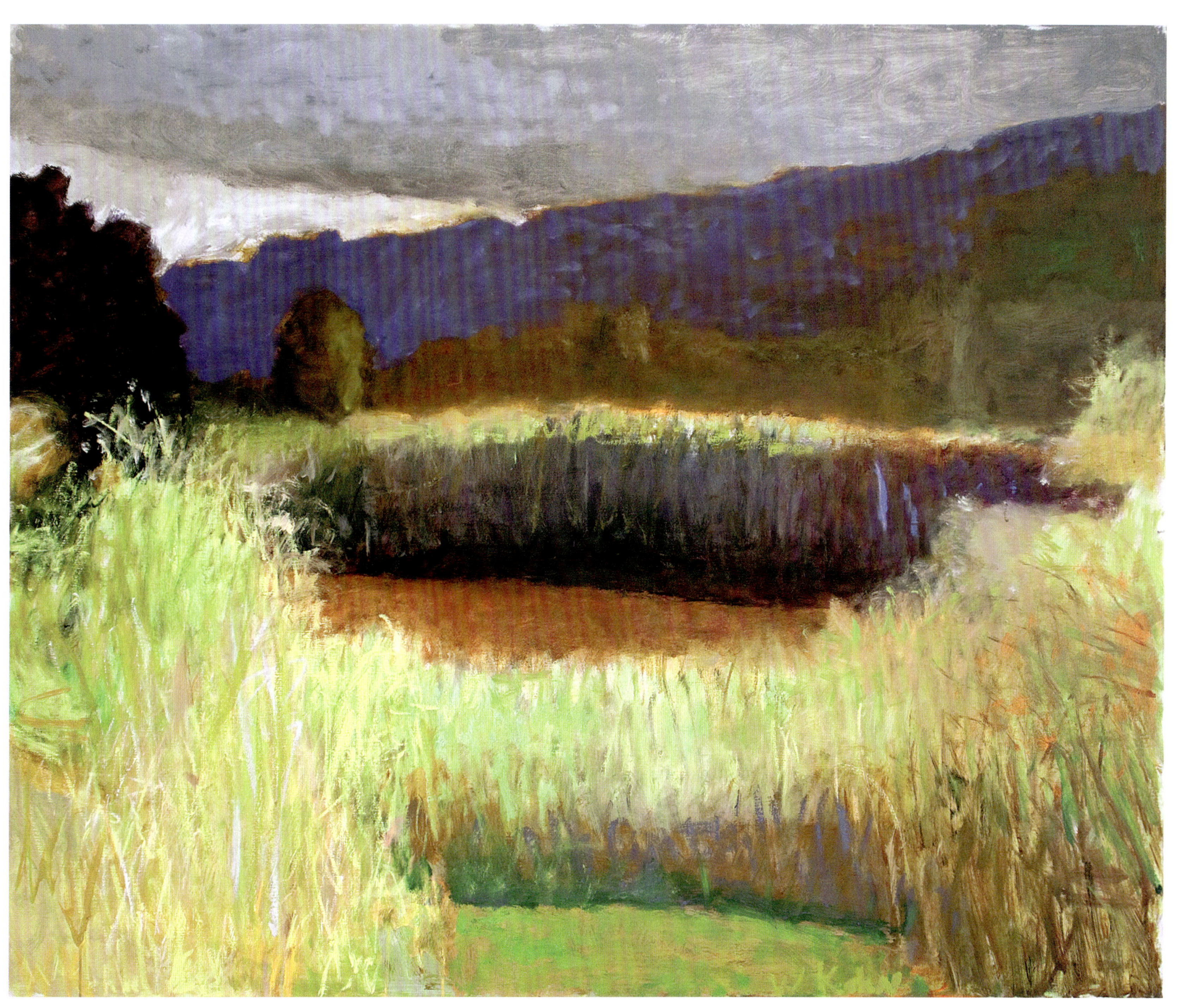

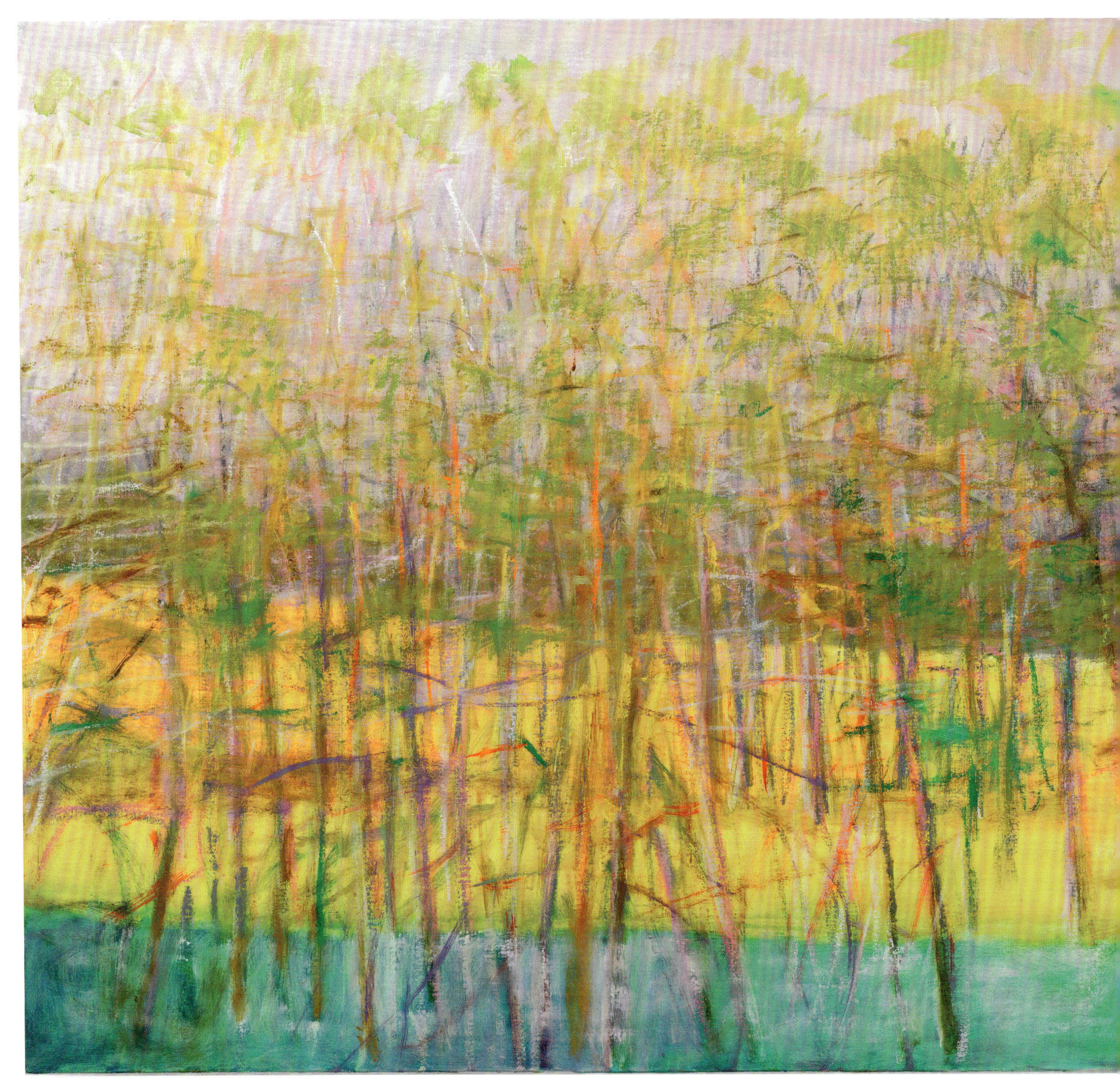

Horizontal Tangle
2010
oil on canvas
36 x 80 inches

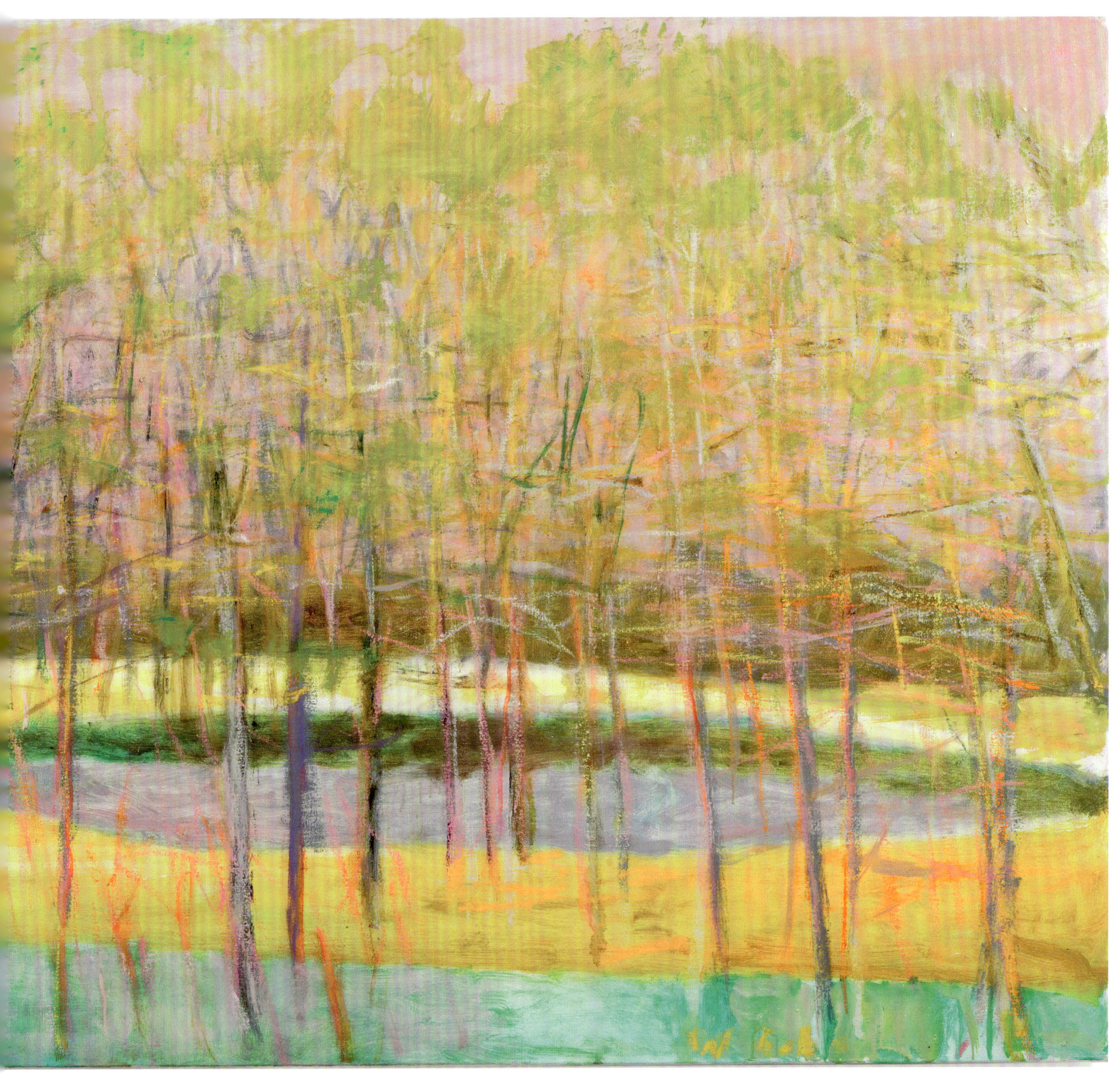

Spring Tree Tangle
2010
oil on canvas
52 x 76 inches

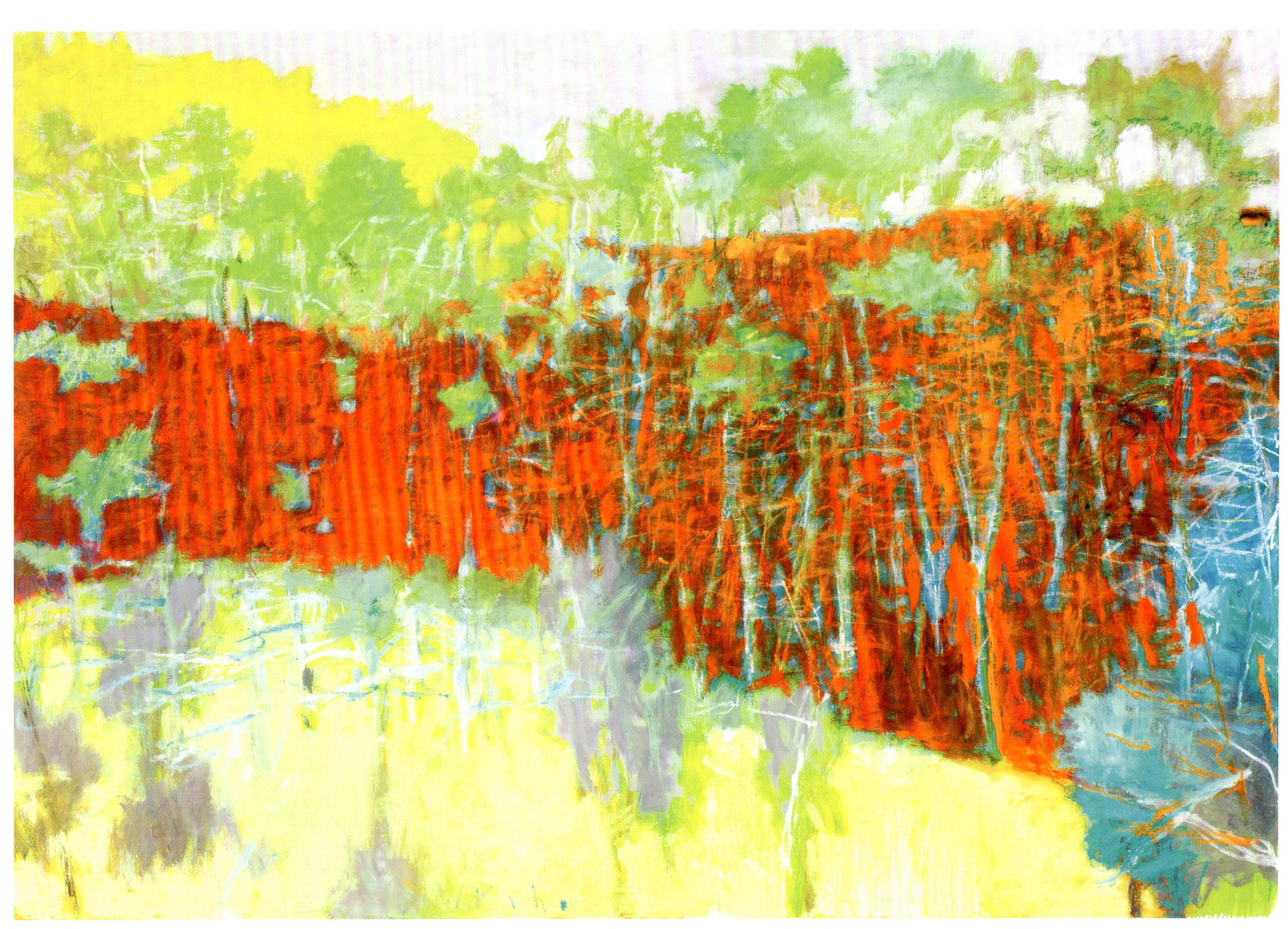

Pale Pink and Gray
2010
oil on canvas
32 x 40 inches

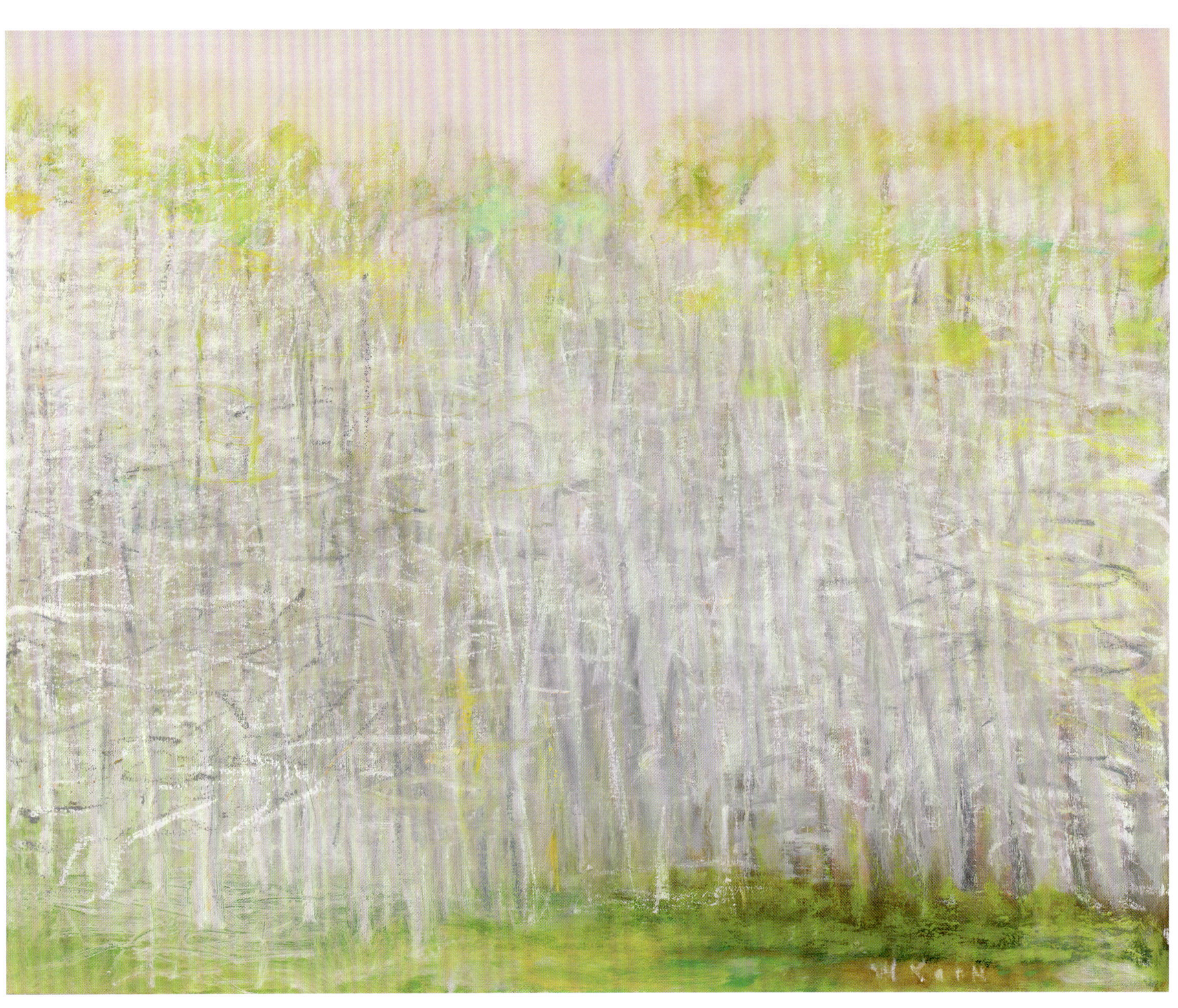

Counterpoint
2010
oil on canvas
40 x 52 inches

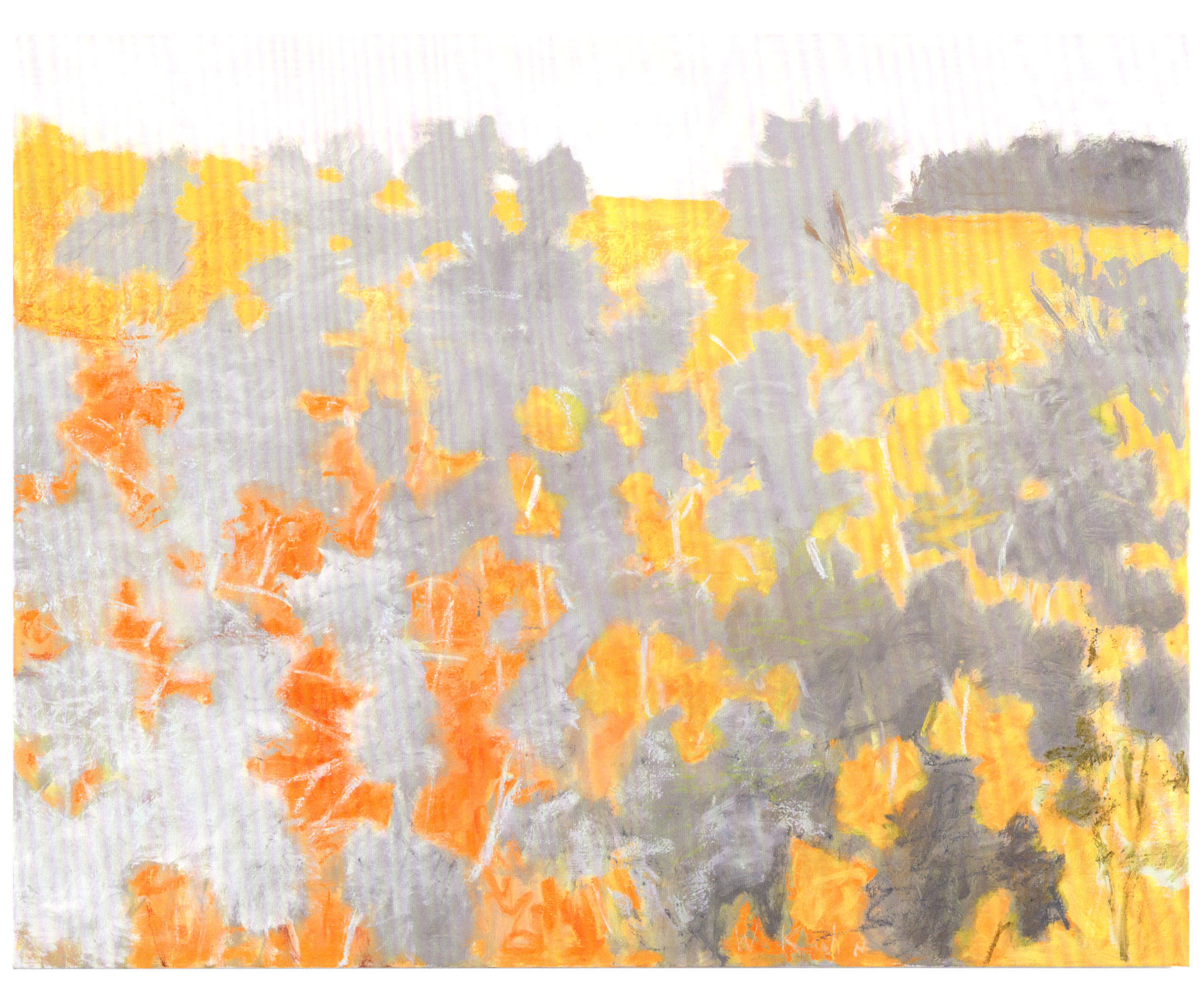

Yellow Slope
(Small Version)
2011
oil on canvas
25 x 28 inches

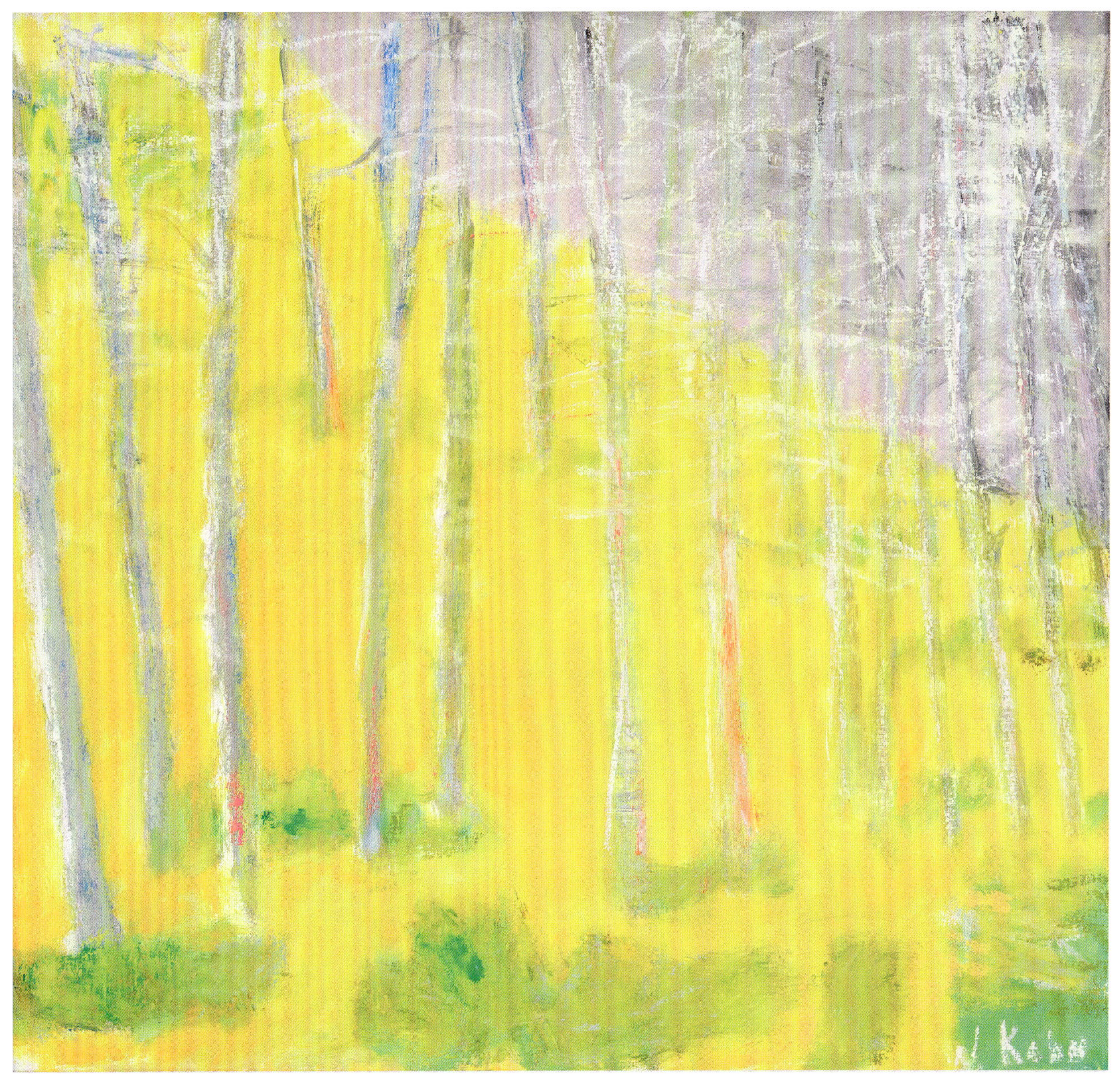

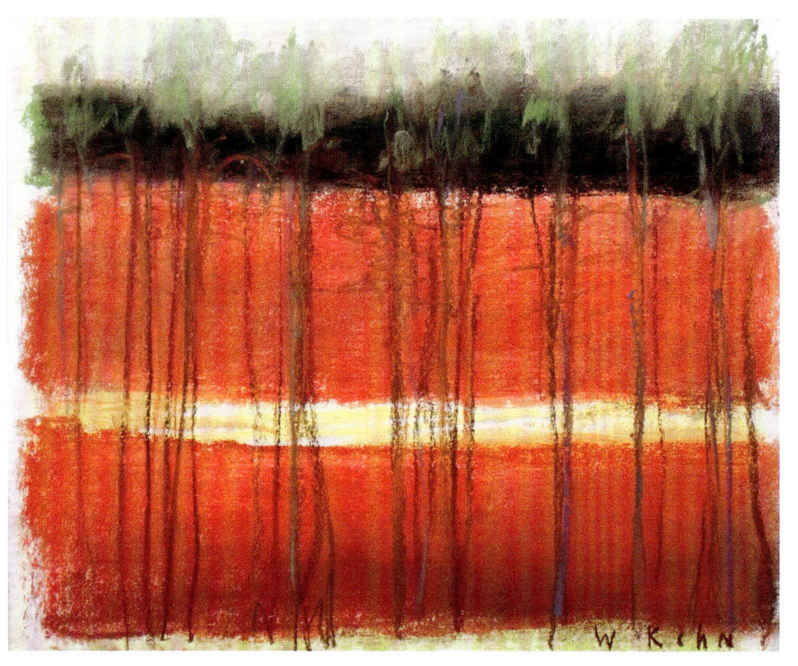

Yellow Stripe
2011
pastel on paper
11 x 14 inches

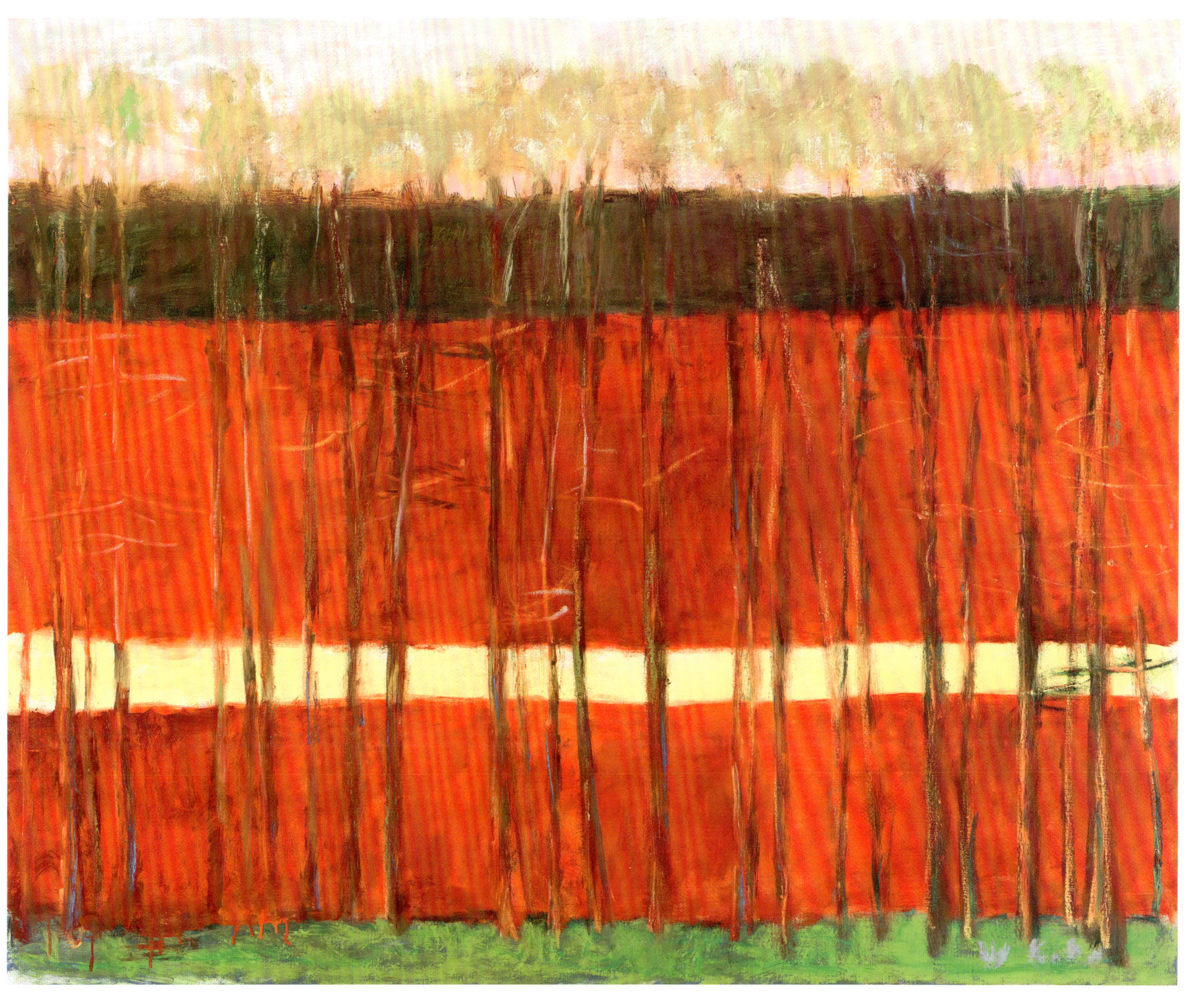

Yellow Stripe
(Large Version)
2011
oil on canvas
40 x 50 inches

Midsummer Madness
2011
oil on canvas
36 x 52 inches

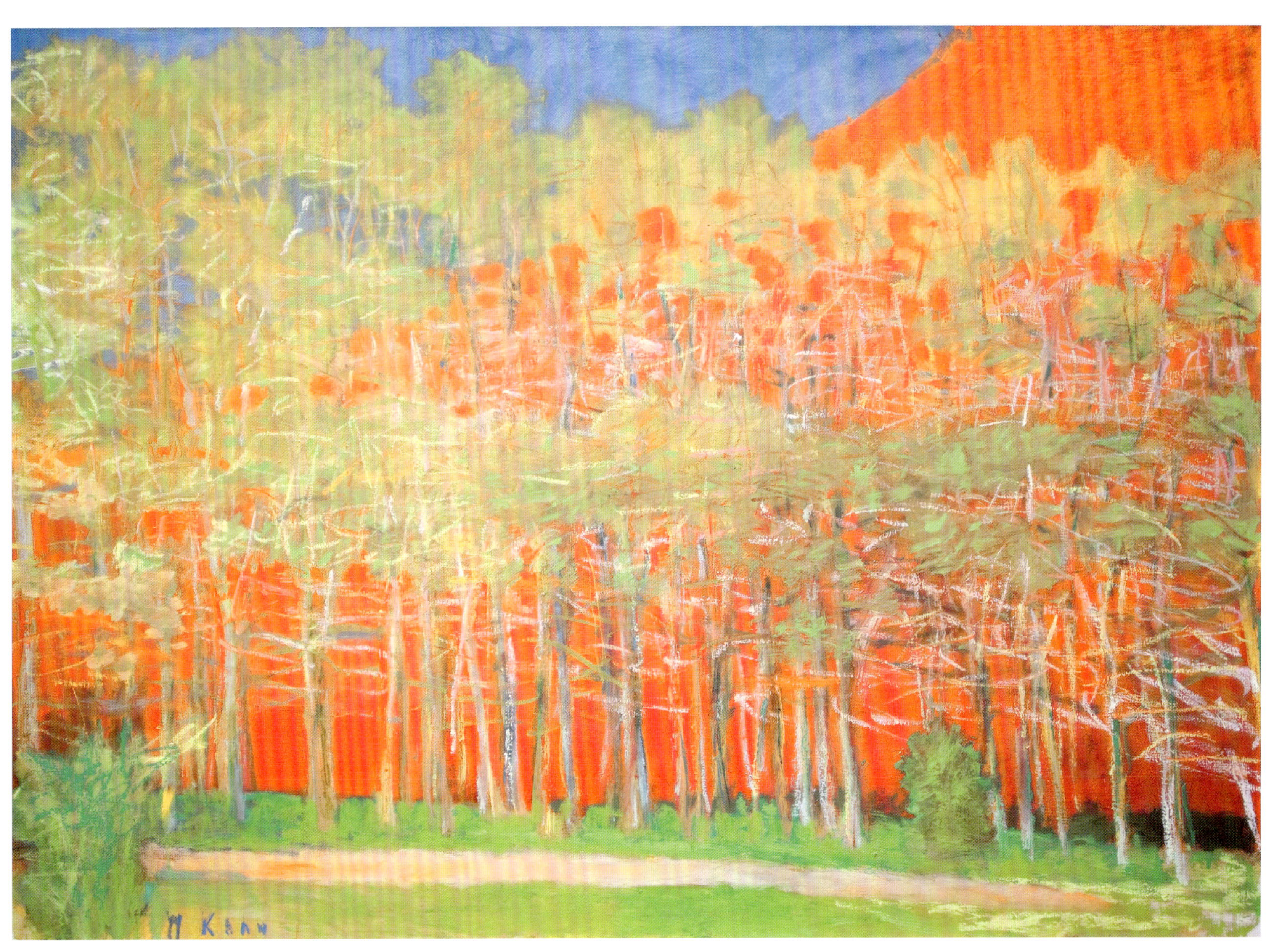

Green to Gold
2011
oil on canvas
30 x 40 inches

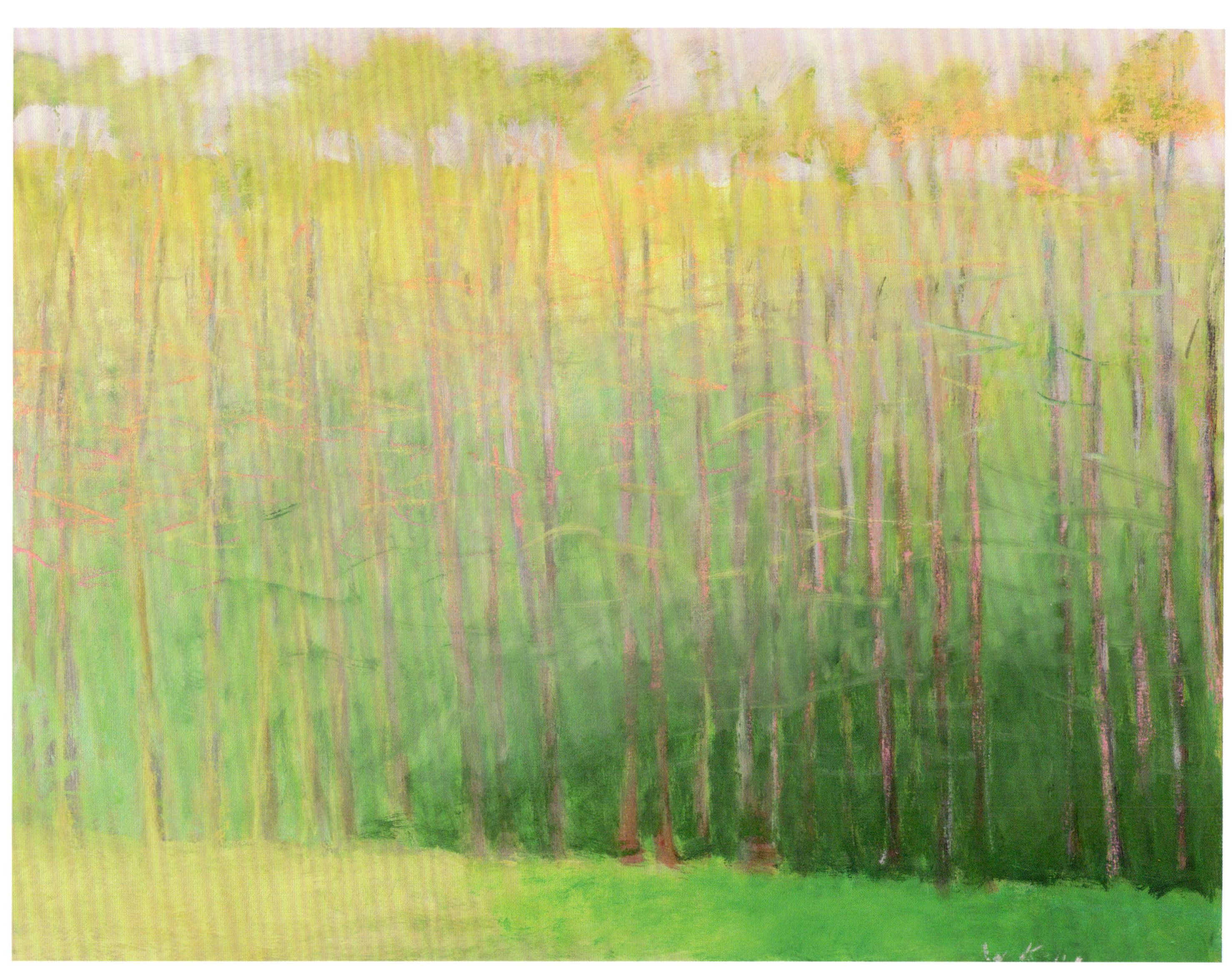

Celebrating Green
2011
oil on canvas
52 x 66 inches

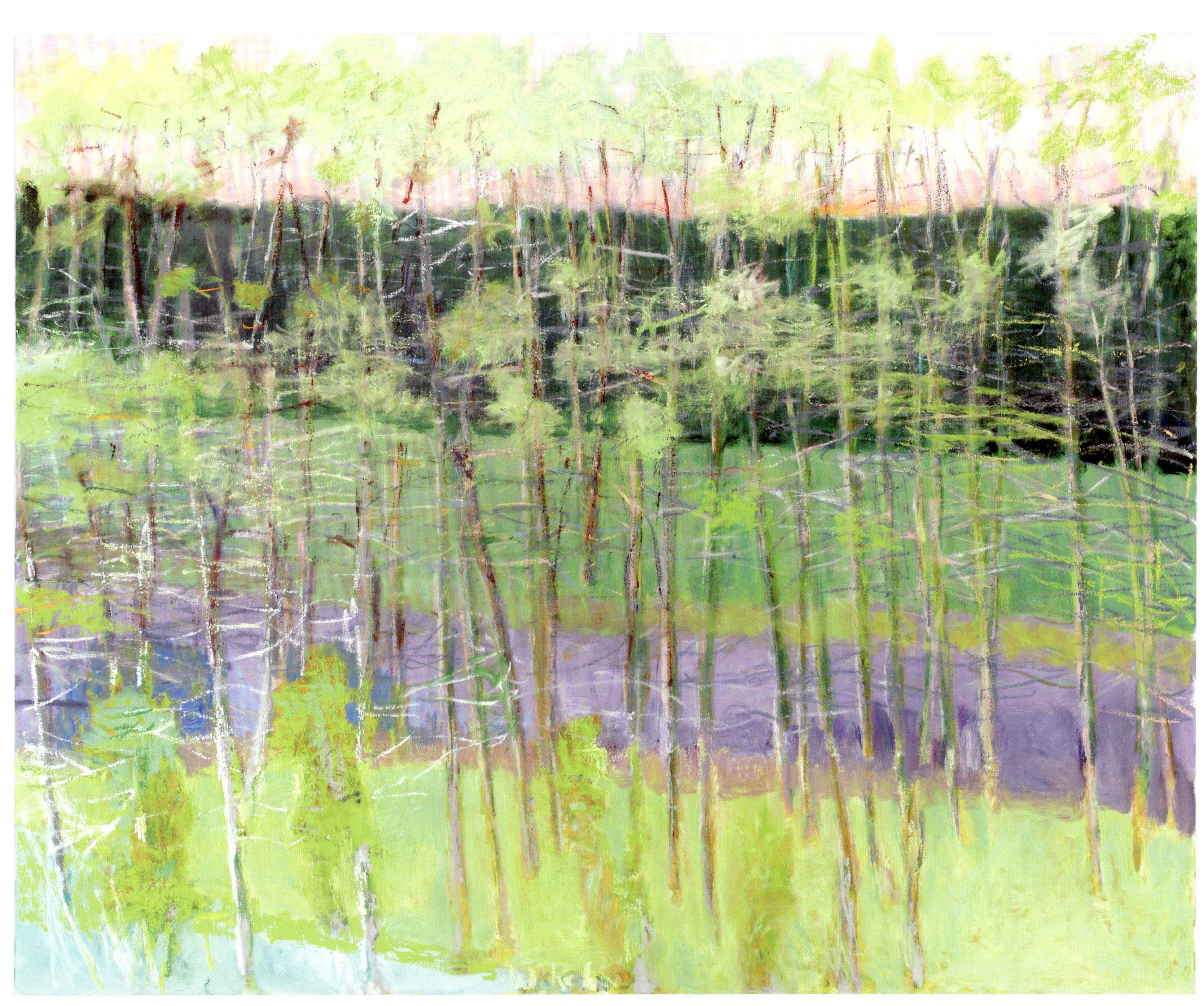

Wooded Slice of Nature
2011
oil on canvas
52 x 52 inches

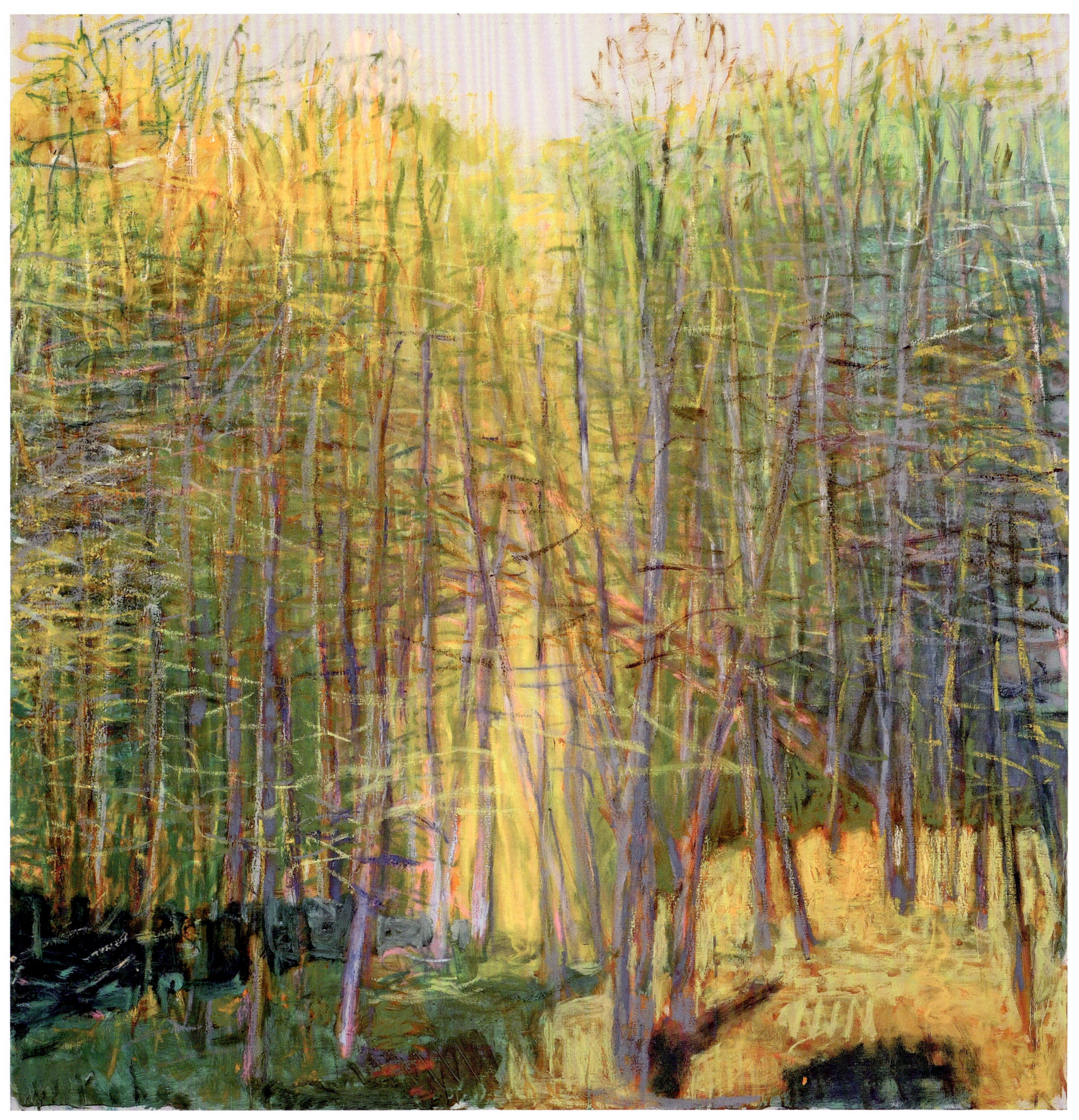

In a Village
2011
oil on canvas
52 x 72 inches

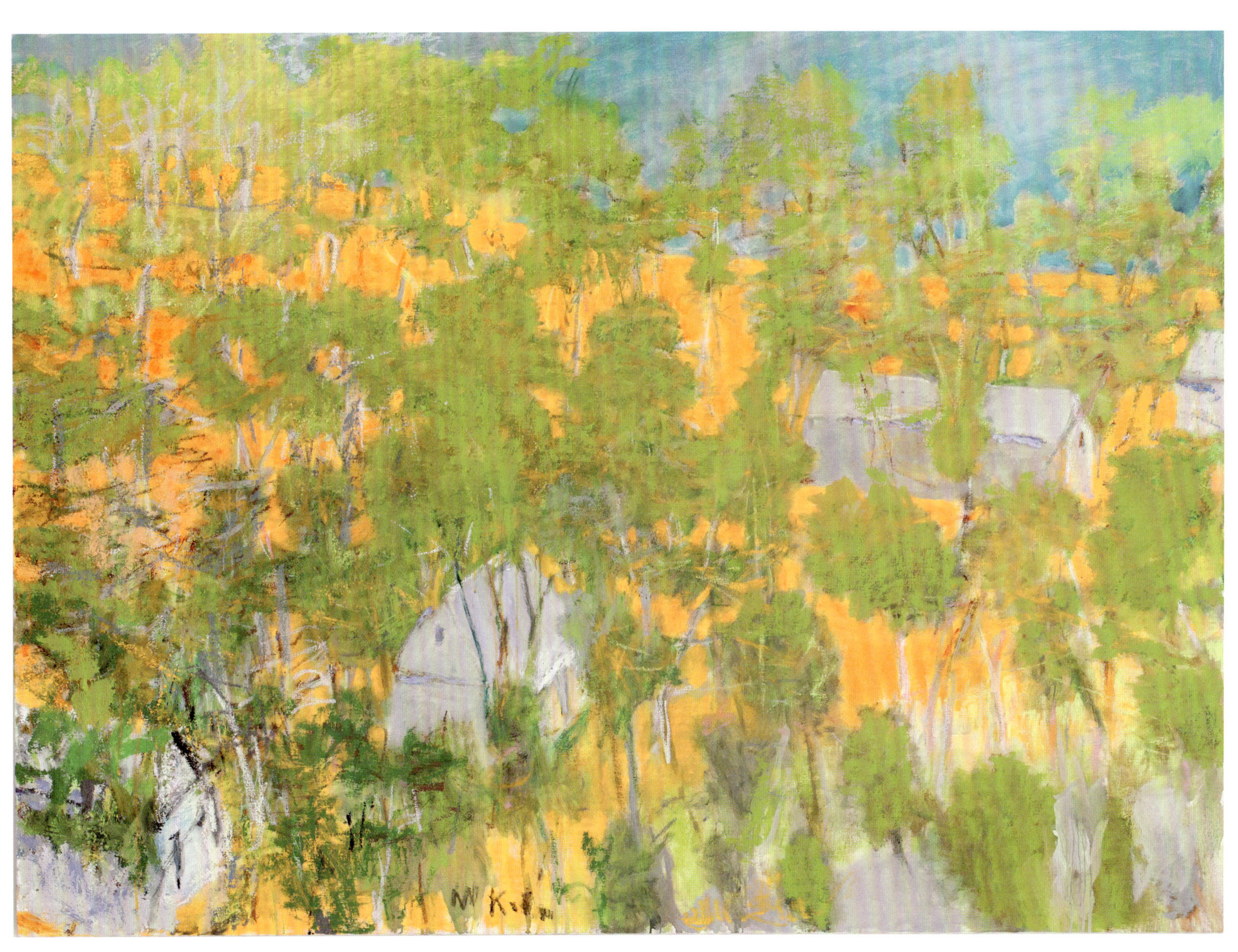

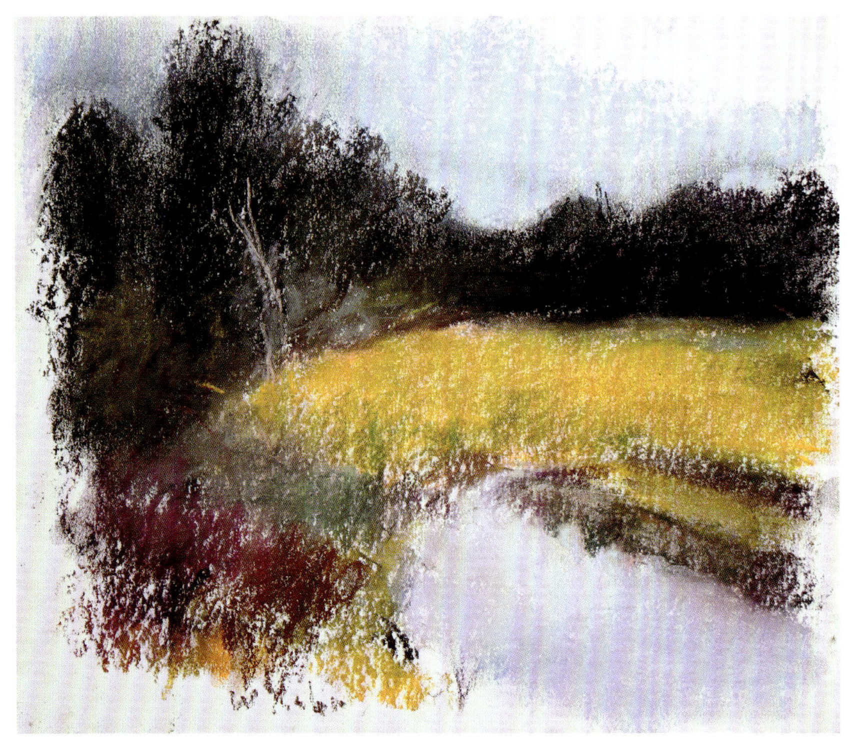

Phil's Pond
2011
pastel on paper
14 x 16½ inches

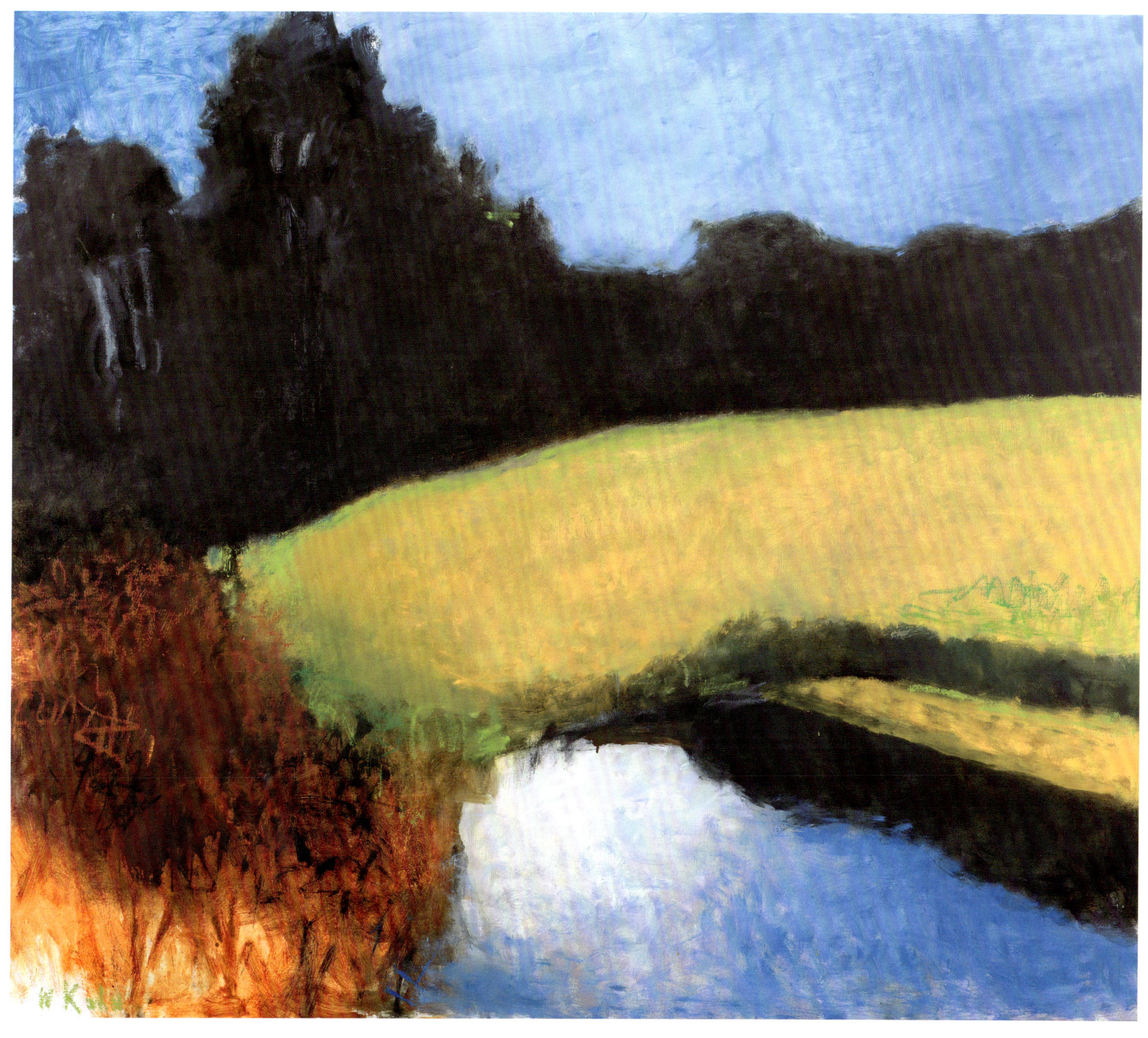

Pond off Barrow Road
2011
oil on canvas
52 x 60 inches

Orange Edges
2011
oil on canvas
30 x 42 inches

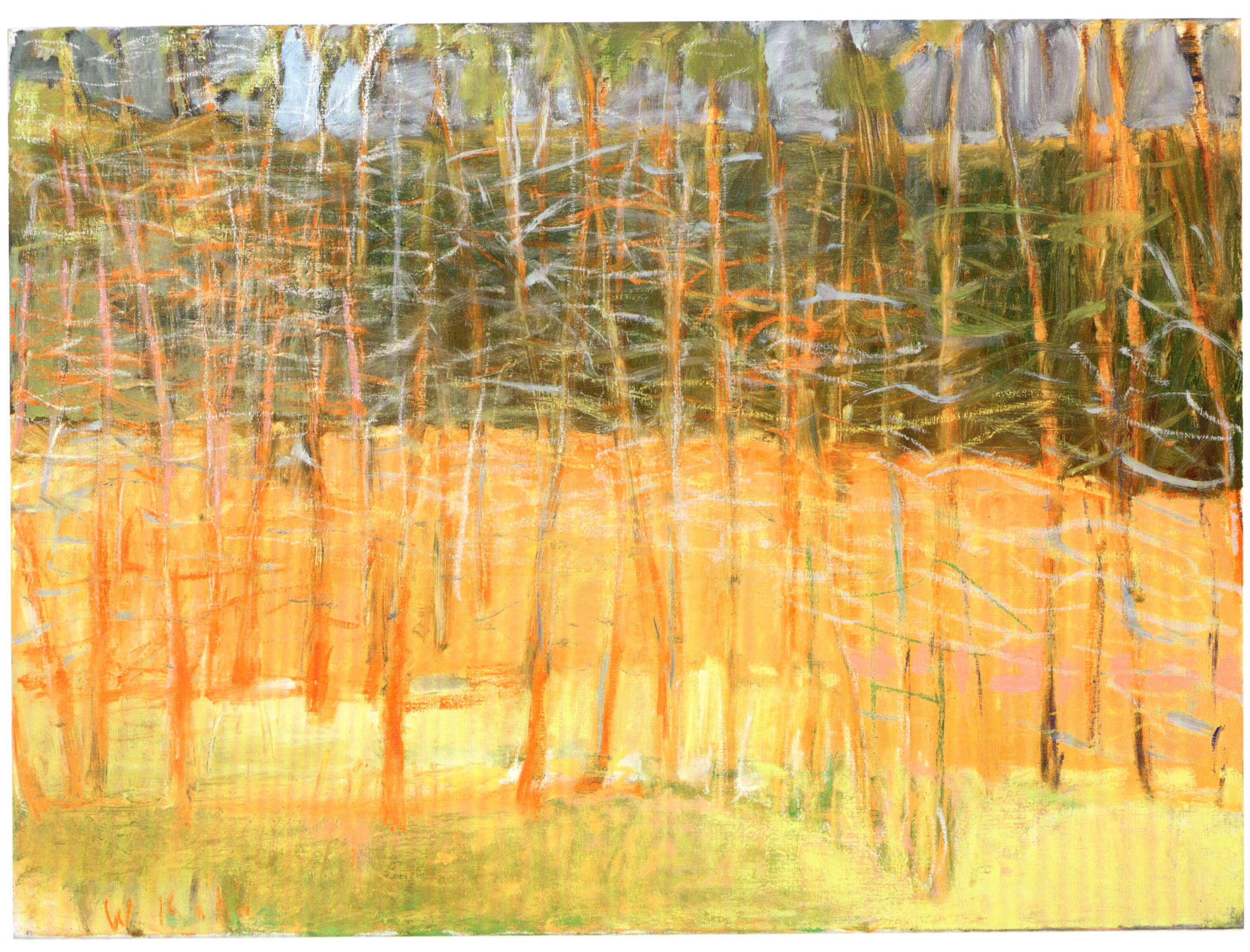

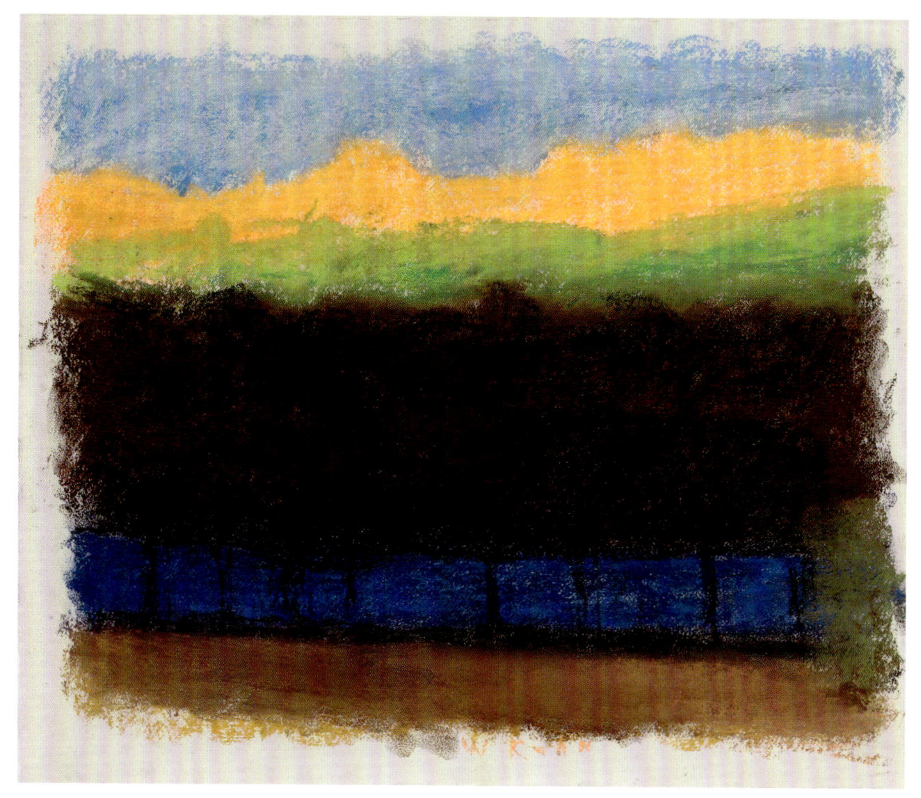

Study for Furthest Glow
2011
pastel on paper
17 x 20 inches

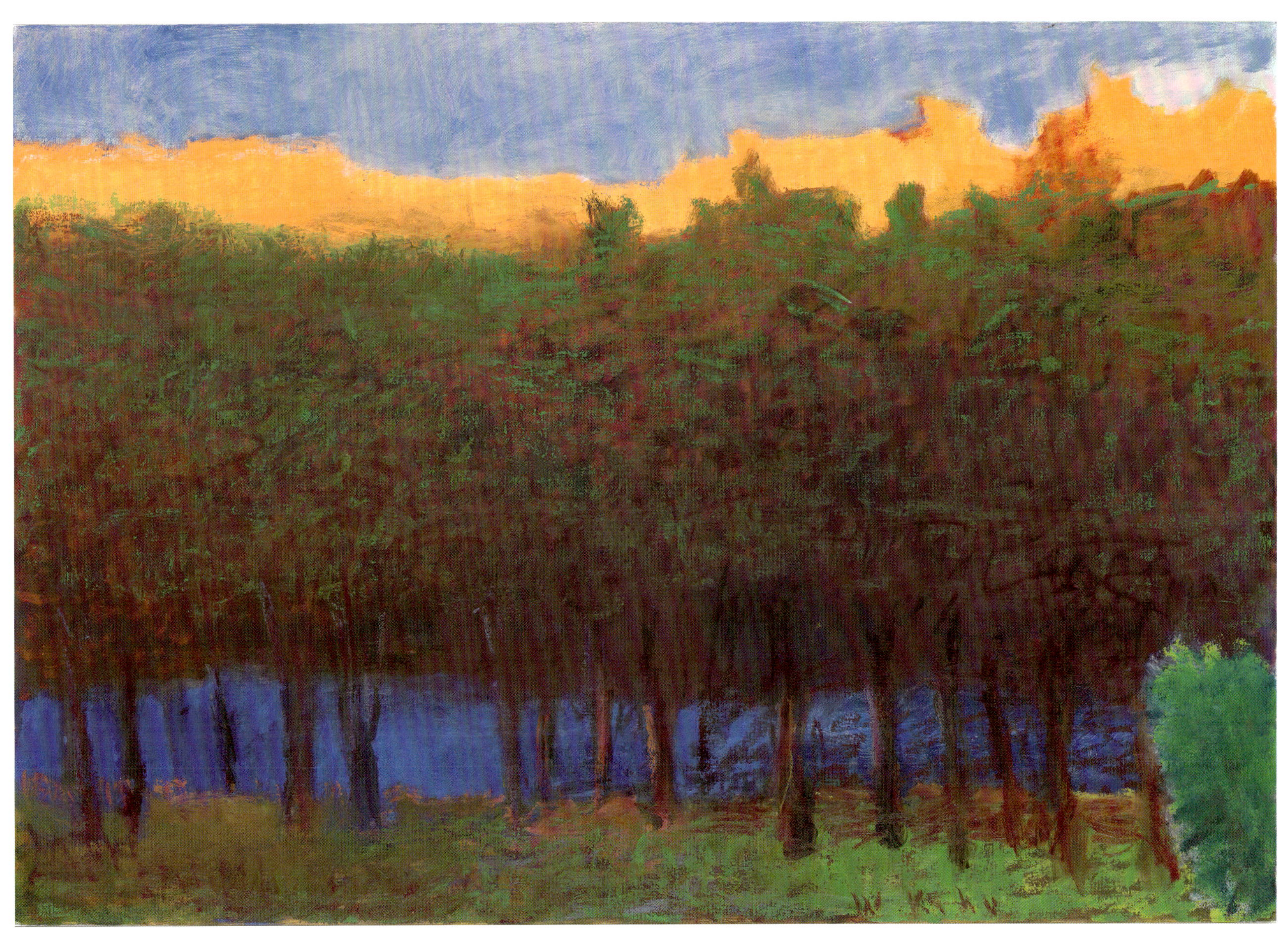

Furthest Glow
2011
oil on canvas
36 x 52 inches

On the Kafka Place
2012
oil on canvas
52 x 60 inches

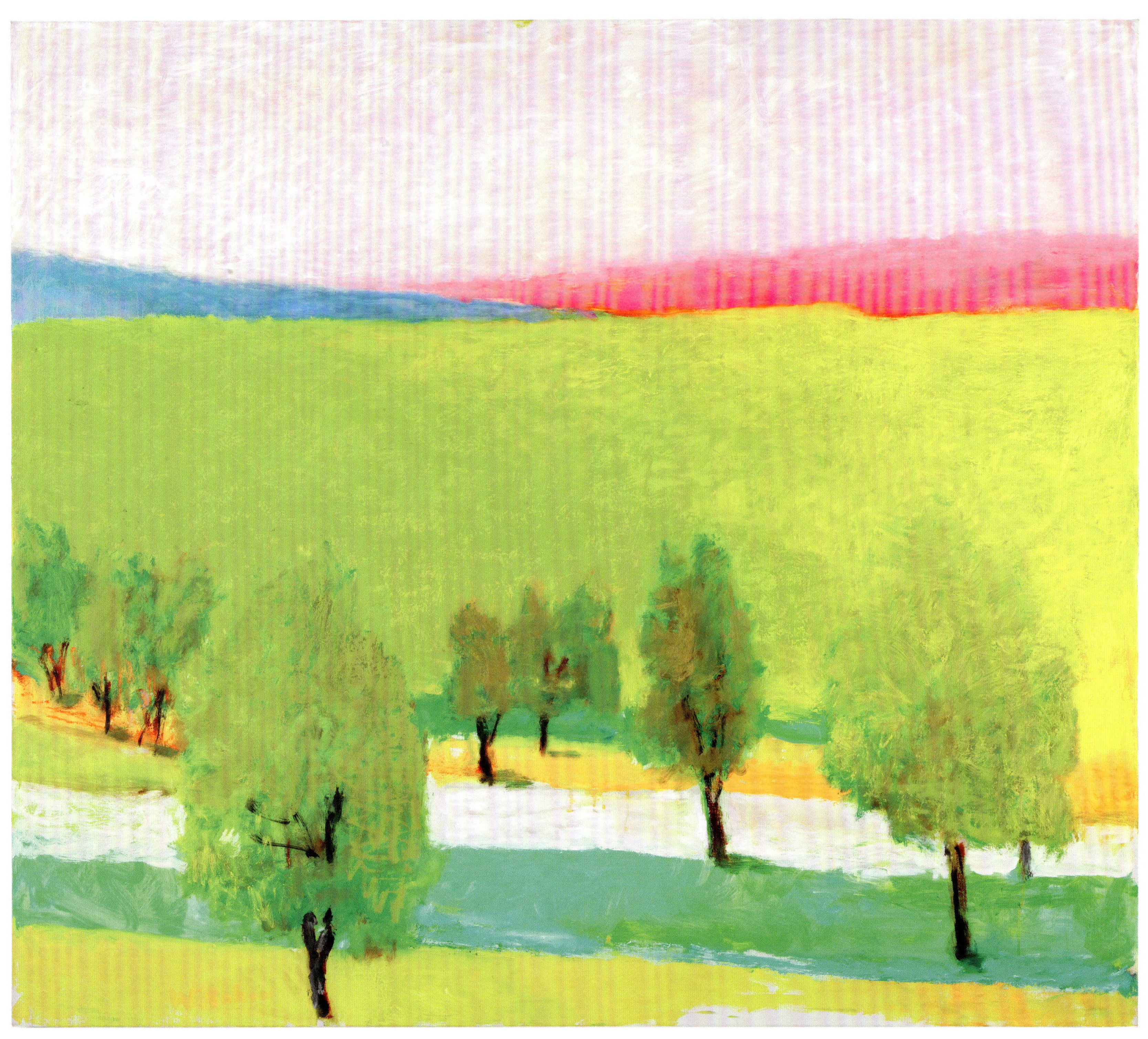

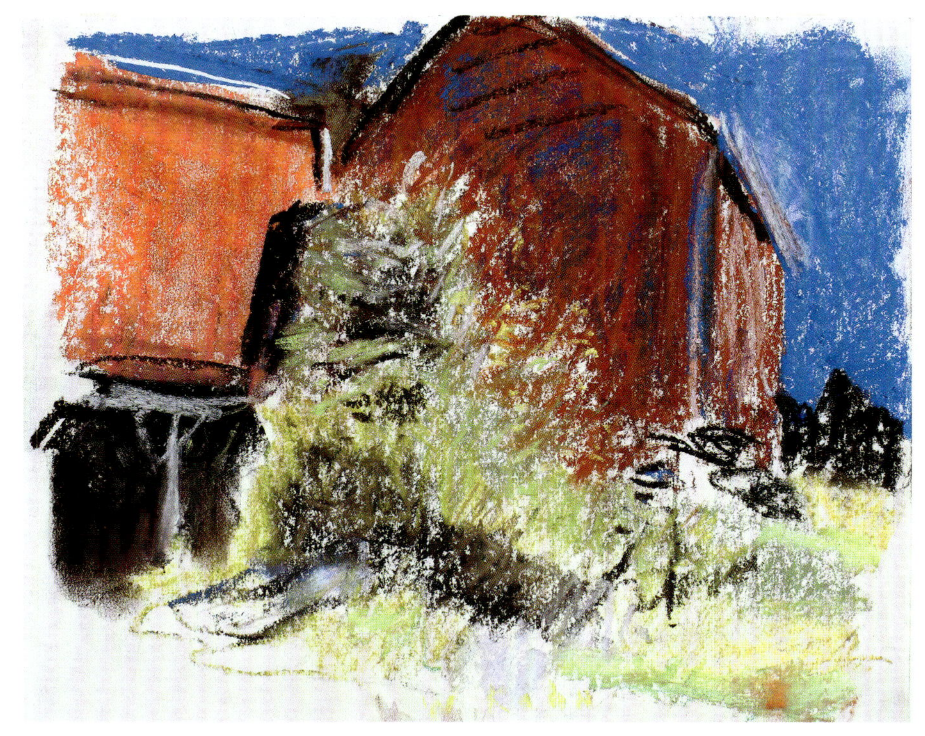

Barn in West Chesterfield, New Hampshire
2011
pastel on paper
9 x 12 inches

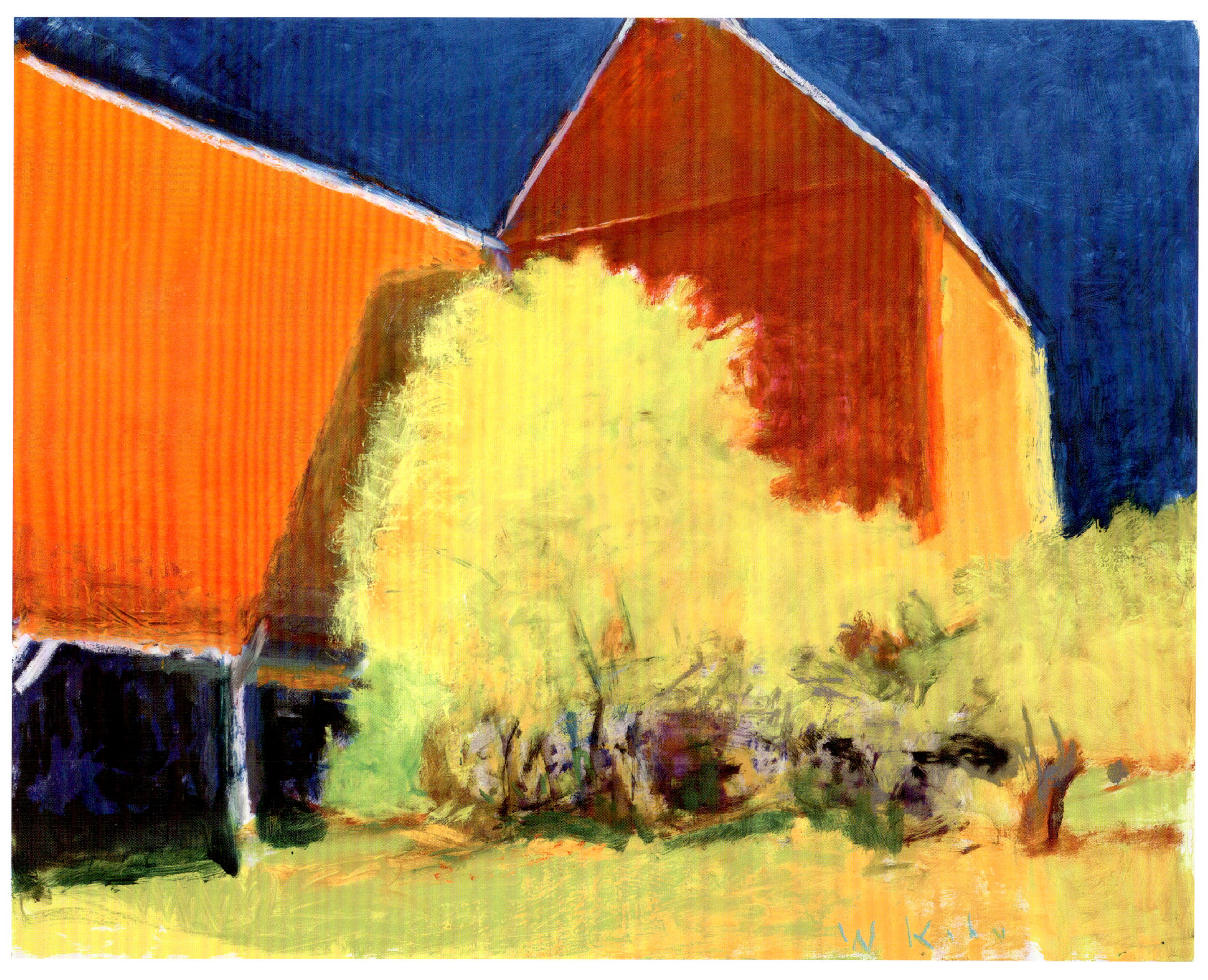

Barn in West Chesterfield
2012
oil on canvas
40 x 52 inches

Green Landscape
with Greenhouses
2012
oil on canvas
64 x 84 inches

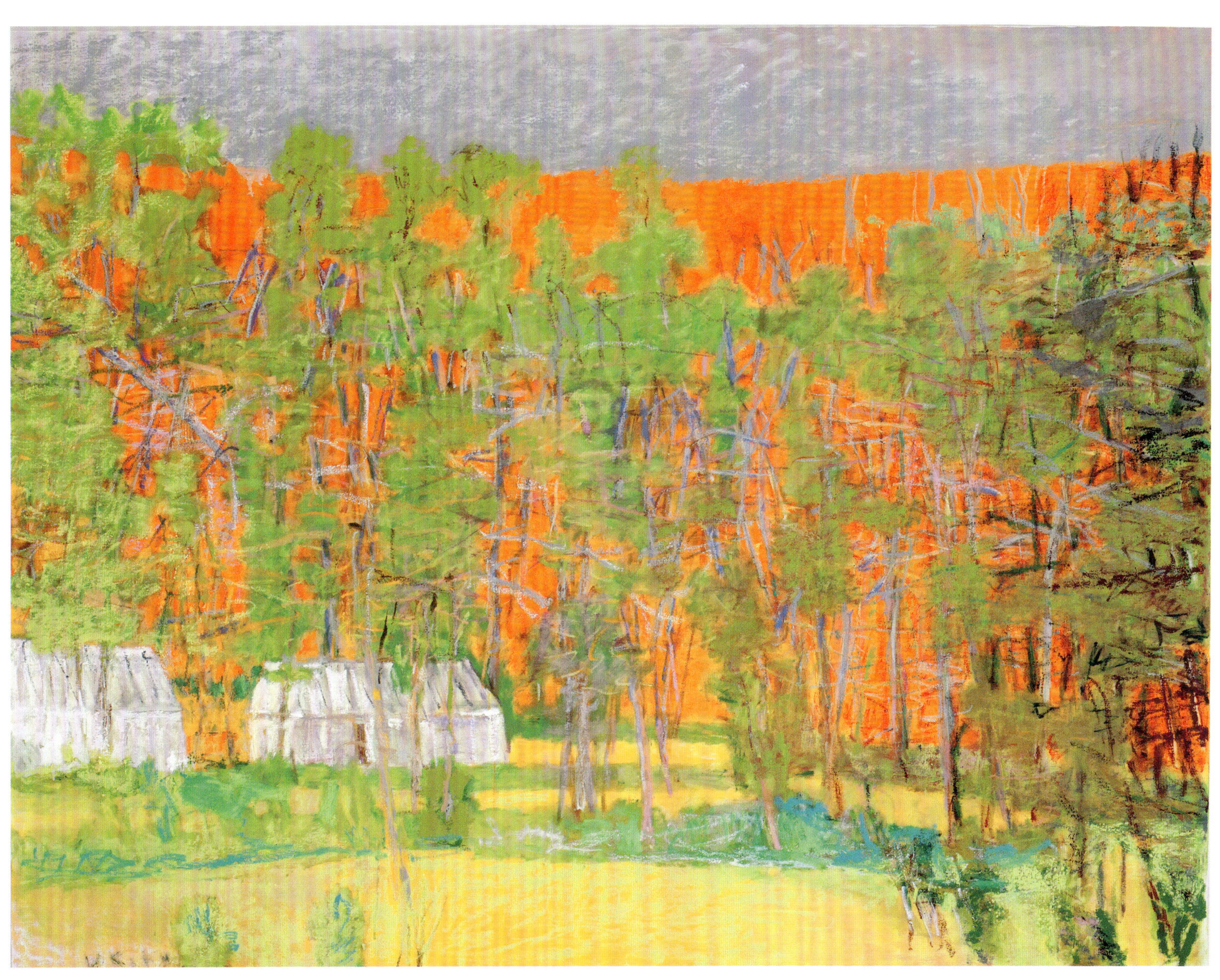

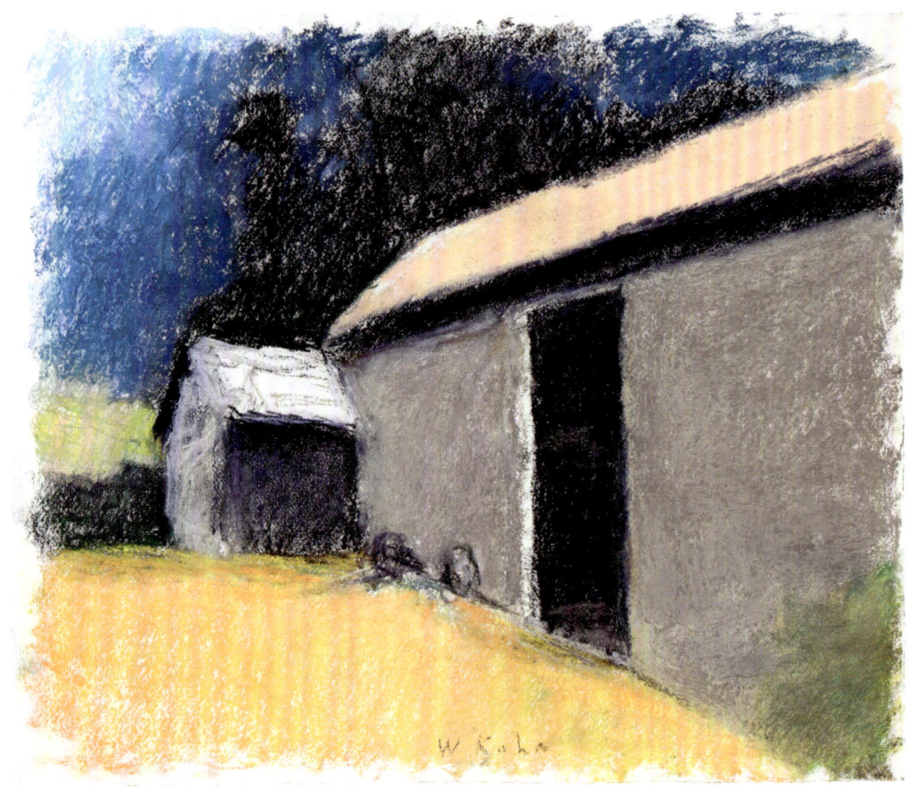

Unused Barn
2012
pastel on paper
17 x 21 inches

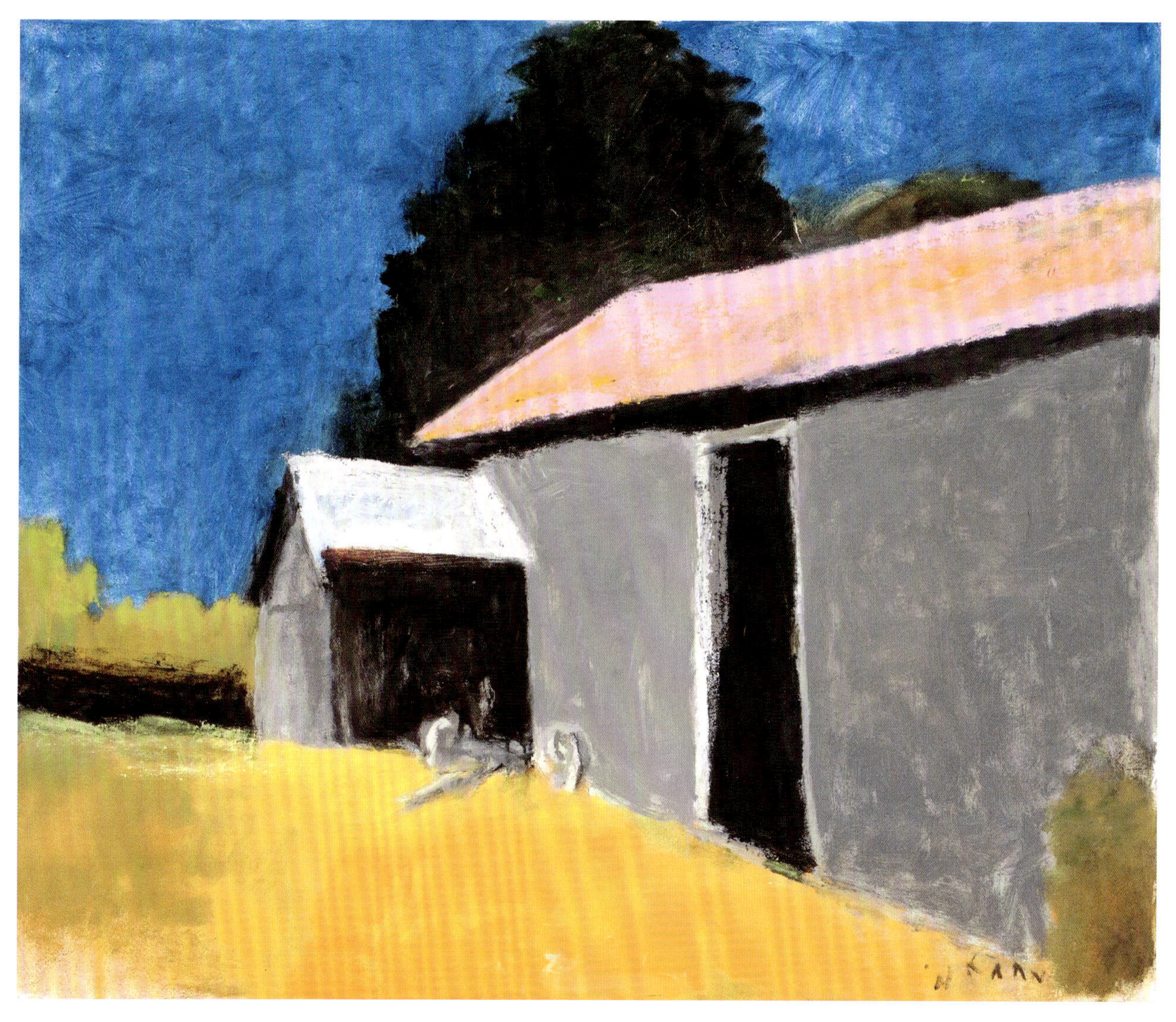

Hewes Barn
2012
oil on canvas
30 x 36 inches

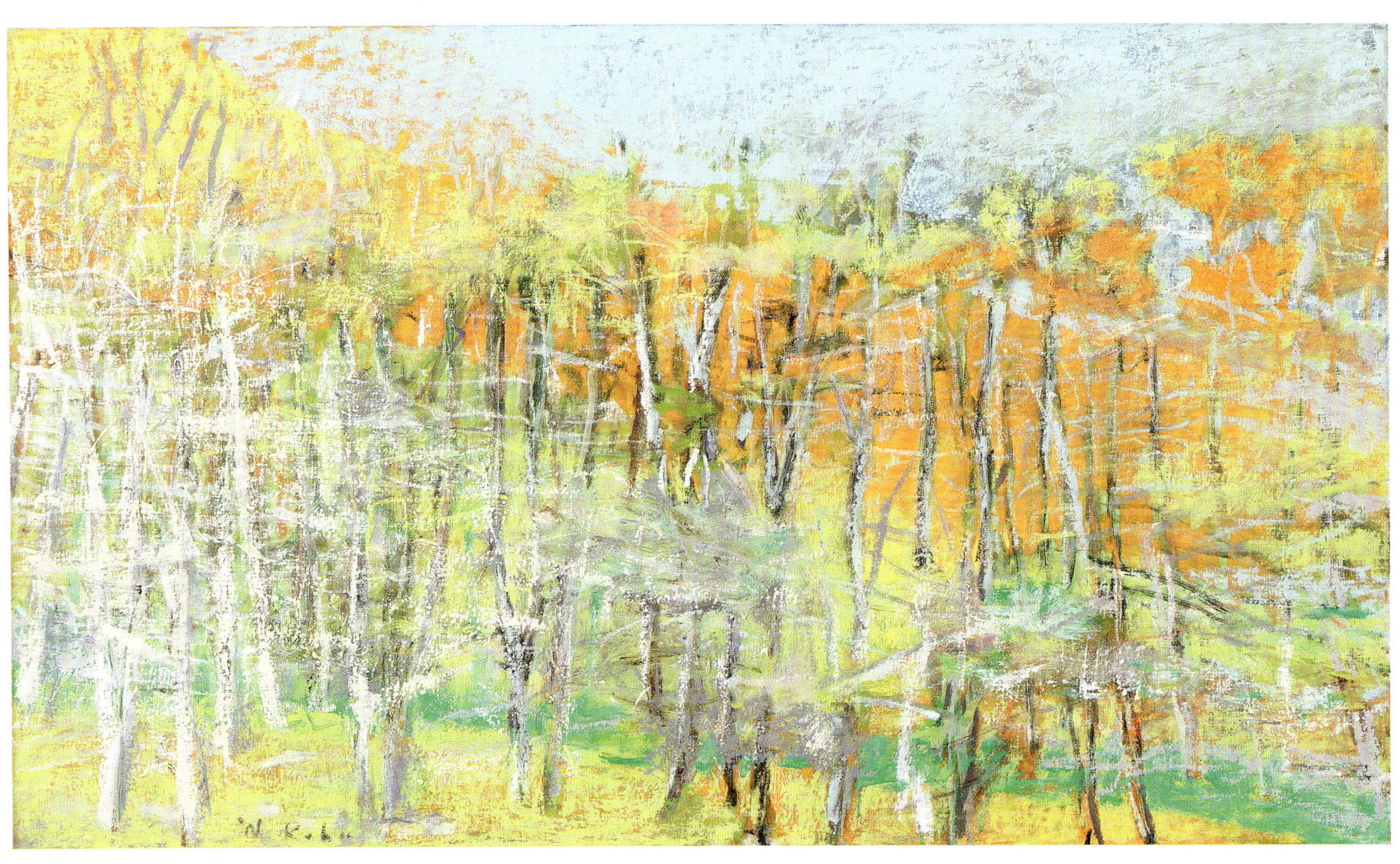

Yellow Predominates
2012
oil on canvas
30 x 52 inches

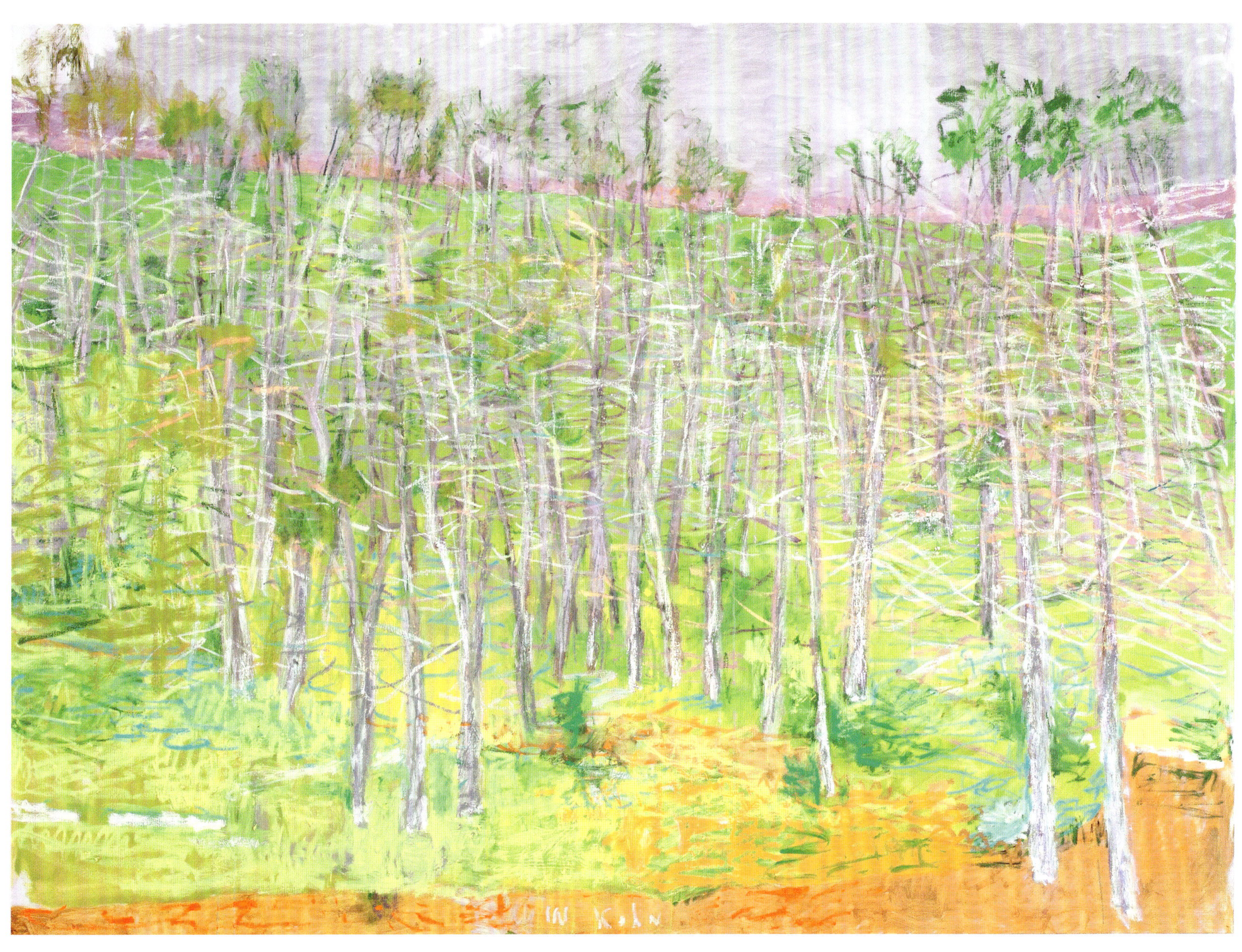

Fine Green Painting
2012
oil on canvas
52 x 72 inches

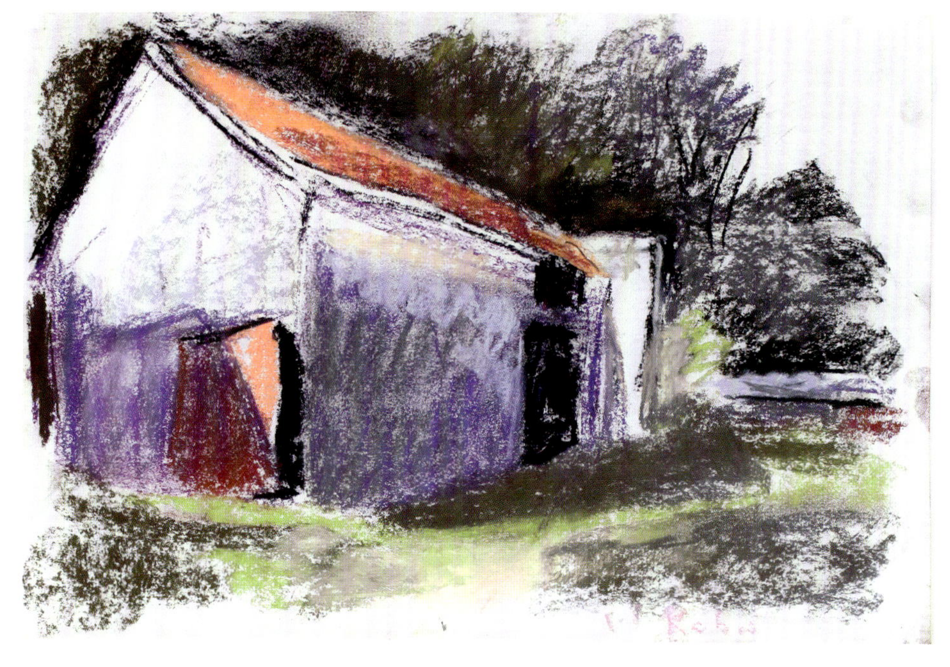

Neglected Barn II
2012
pastel on paper
12 x 18 inches

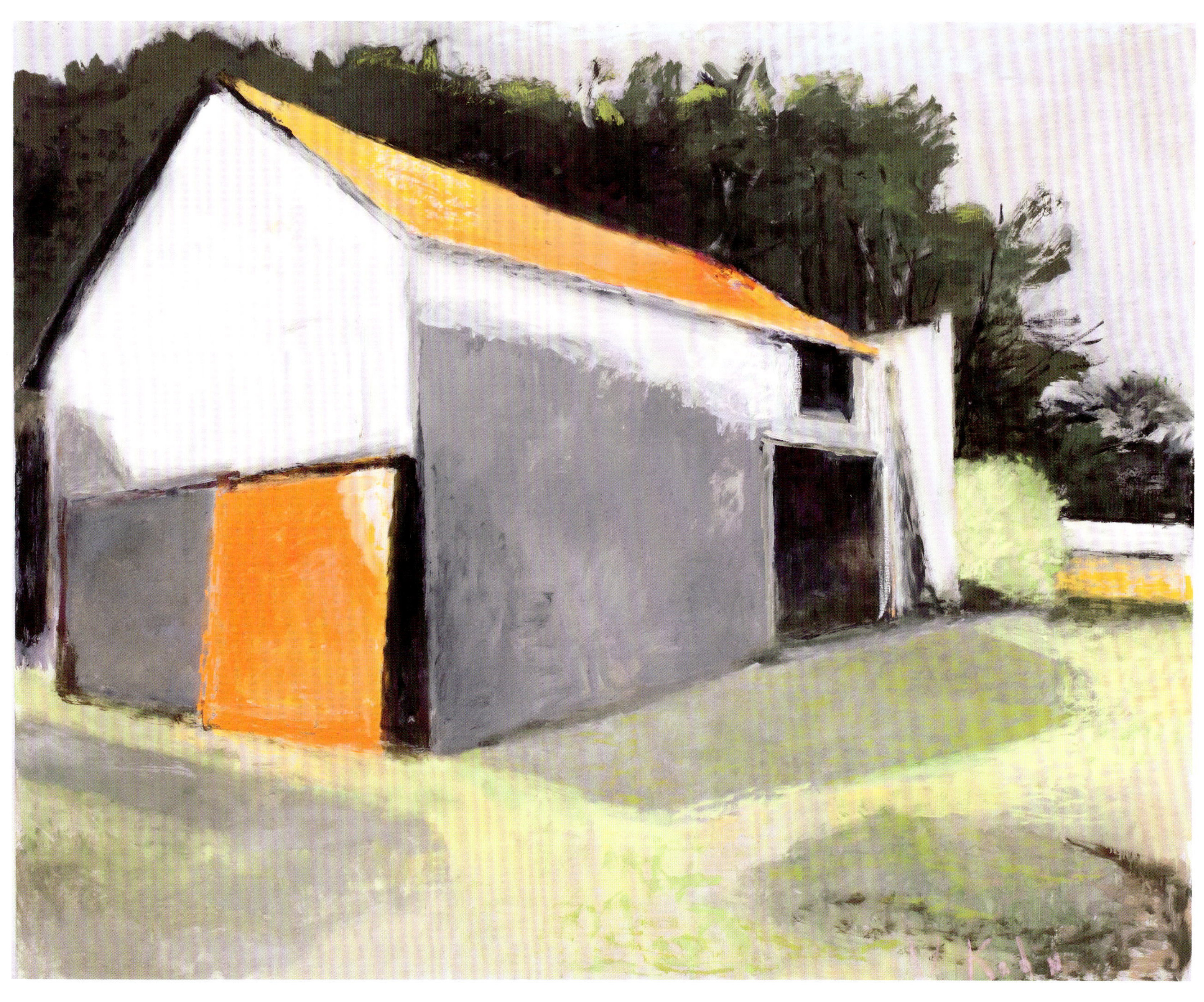

On the Carpenter Farm
2012
oil on canvas
52 x 66 inches

On a Base of Red
2012
oil on canvas
30 x 52 inches

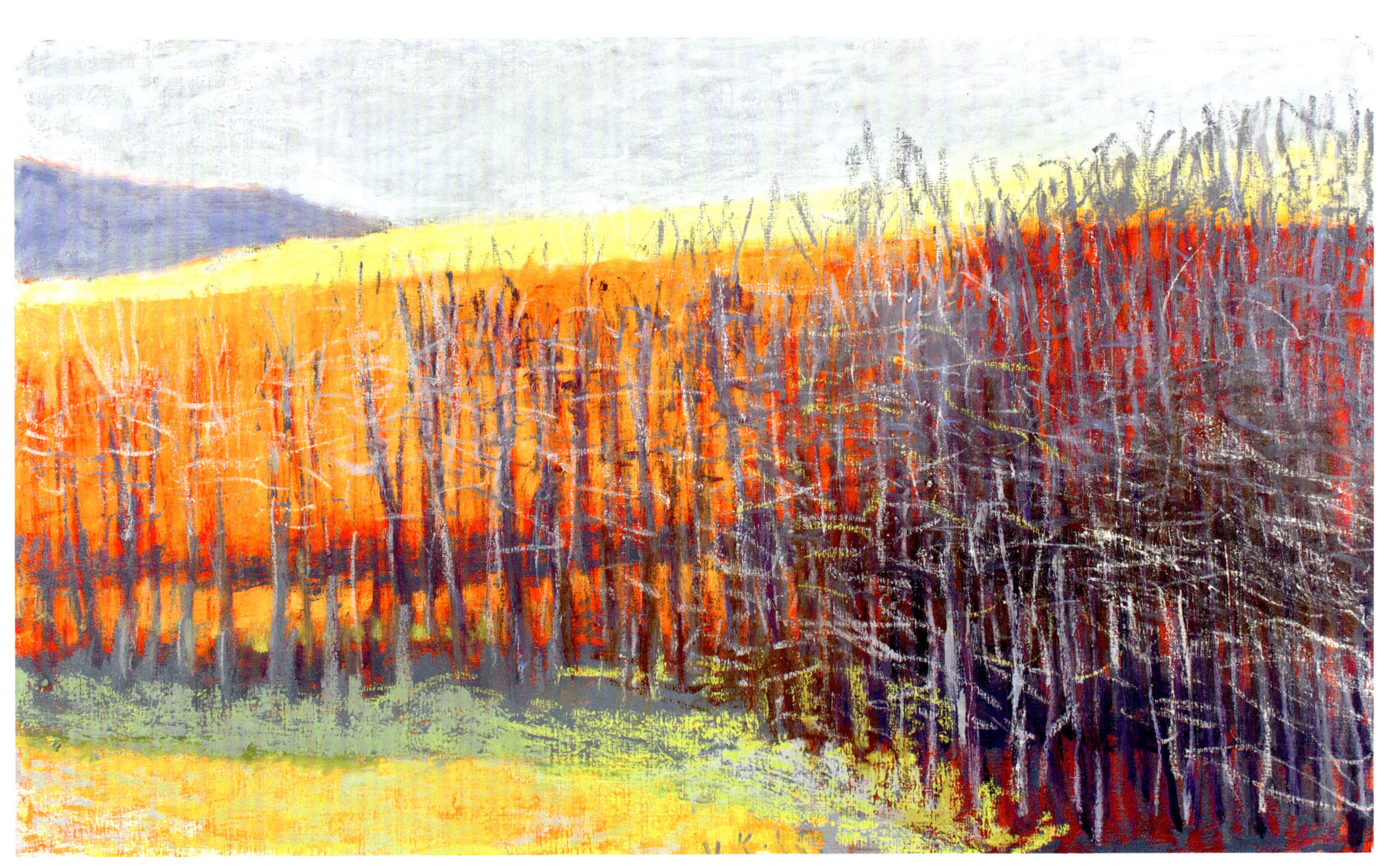

About Sunshine
2013
oil on canvas
32 x 40 inches

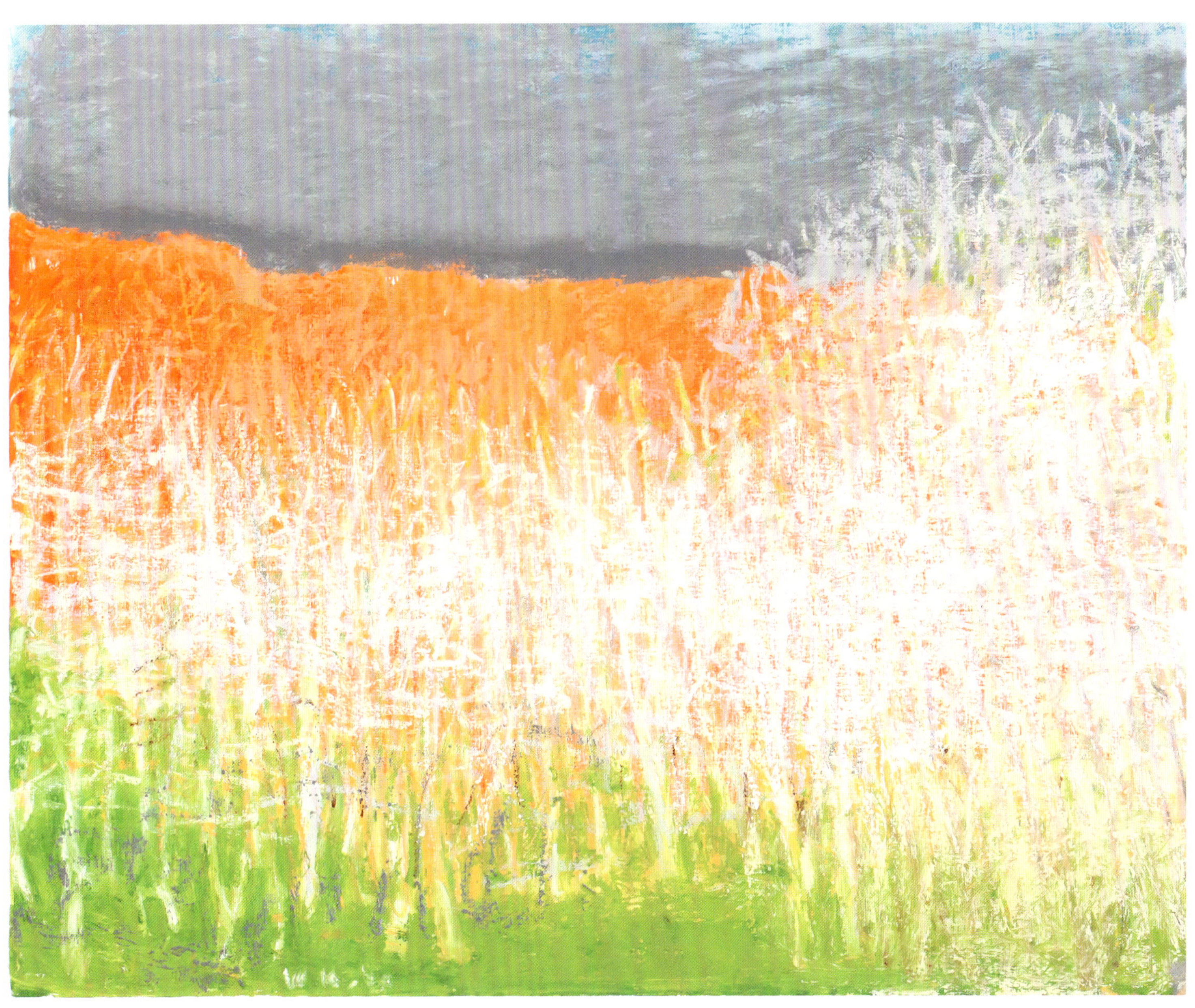

River Through a Yellow Meadow
2013
oil on canvas
32 x 52 inches

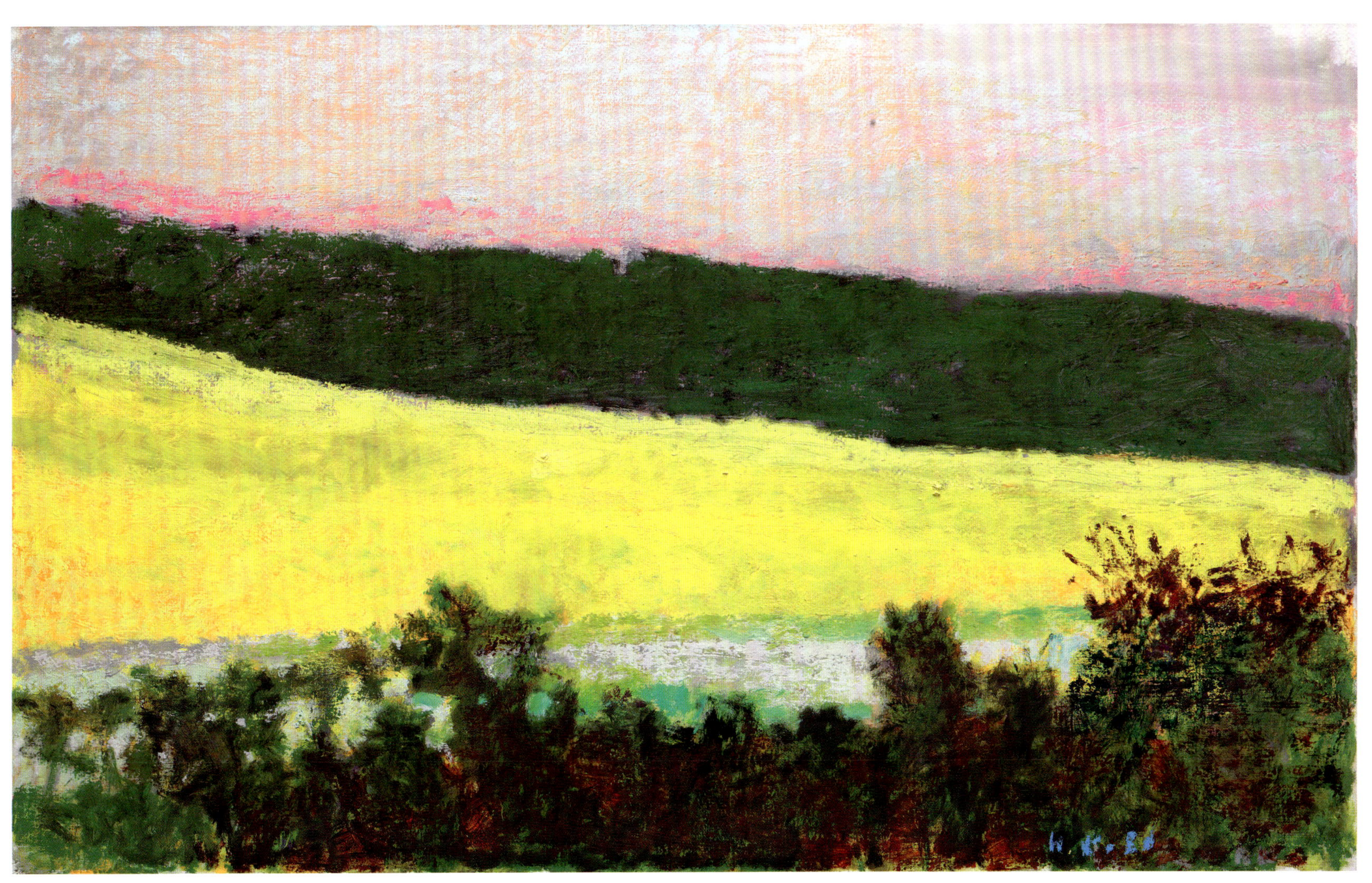

Blue Distance
2013
oil on canvas
36 x 52 inches

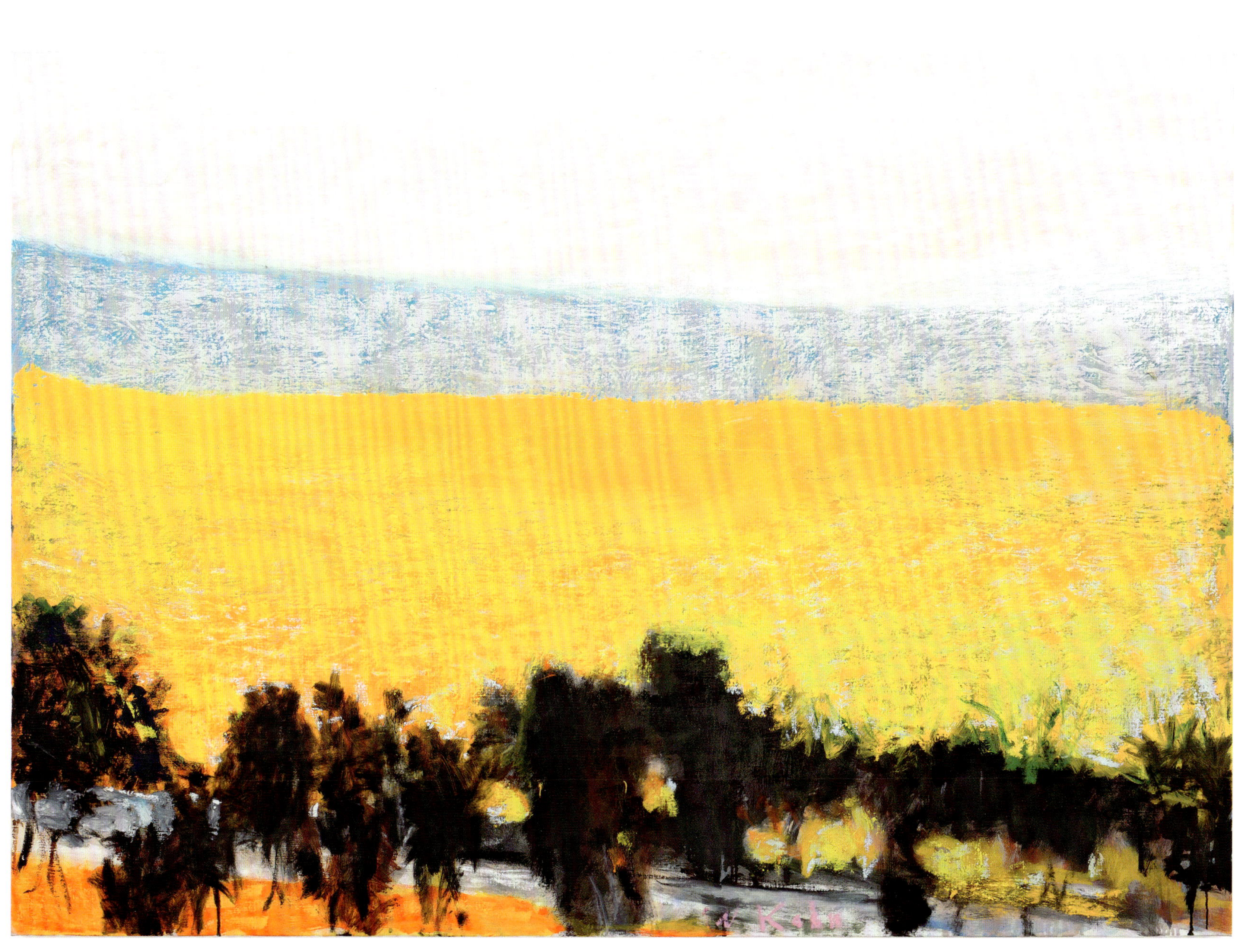

Density
2013
oil on canvas
52 x 66 inches

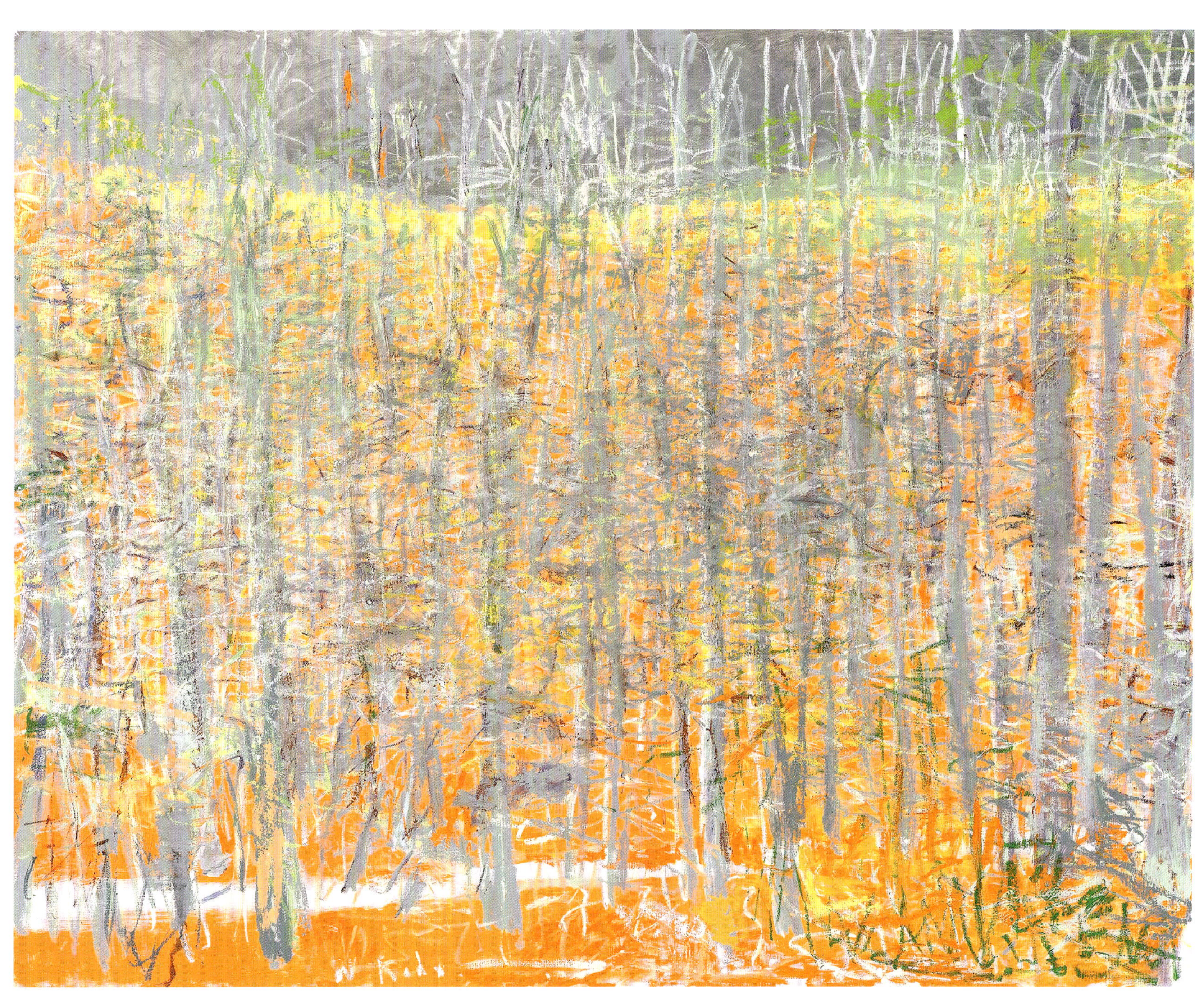

Dark Corner
2013
oil on canvas
36 x 68 inches

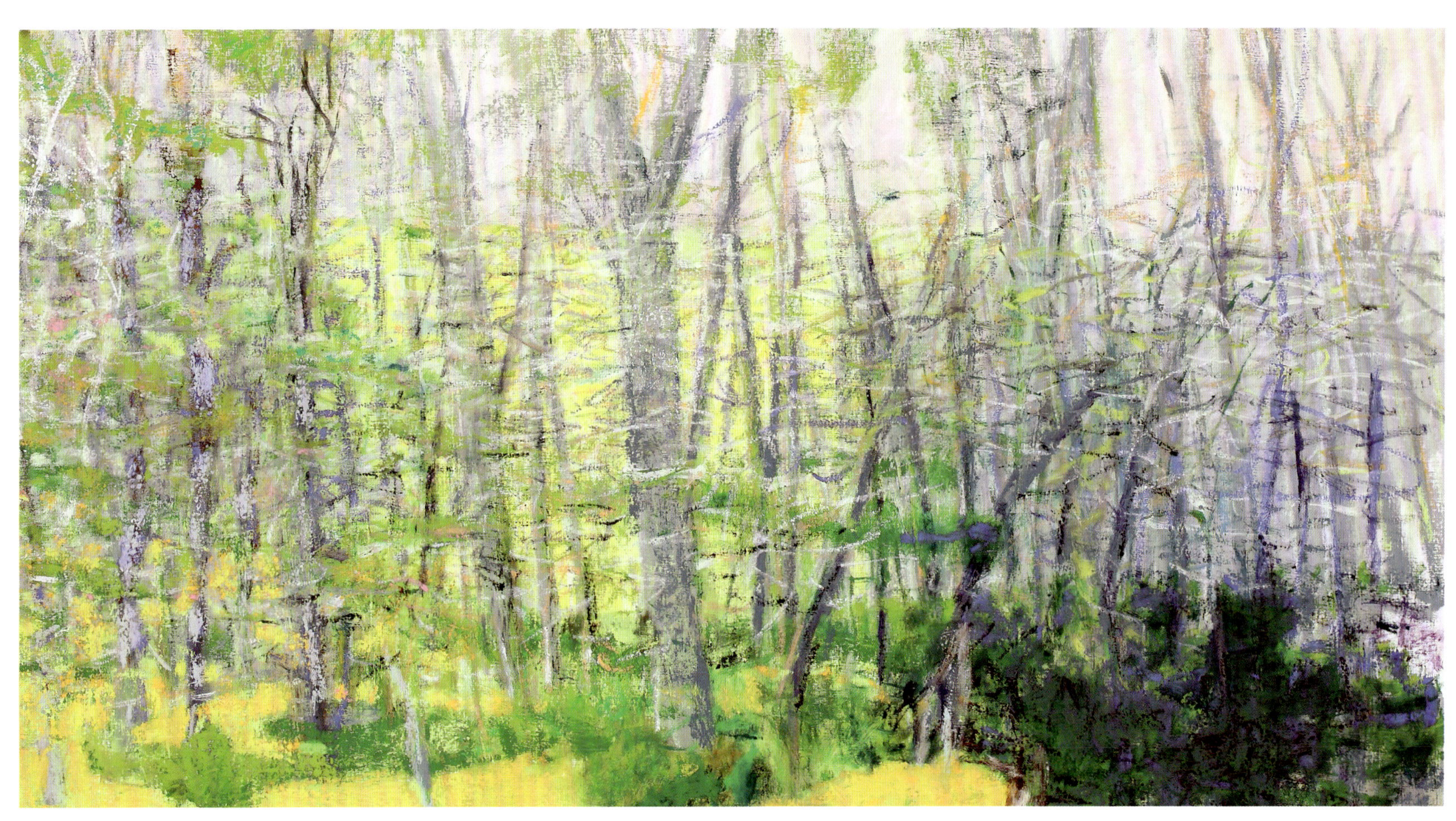

Against a Yellow Rise
2013
oil on canvas
64 x 84 inches

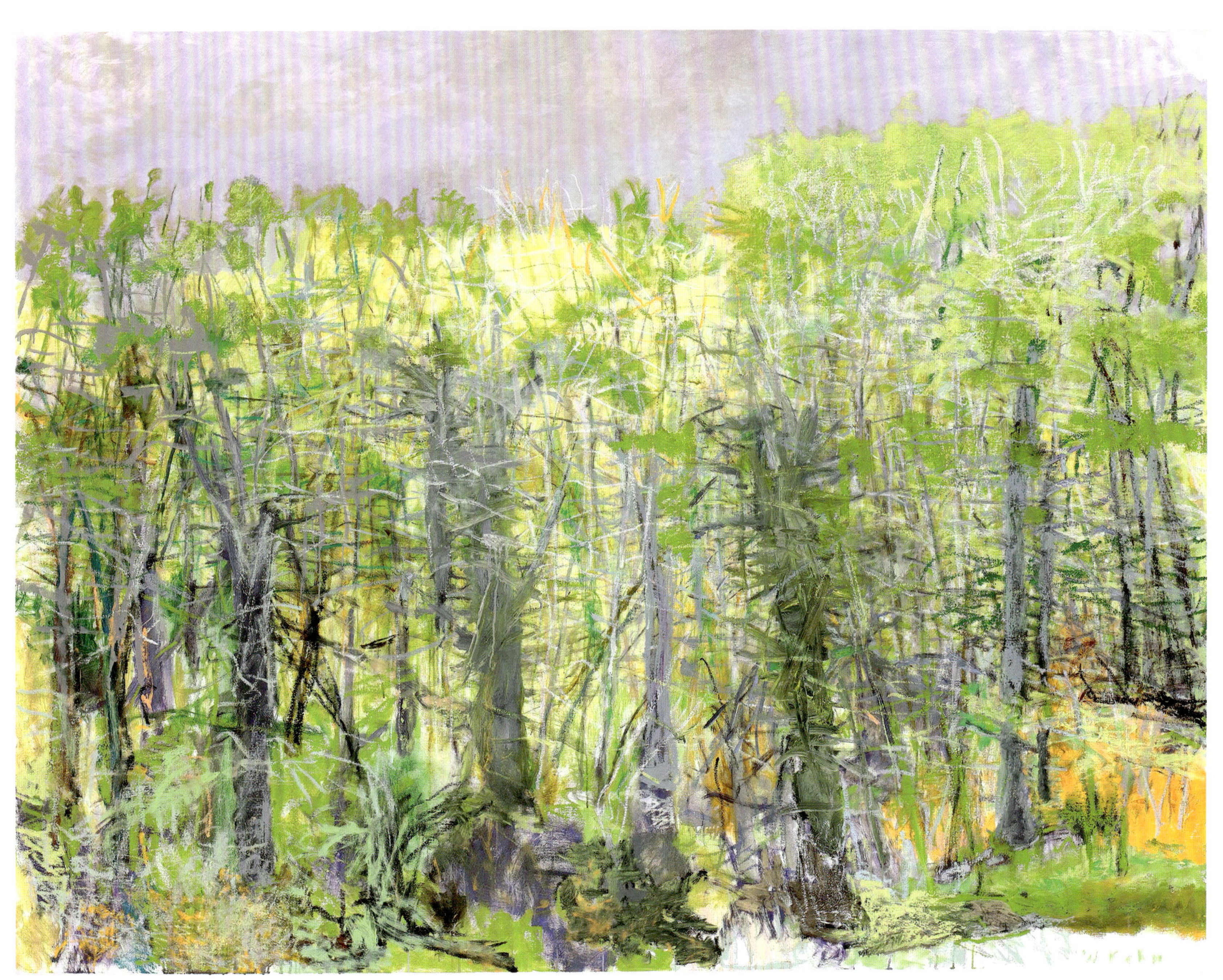

Textured
2013
oil on canvas
32 x 44 inches

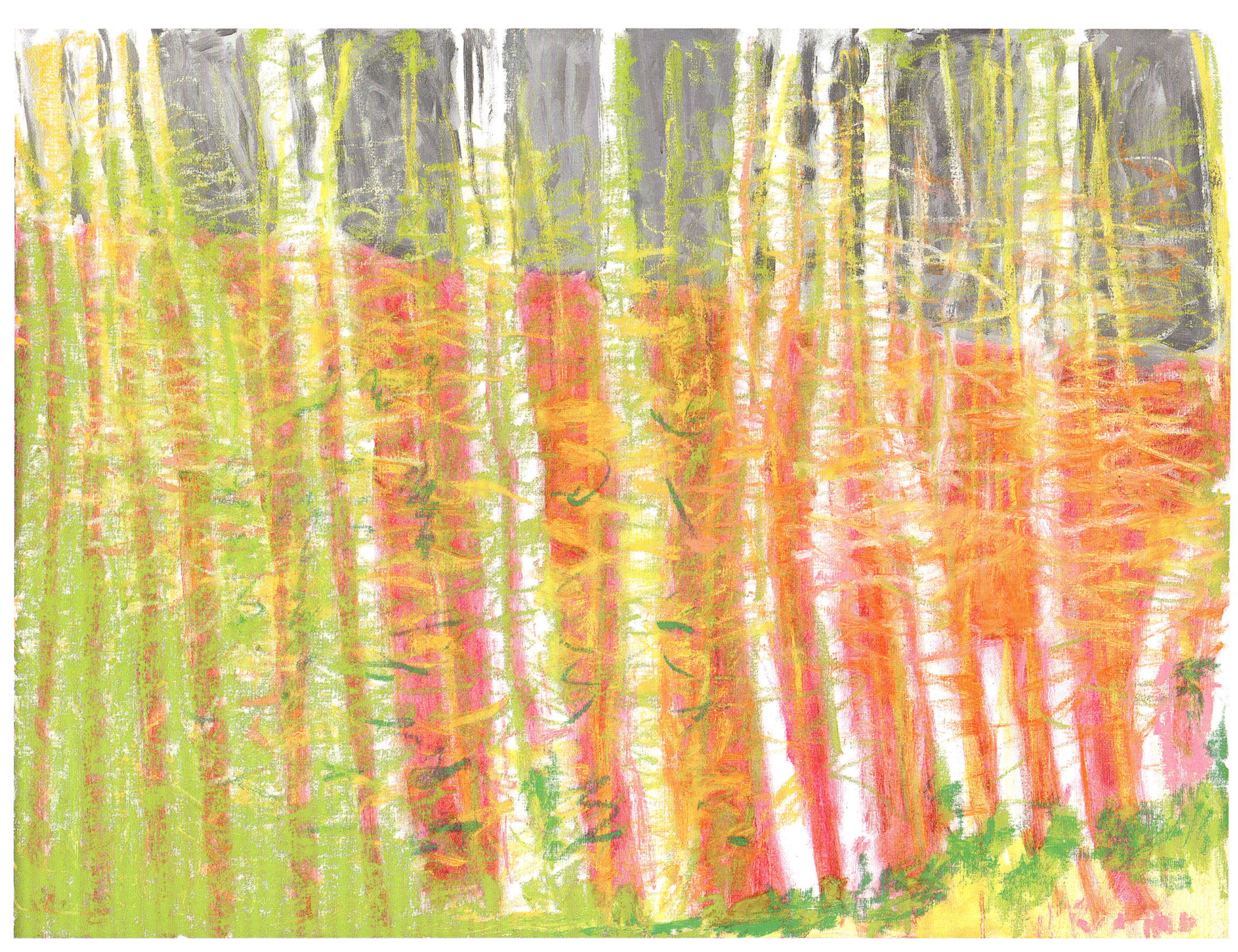

Translucent
2013
oil on canvas
30 x 52 inches

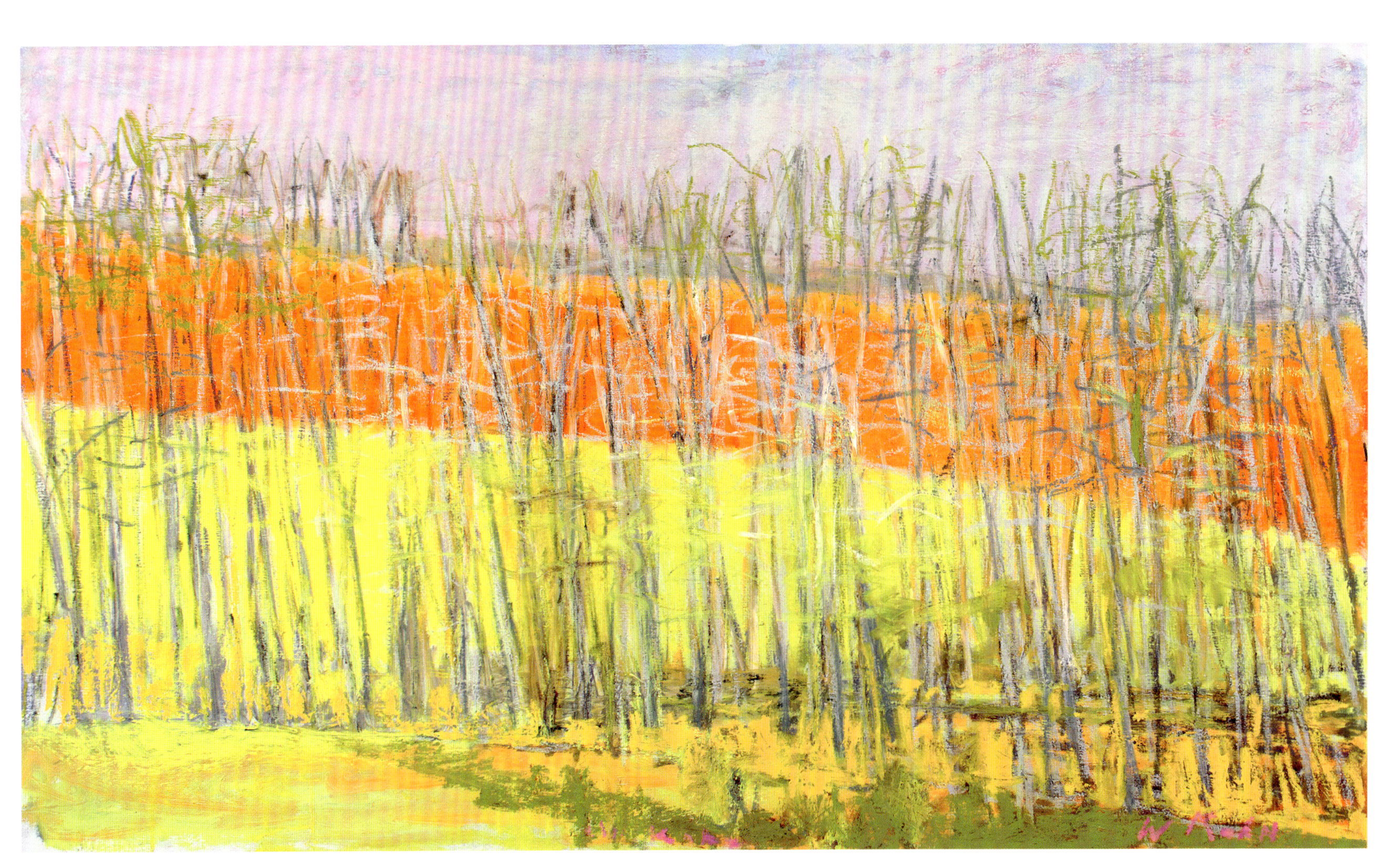

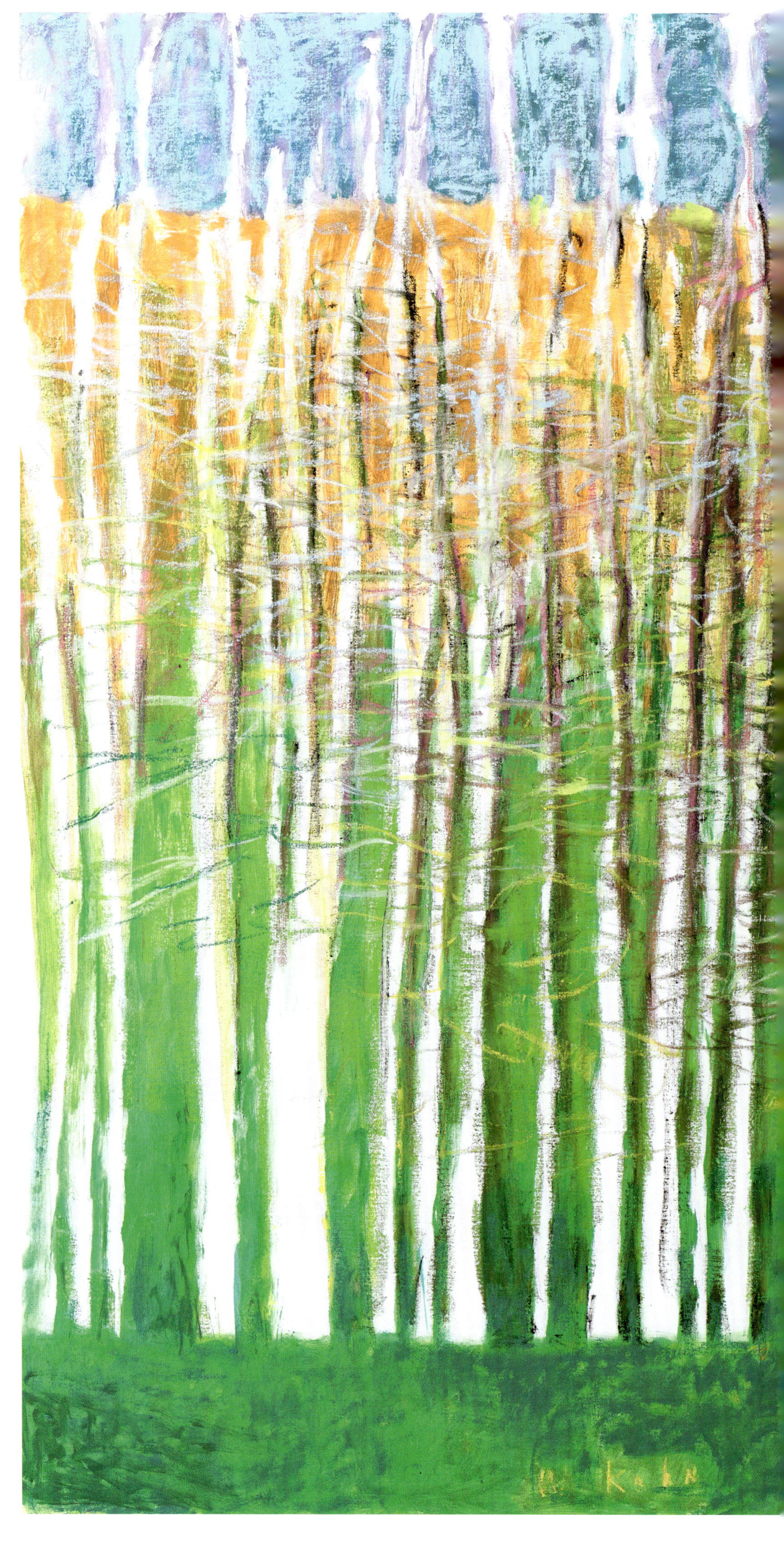

Large Tree Parade
2013
oil on canvas
64 x 90 inches

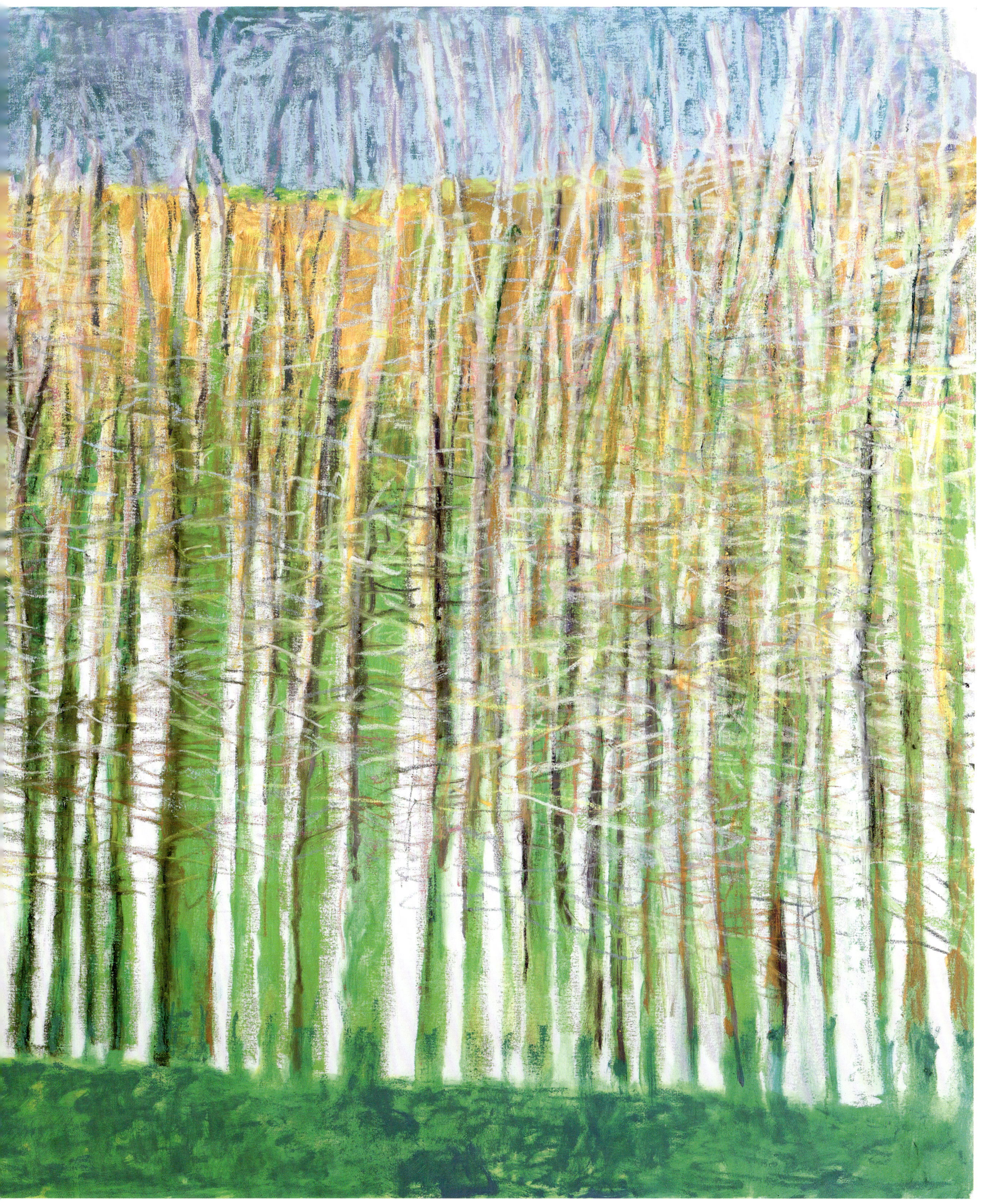

Red Barns
2013
oil on canvas
36 x 52 inches

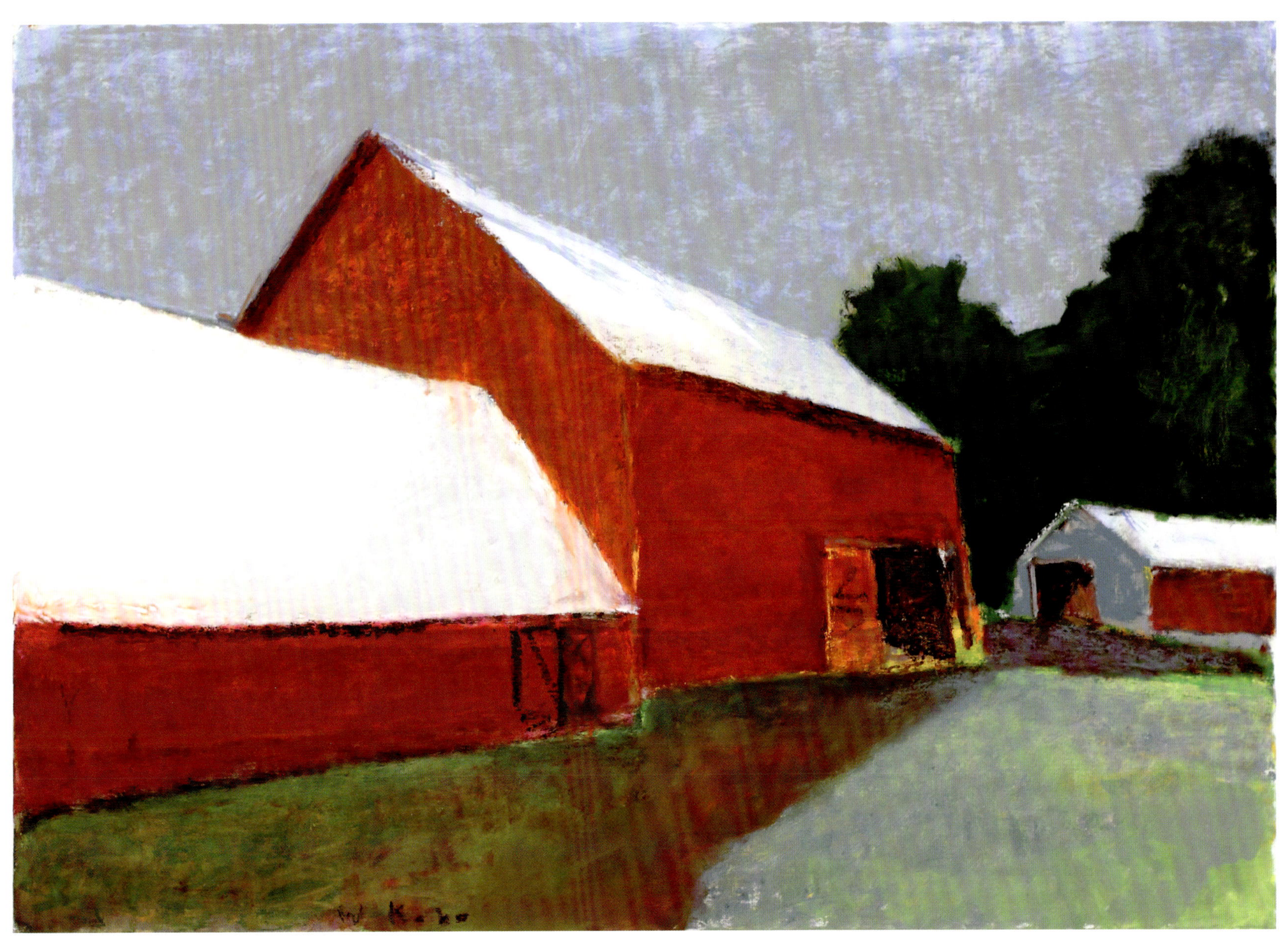

Celebrating Blue Gray
(Large Version)
2013
oil on canvas
52 x 52 inches

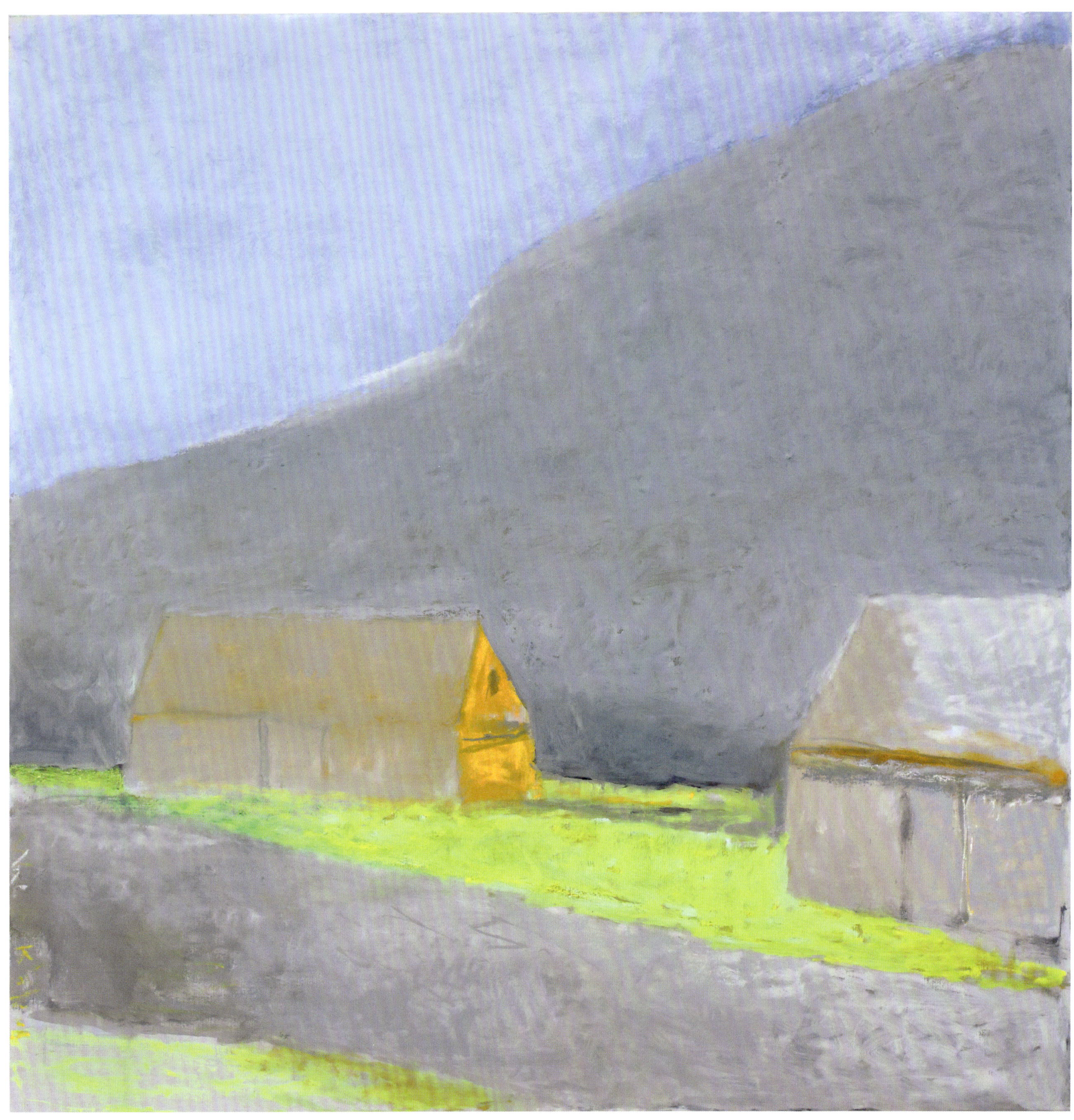

On the Leyden Road
(Large Version)
2013
oil on canvas
52 x 76 inches

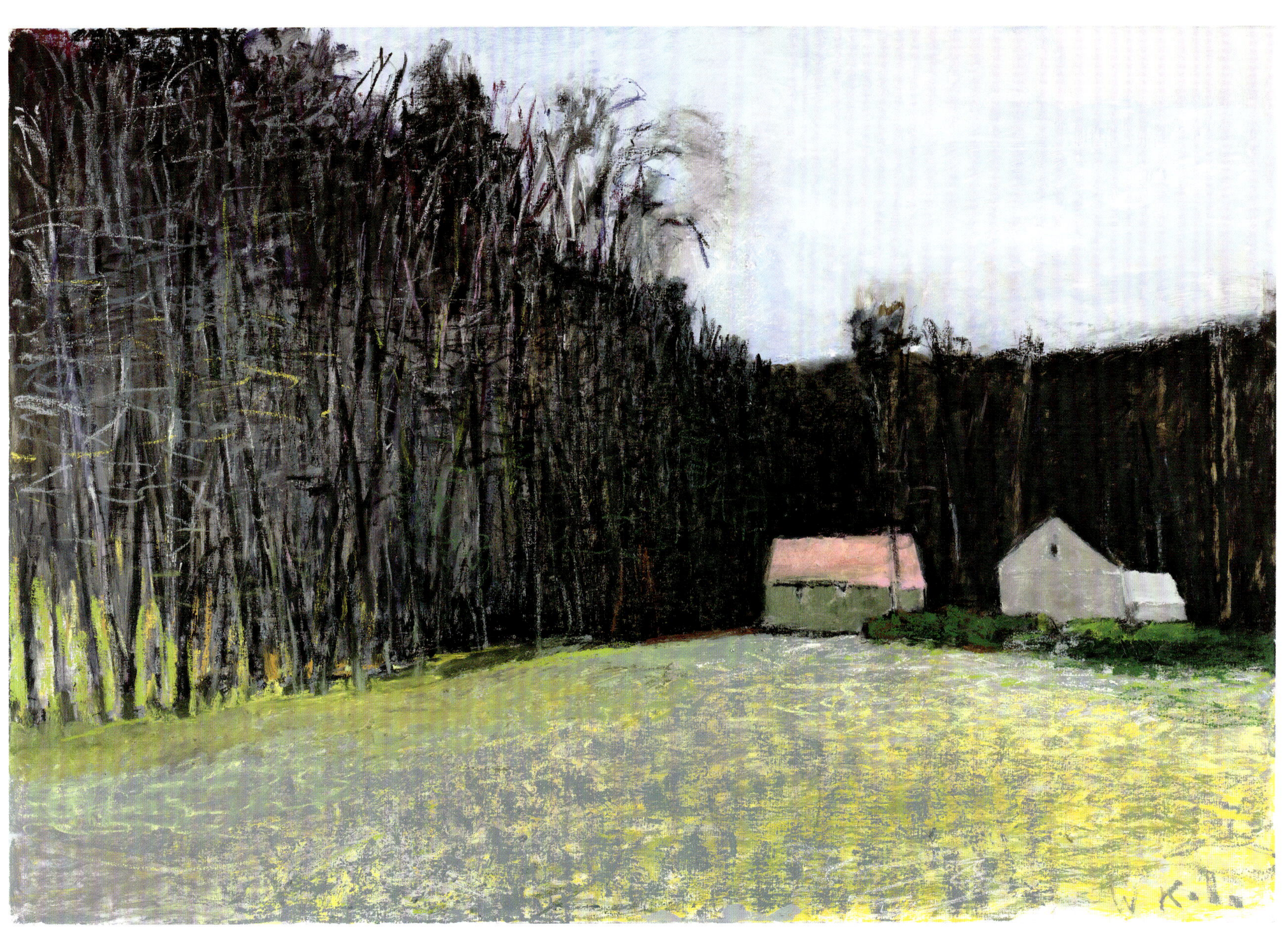

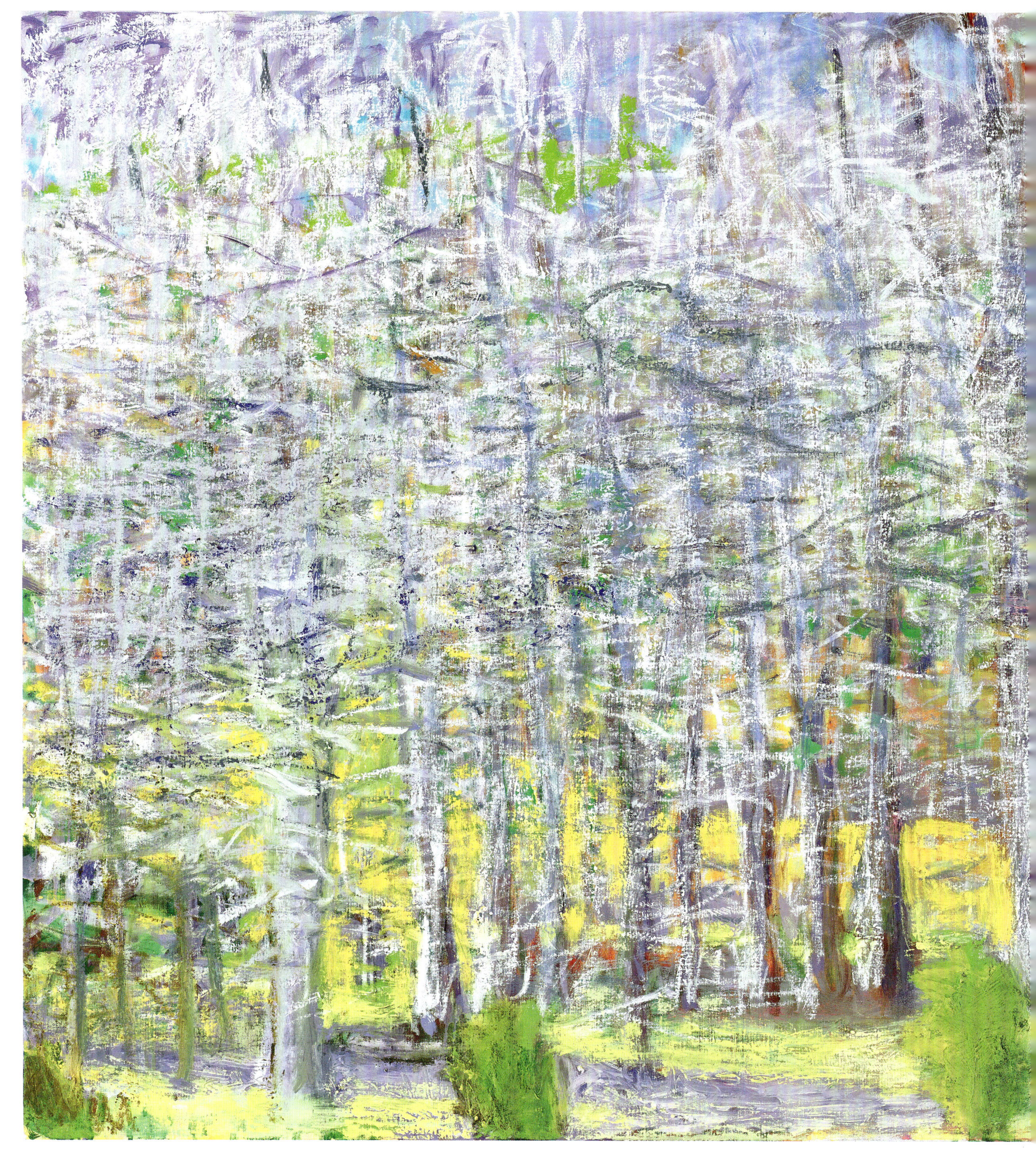

Horizontal/Silvery
2013
oil on canvas
36 x 68 inches

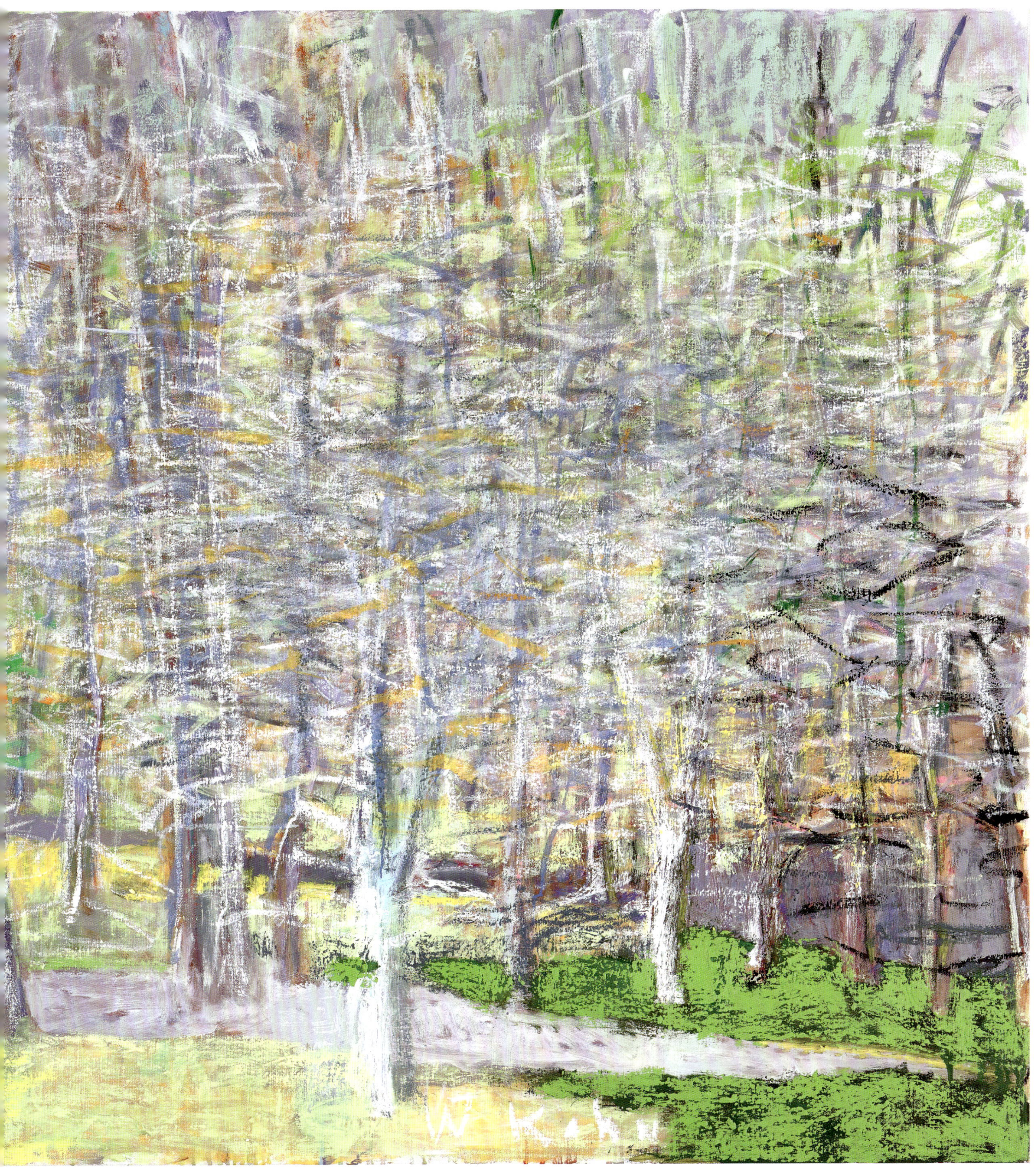
W. Kahn

River Bend
2013
oil on canvas
36 x 44 inches

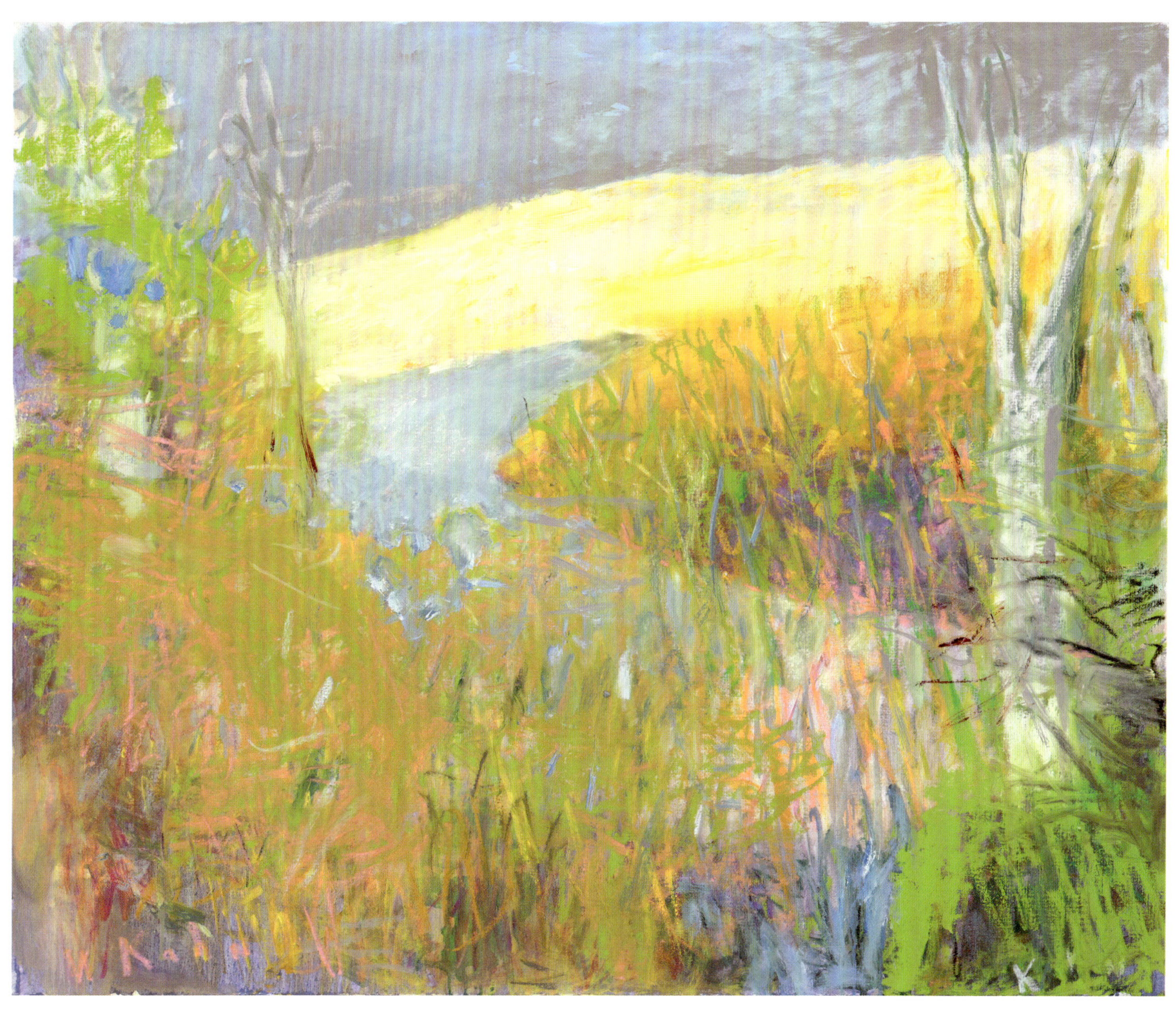

Deserted Barn
2013
oil on canvas
36 x 44 inches

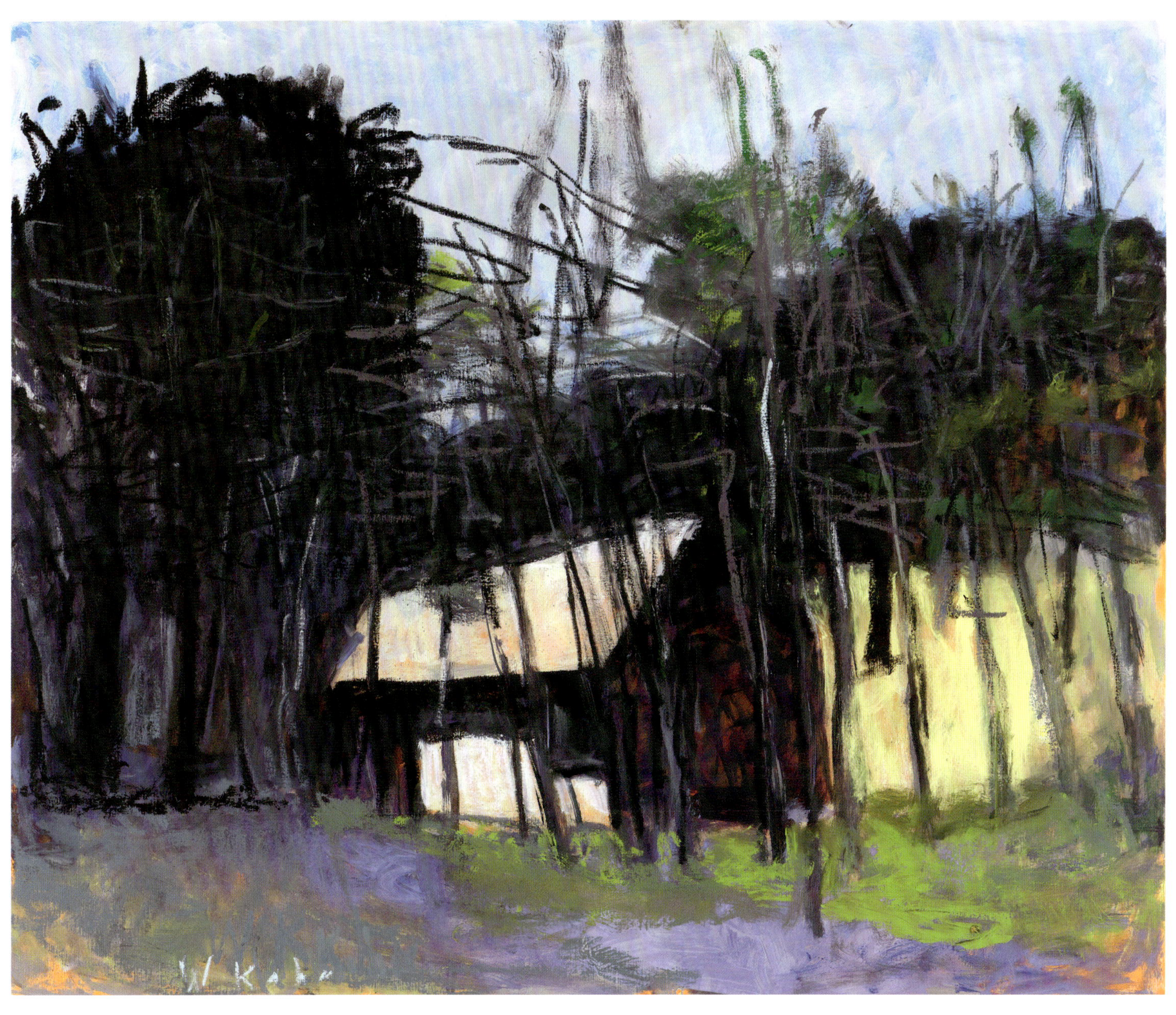

Surprising Blue Background
2014
oil on canvas
52 x 60 inches

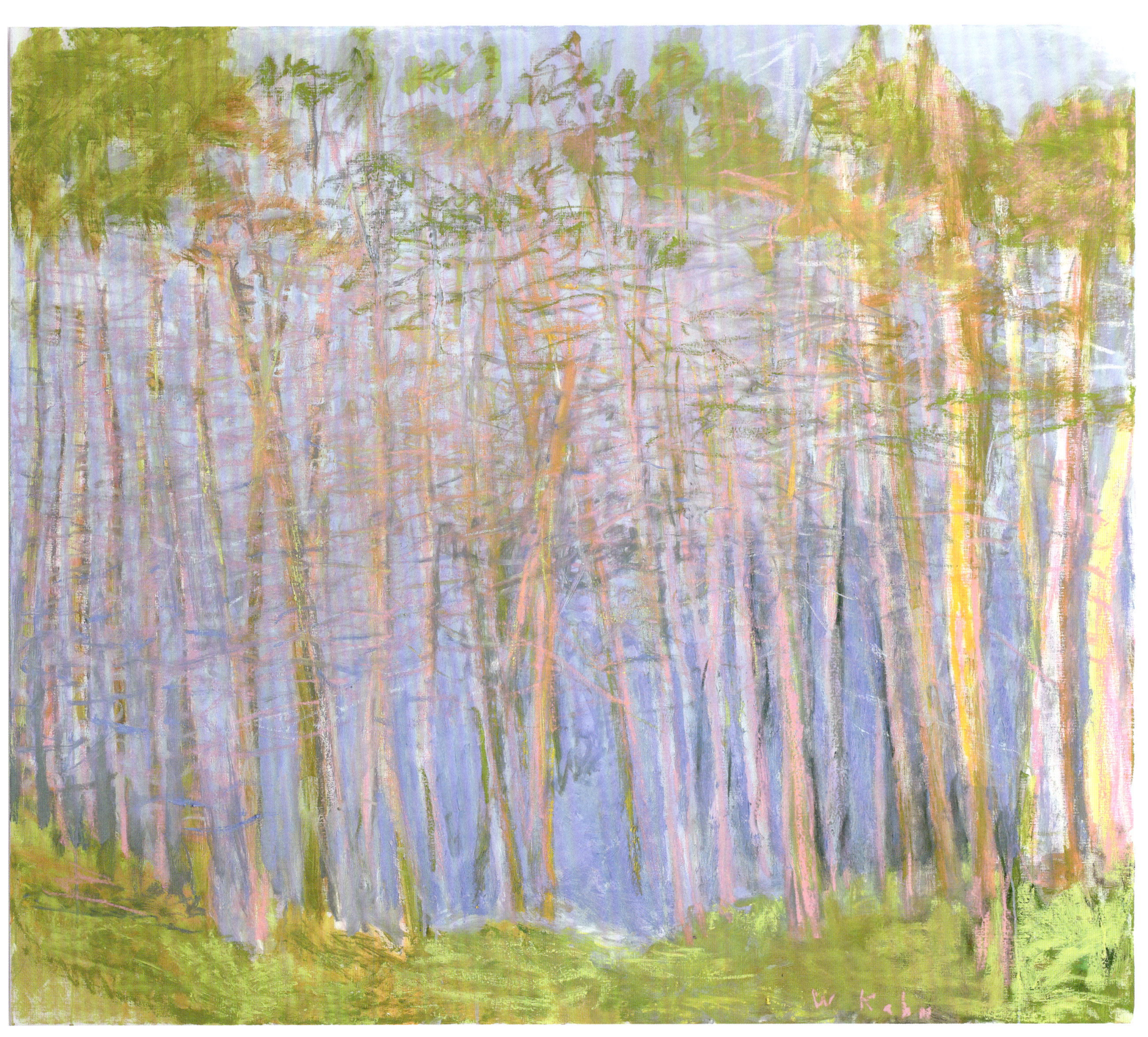
W Kahn

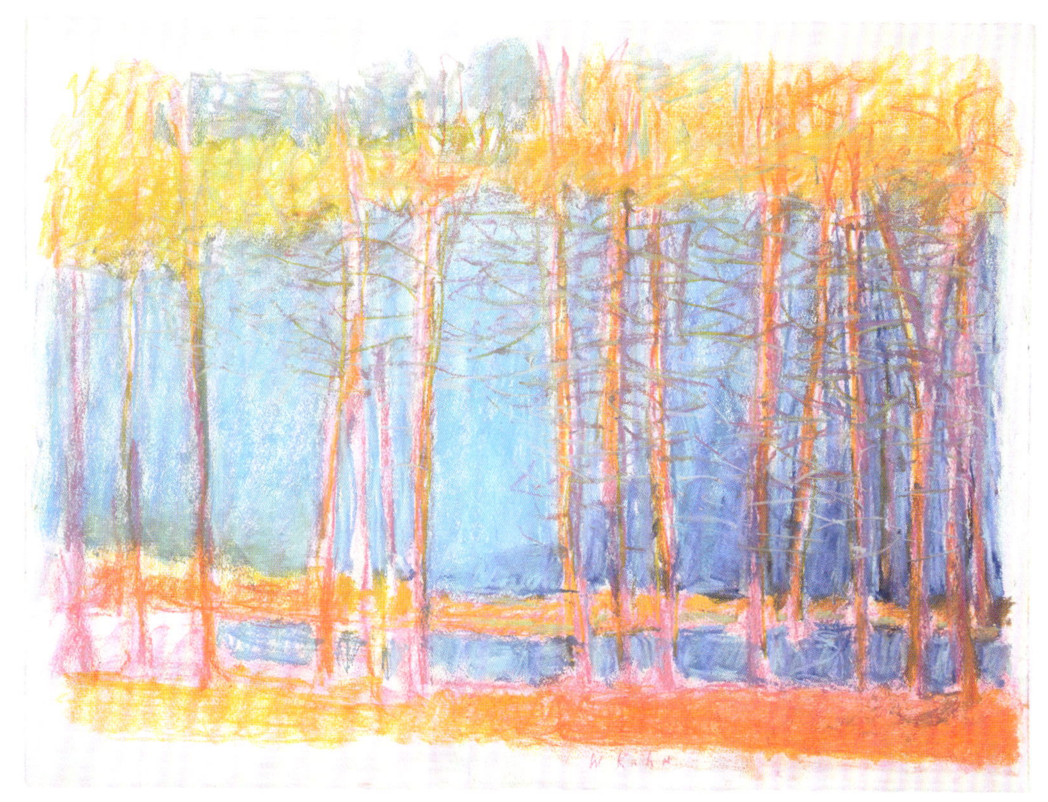

Cove
2014
pastel on paper
22 x 30 inches

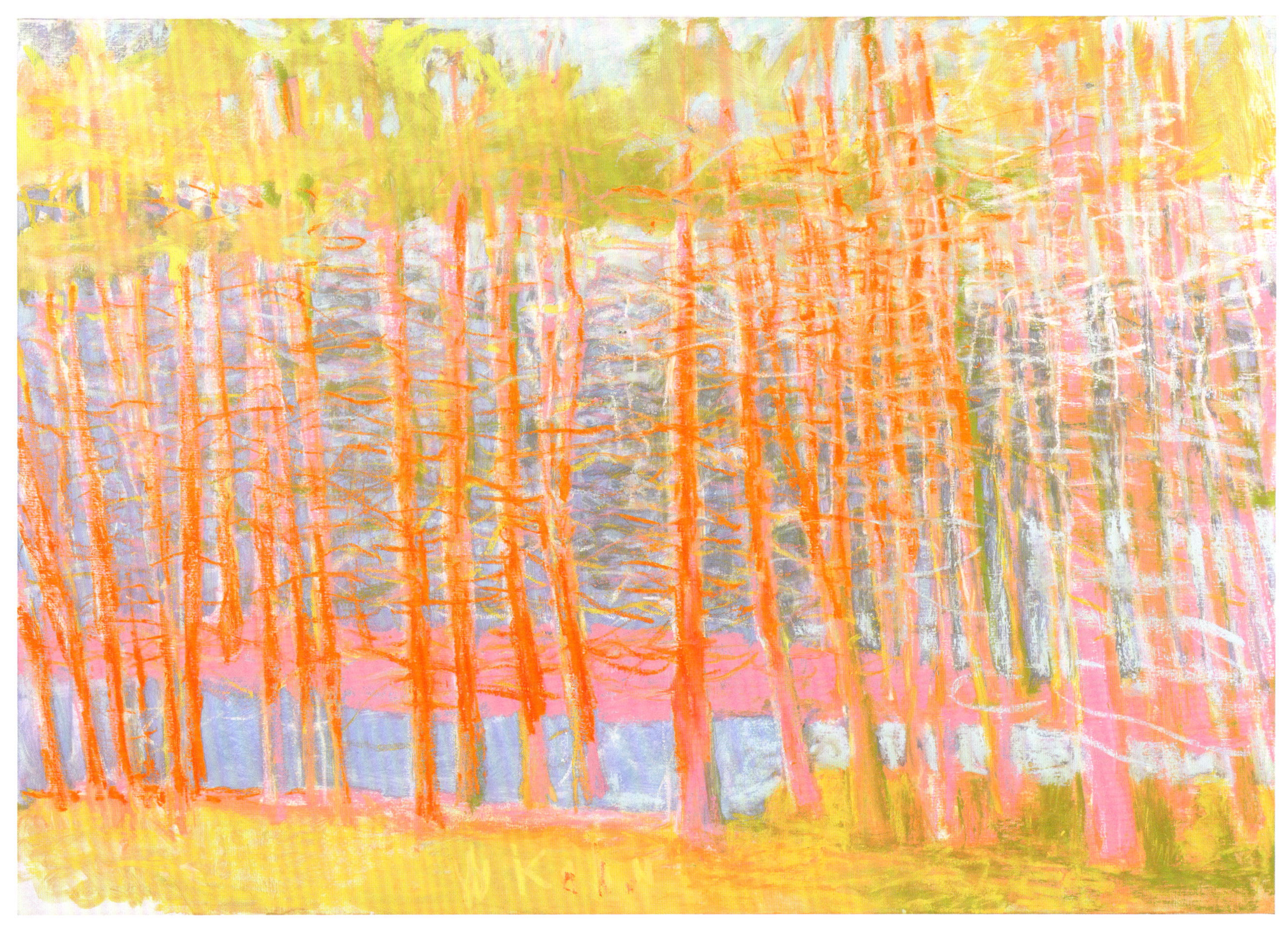

Adopting Rarely Used Reds
2014
oil on canvas
36 x 52 inches

Black Tangle
2014
oil on canvas
52 x 52 inches

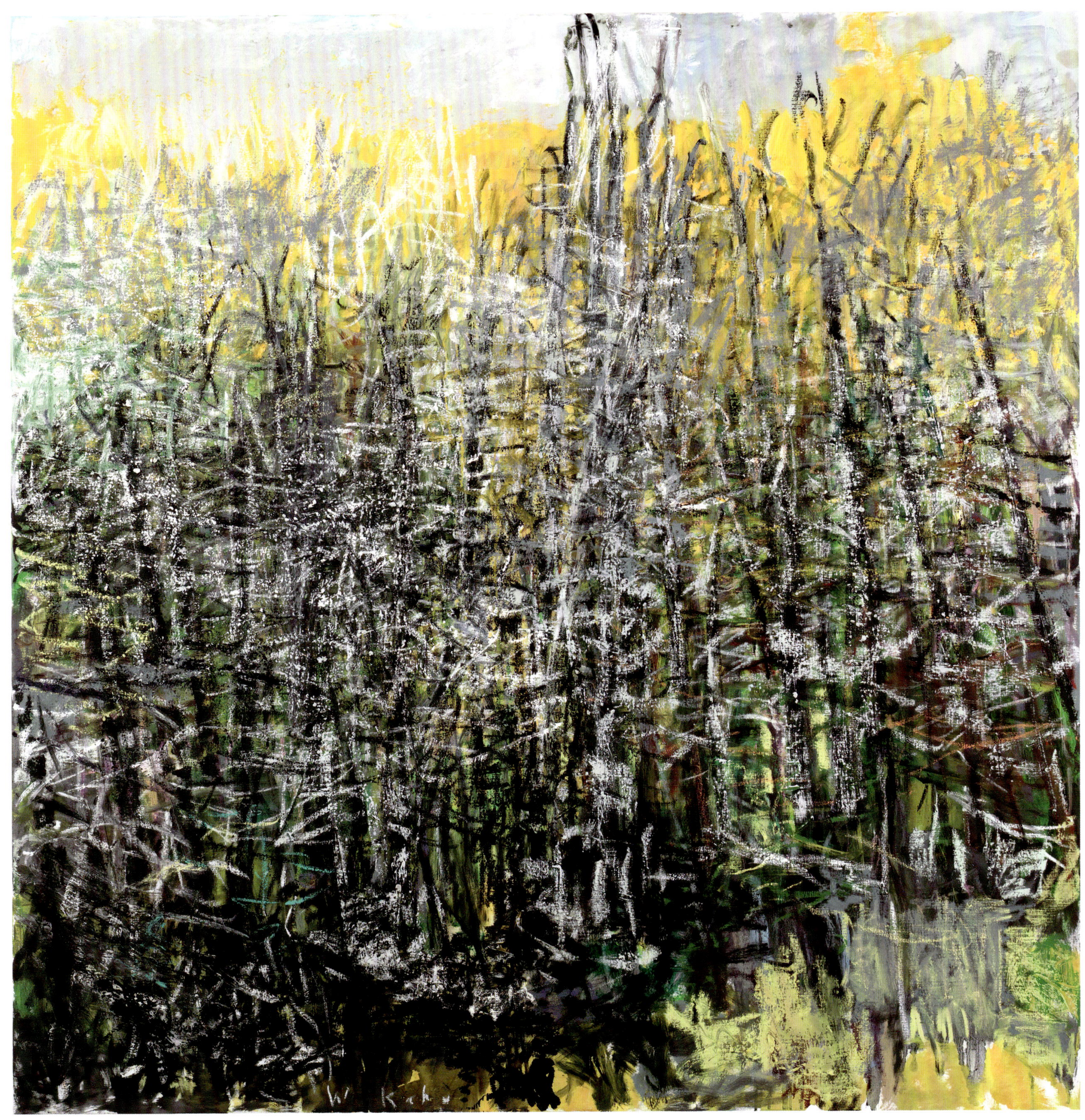

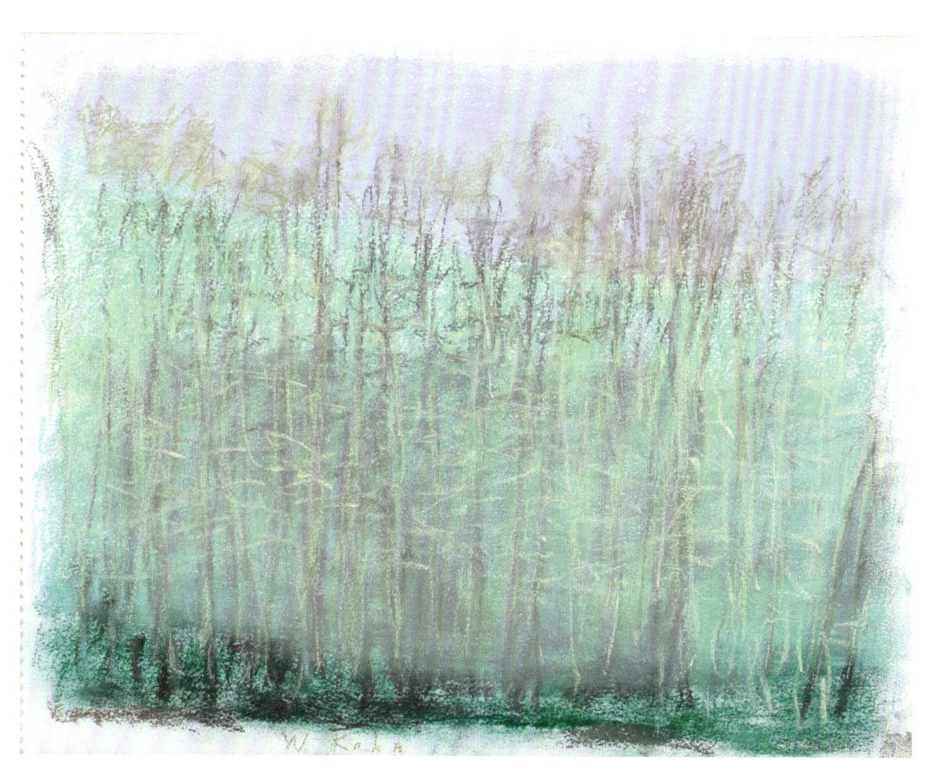

Study for Overall Green
2014
pastel on paper
14 x 18 inches

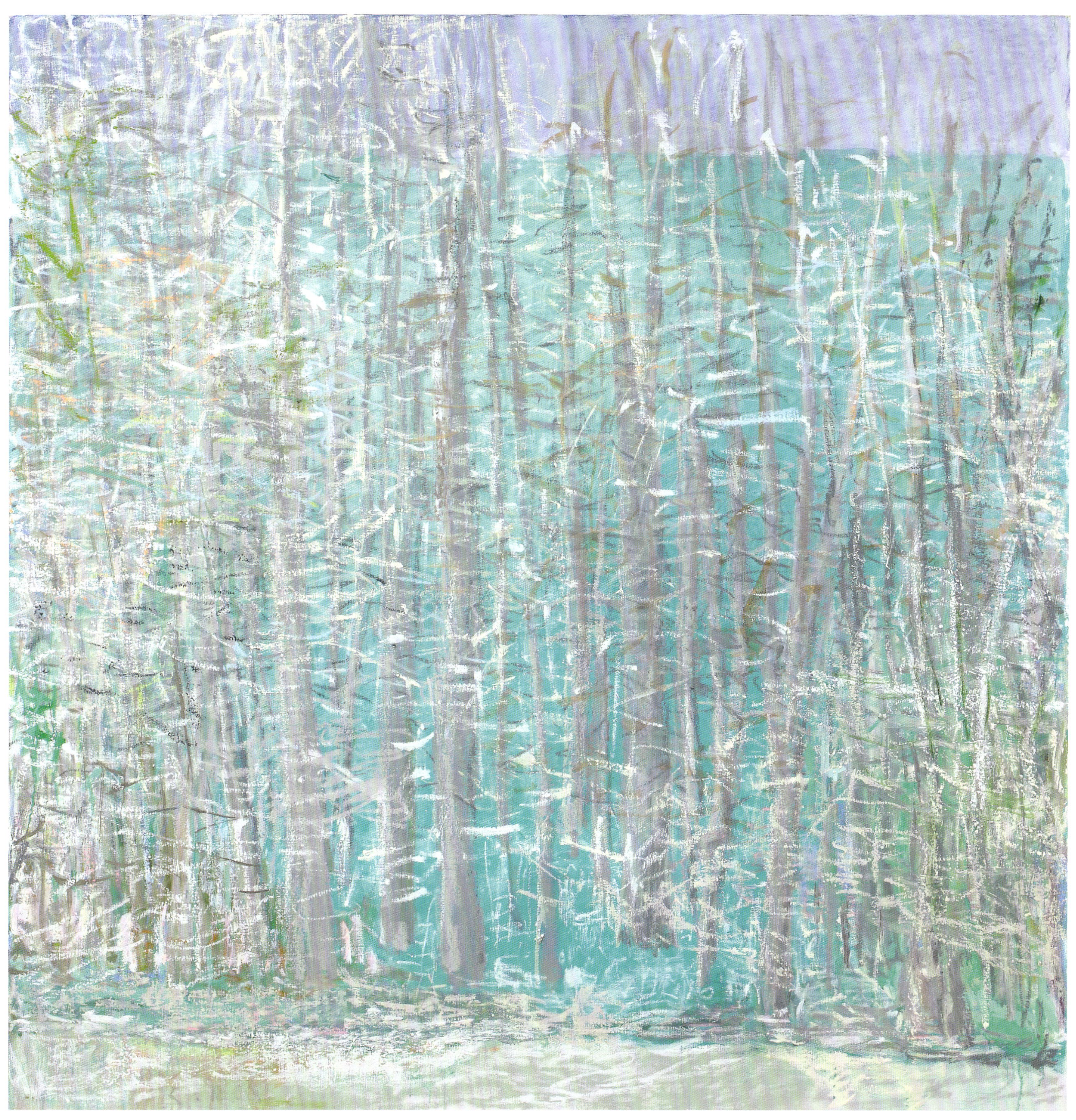

Overall Blue Green
2014
oil on canvas
52 x 52 inches

Green Remains
2014
oil on canvas
66 x 52 inches

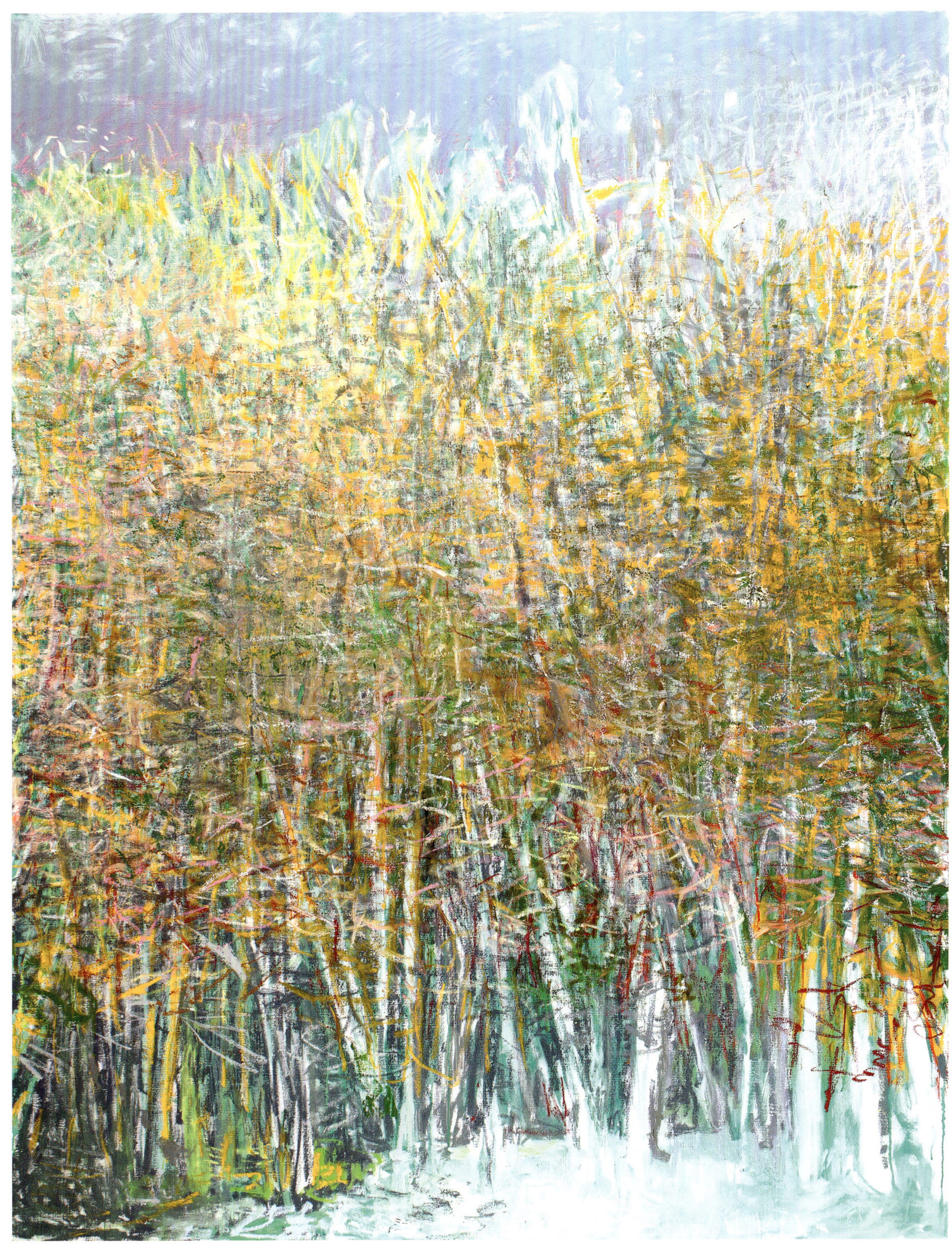

Uphill
2014
oil on canvas
52 x 52 inches

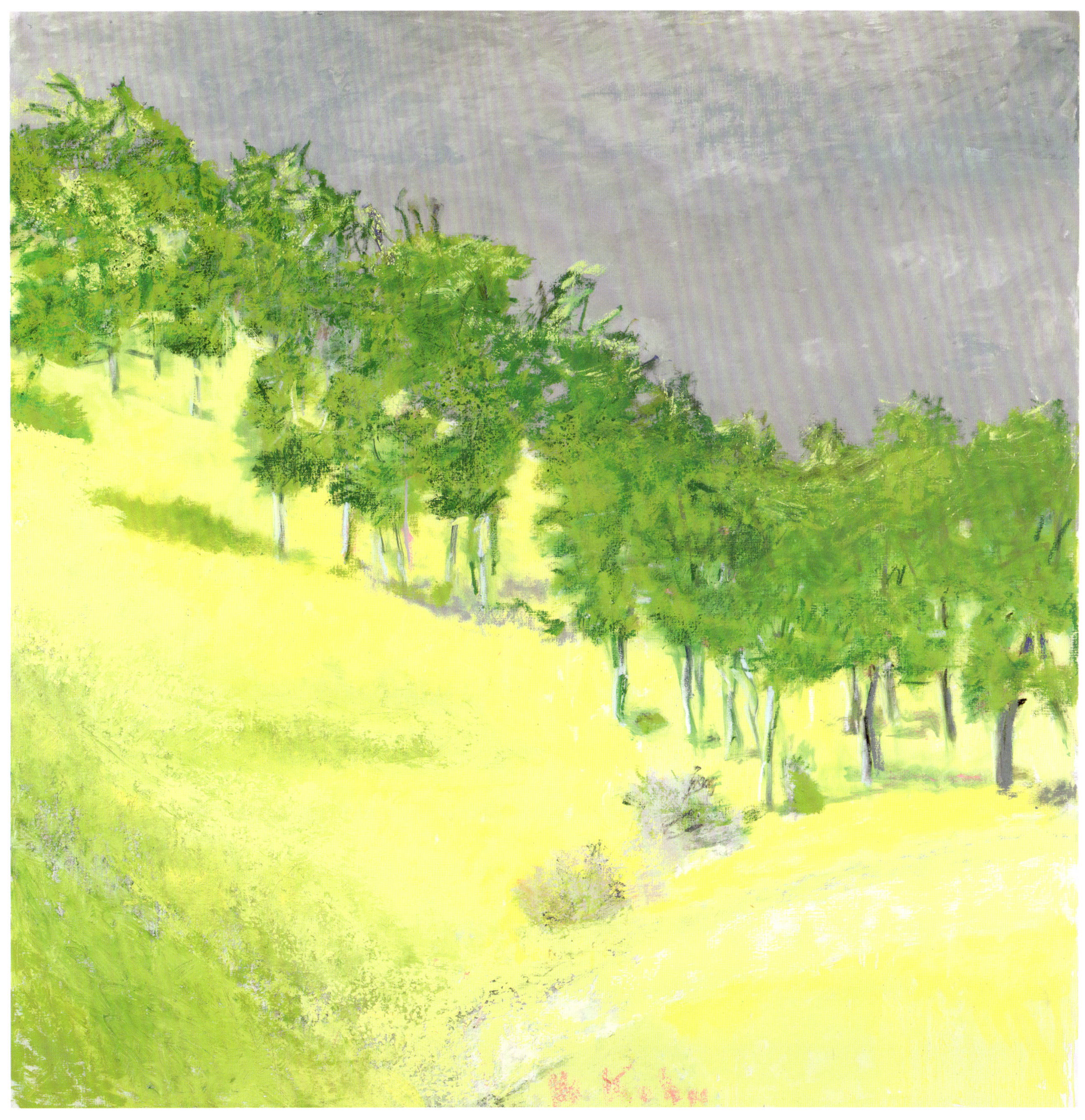

Stand of Trees
2014
oil on canvas
40 x 52 inches

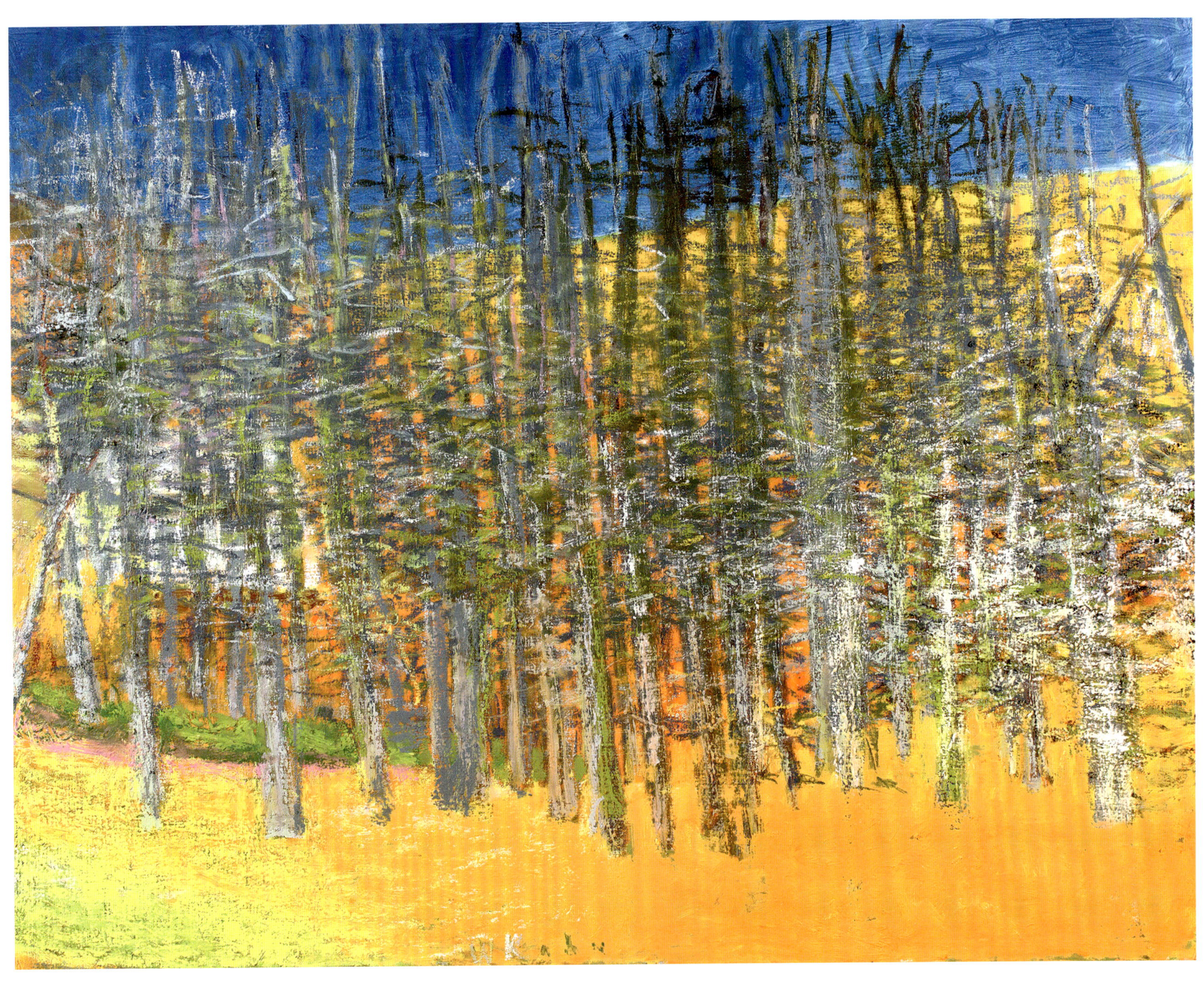

Copse
2014
oil on canvas
36 x 68 inches

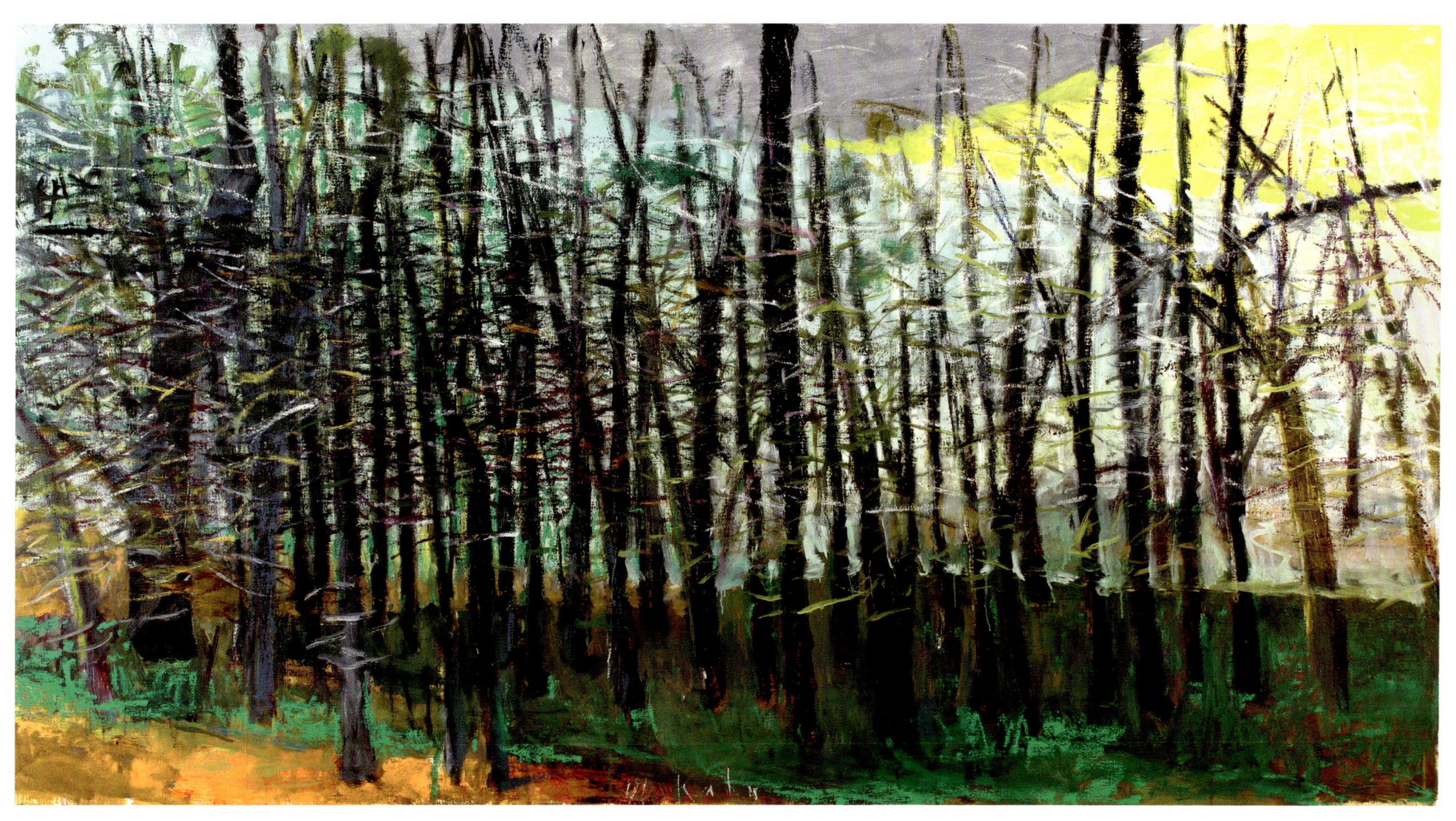

Under a White Sky
2014
oil on canvas
30 x 52 inches

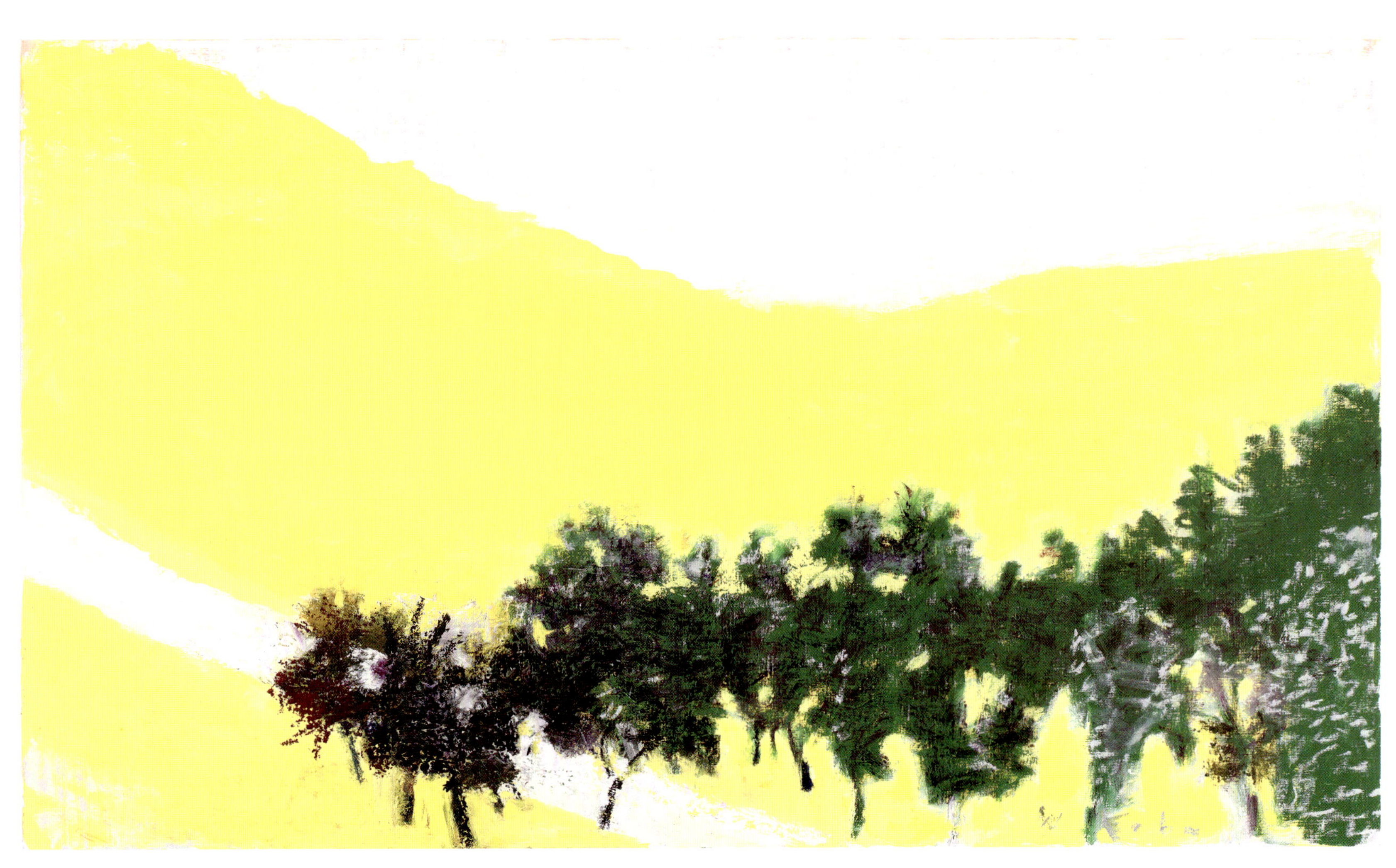

Hidden Greenhouse
2015
oil on canvas
30 x 52 inches

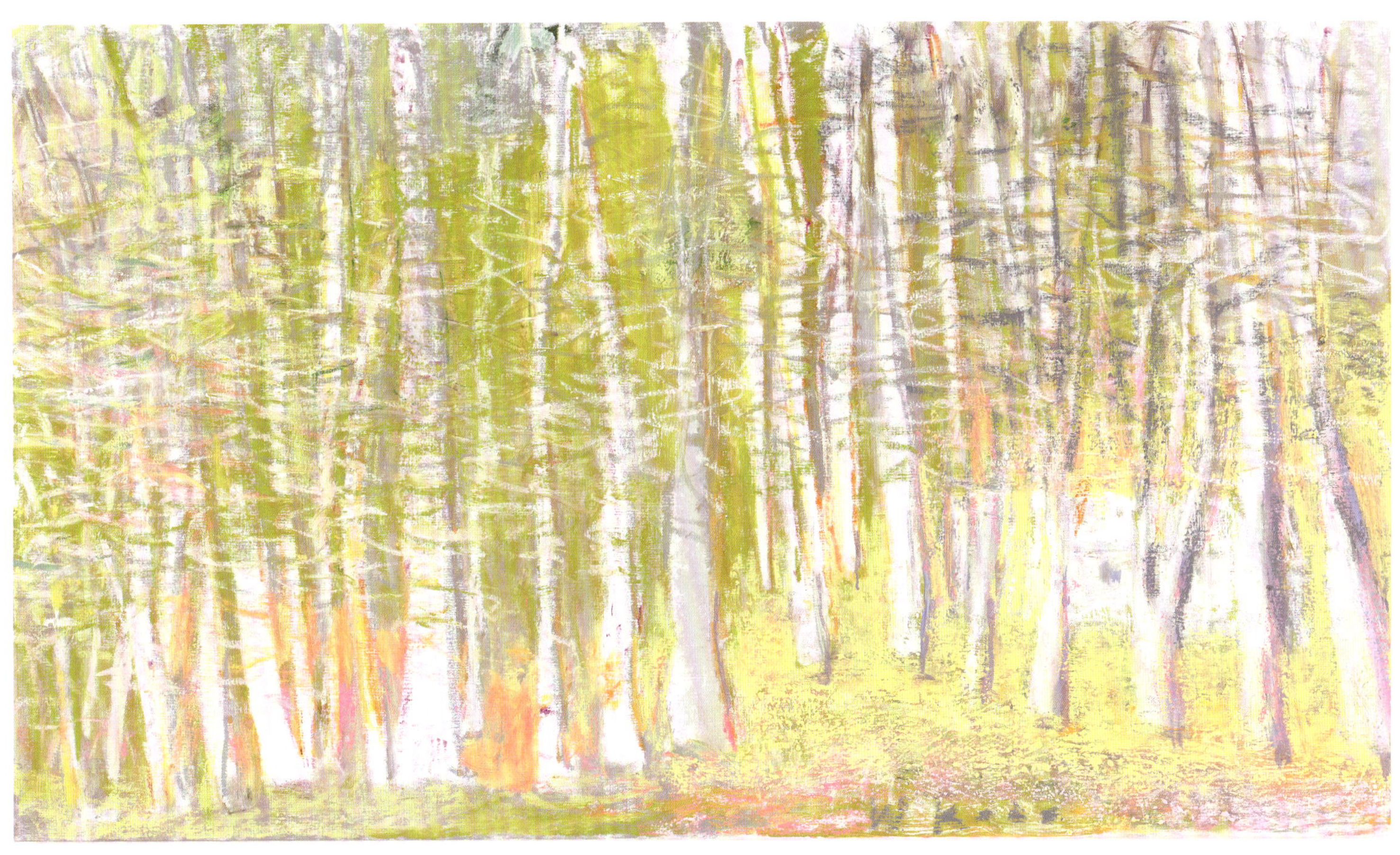

Half Hidden Violet
2015
oil on canvas
52 x 52 inches

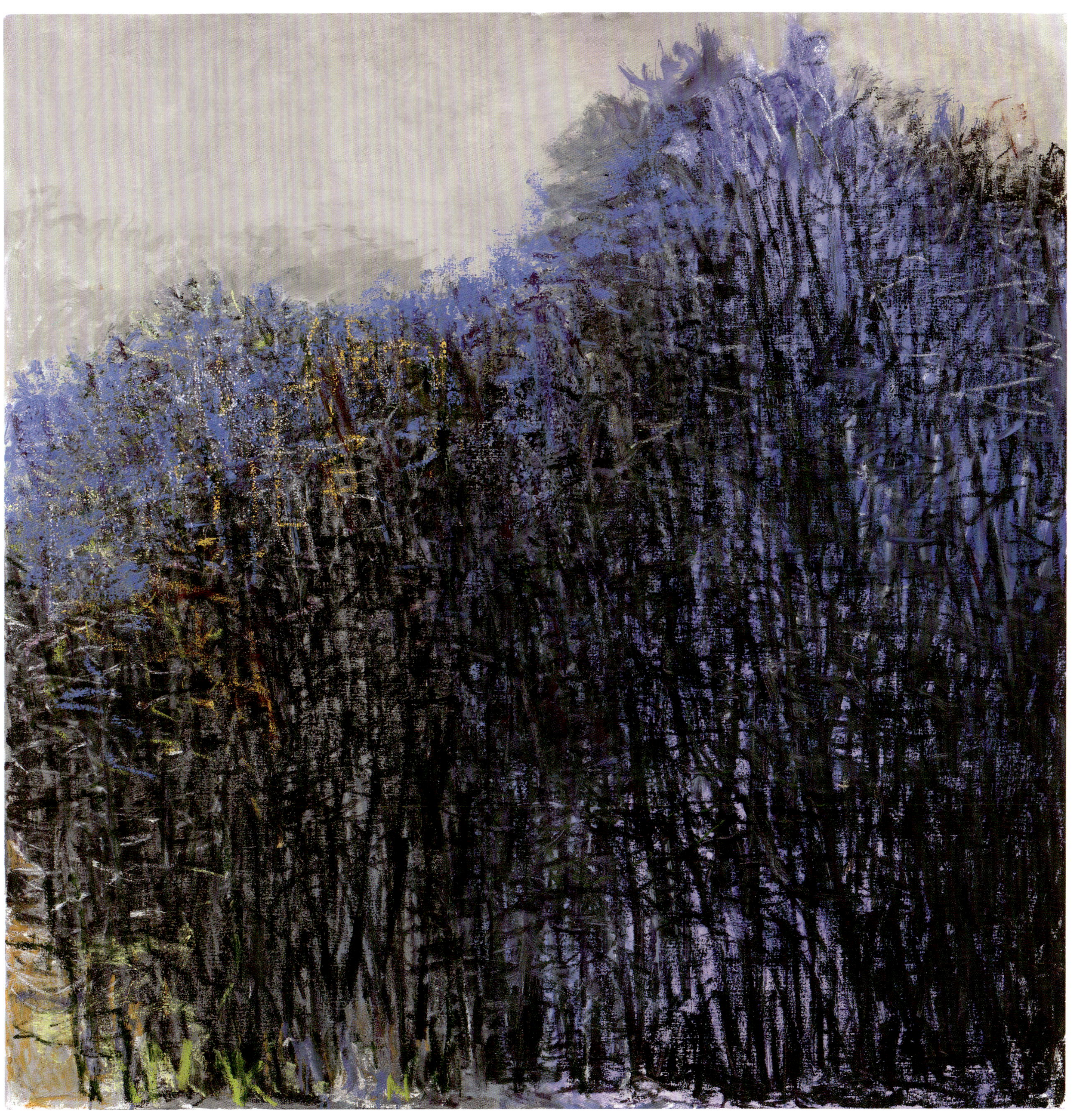

Nearly Opaque
2015
oil on canvas
52 x 52 inches

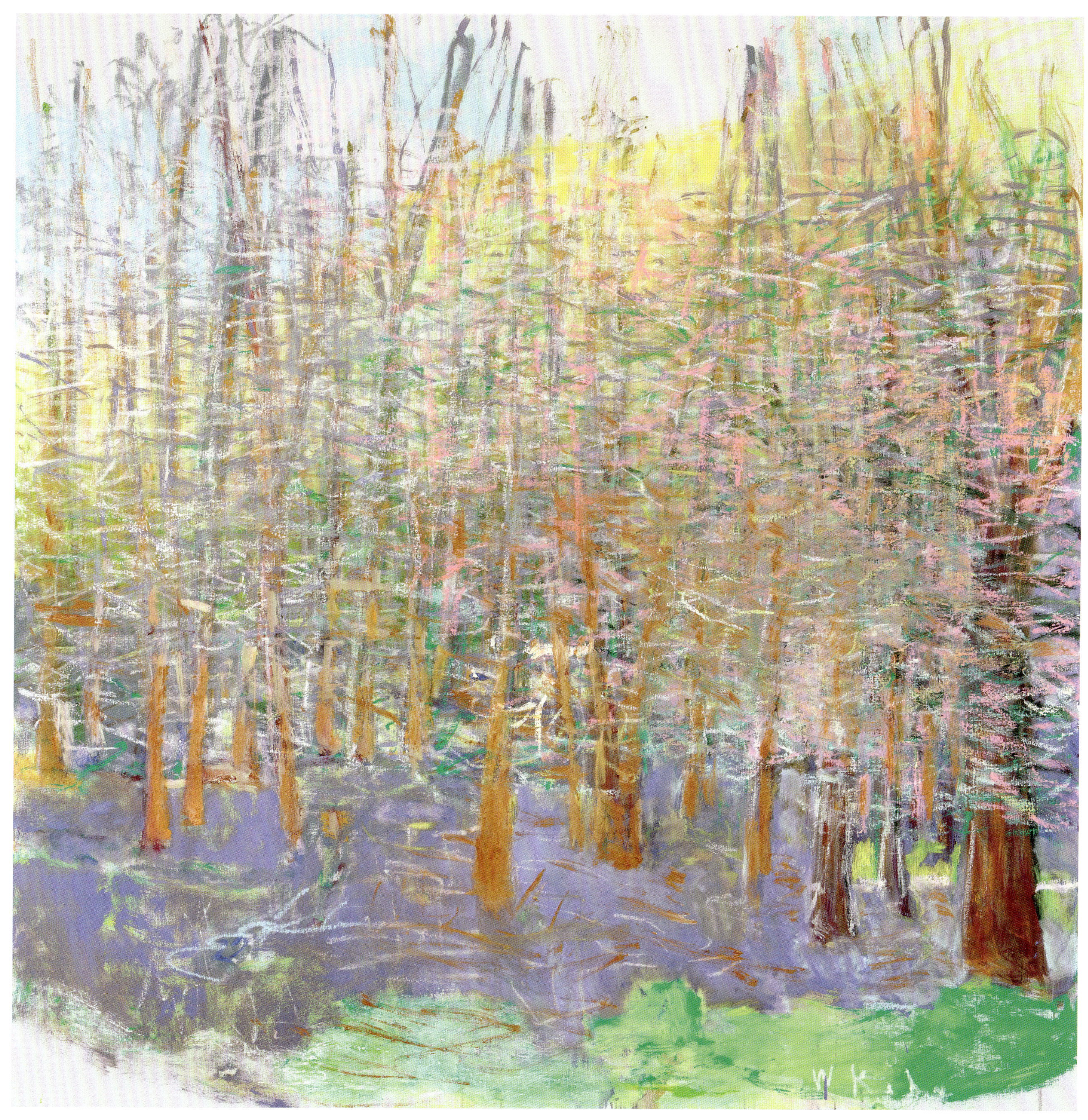

Small Watercourse
2015
oil on canvas
36 x 52 inches

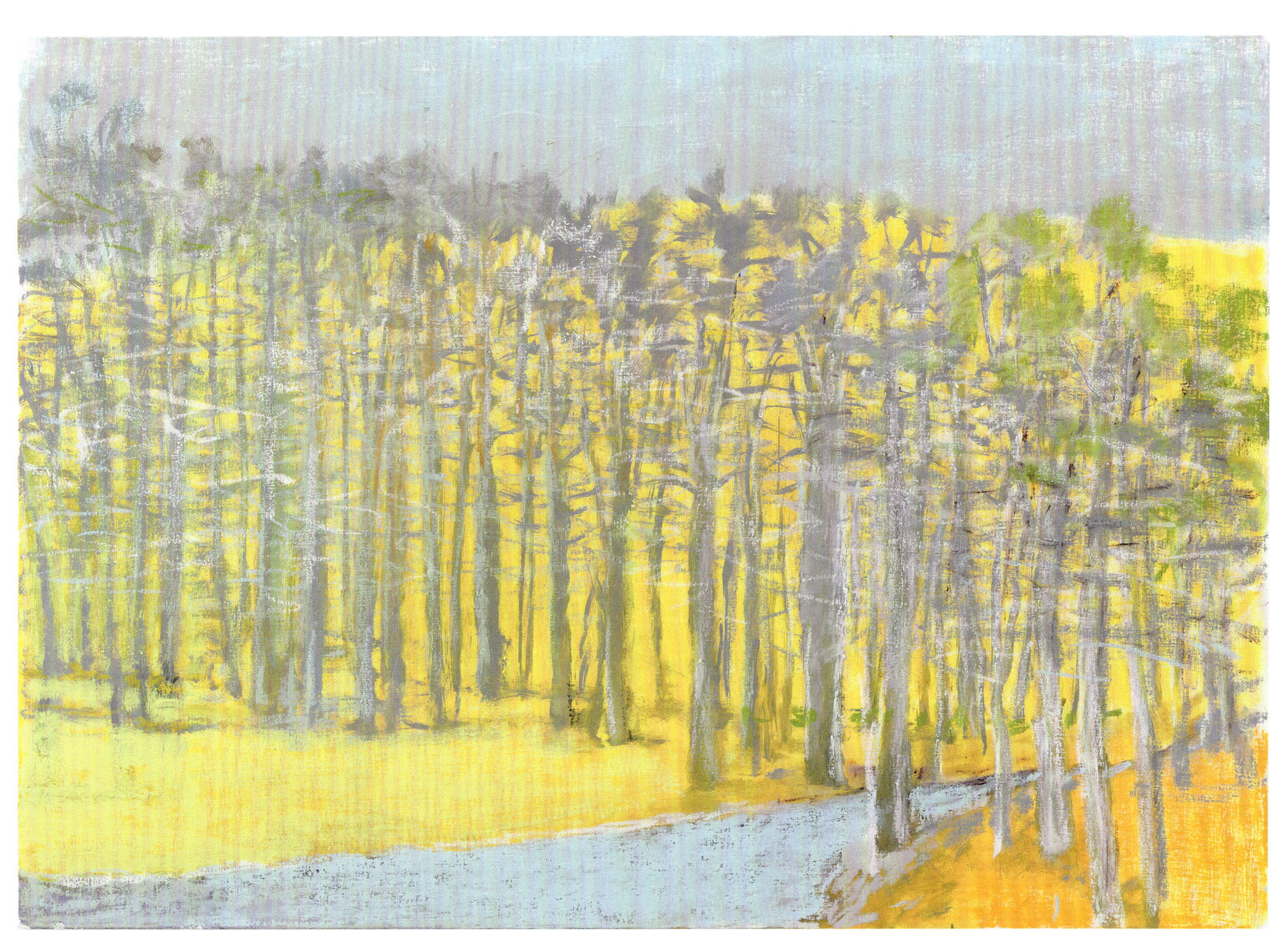

Large Burl
2015
oil on canvas
36 x 52 inches

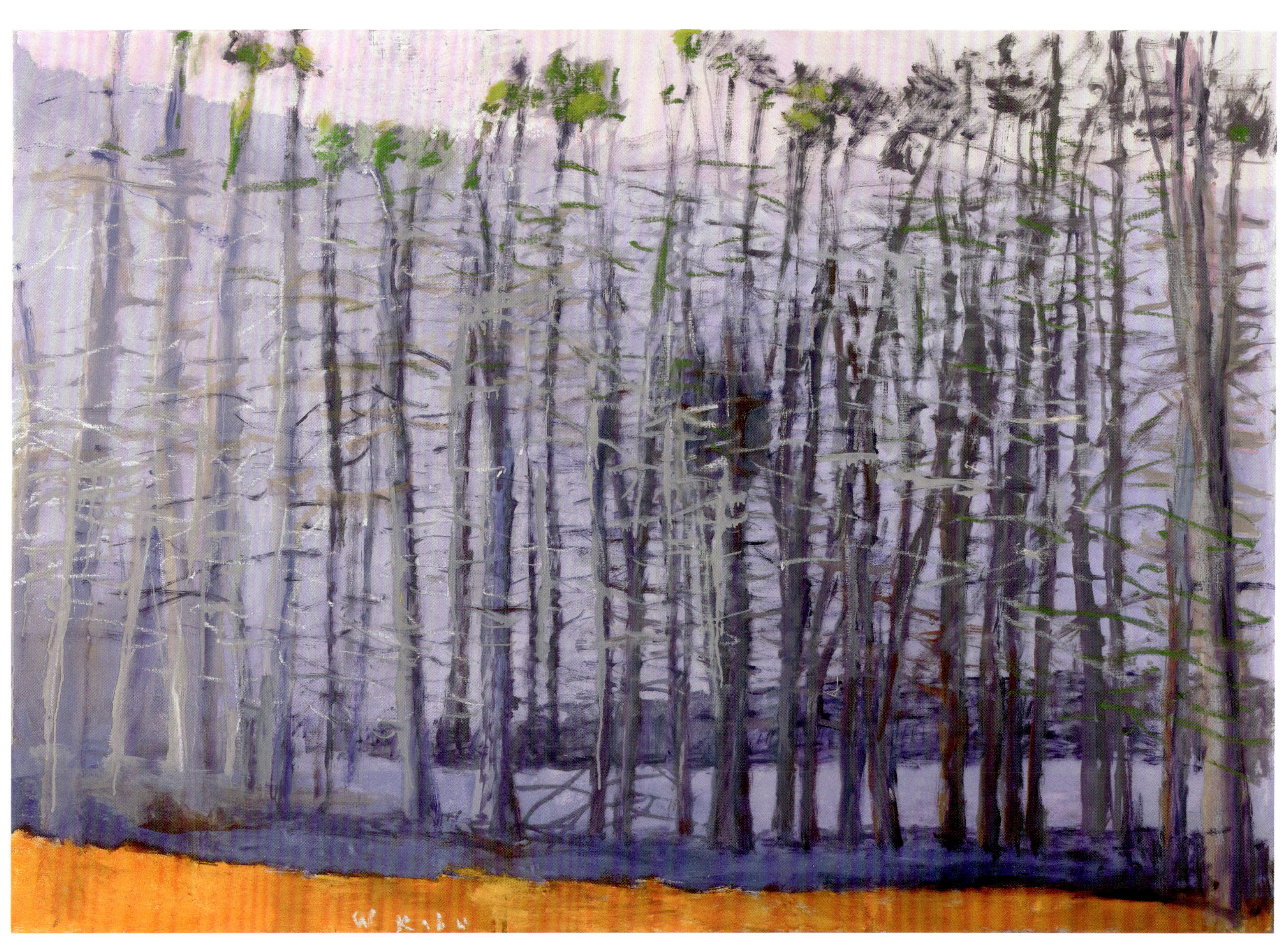

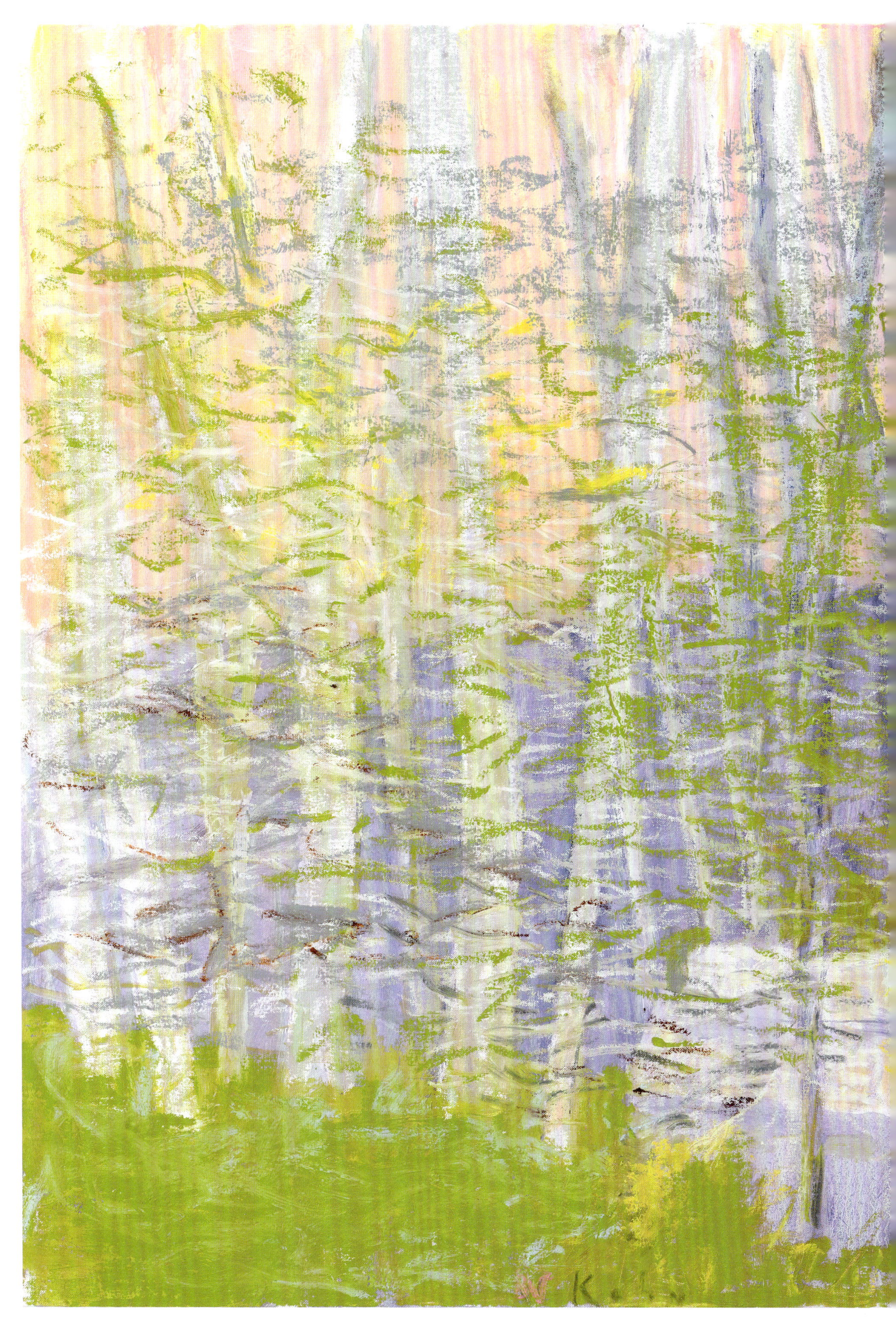

White Barn, White Roof
2015
oil on canvas
36 x 60 inches

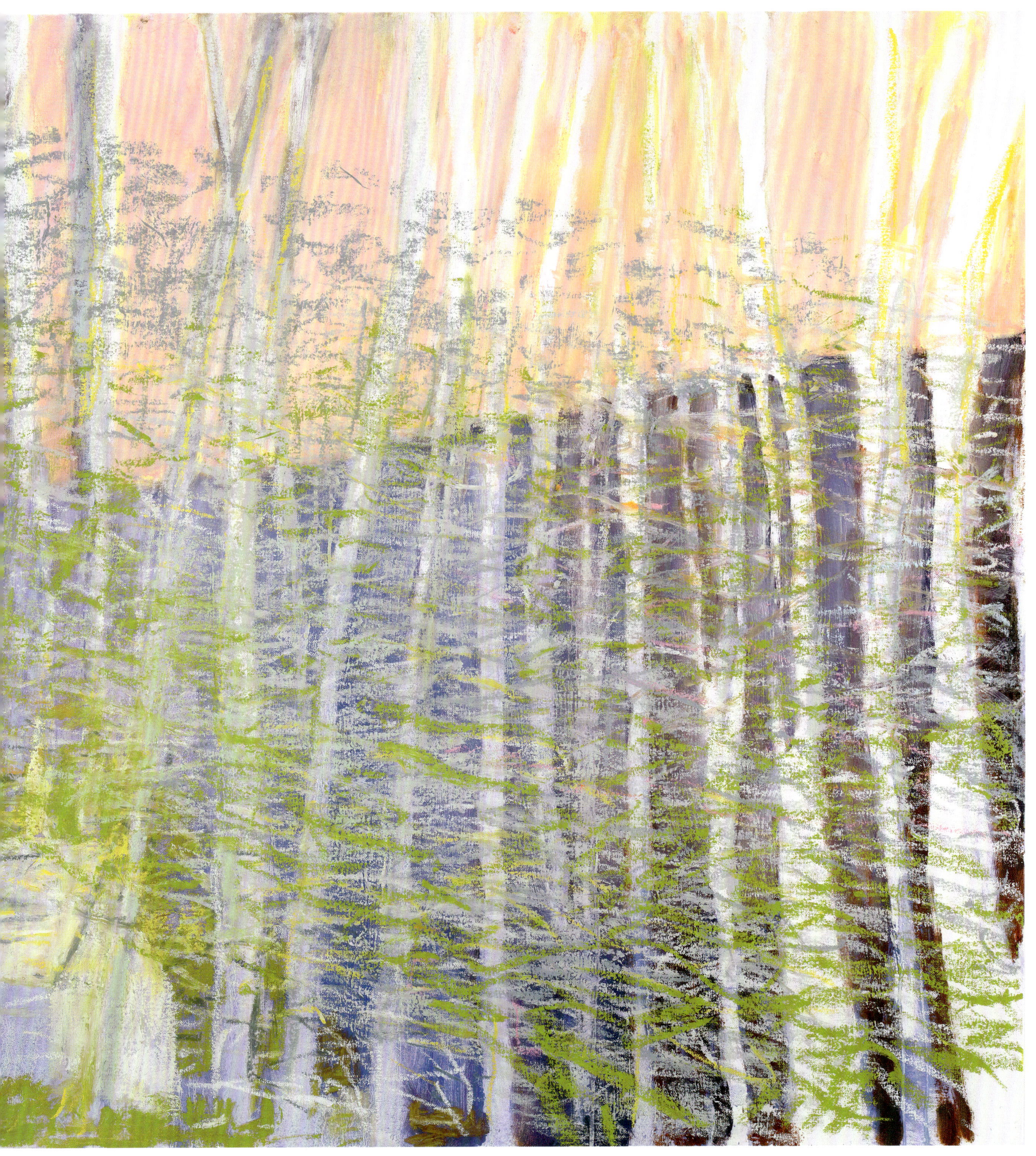

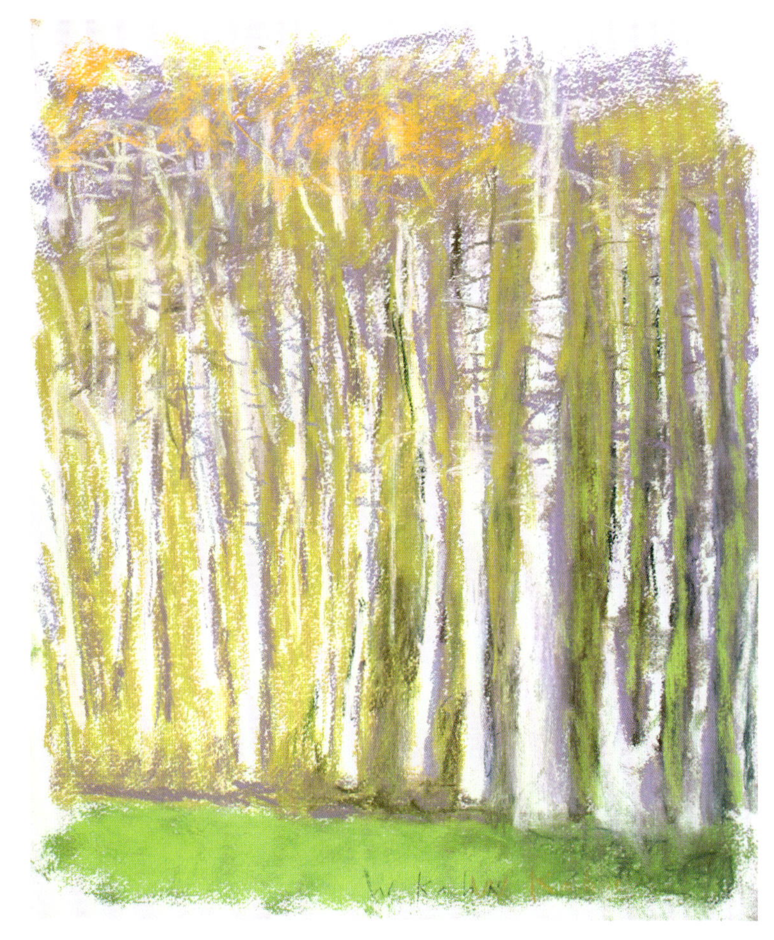

White Background
2014
pastel on paper
17 x 14 inches

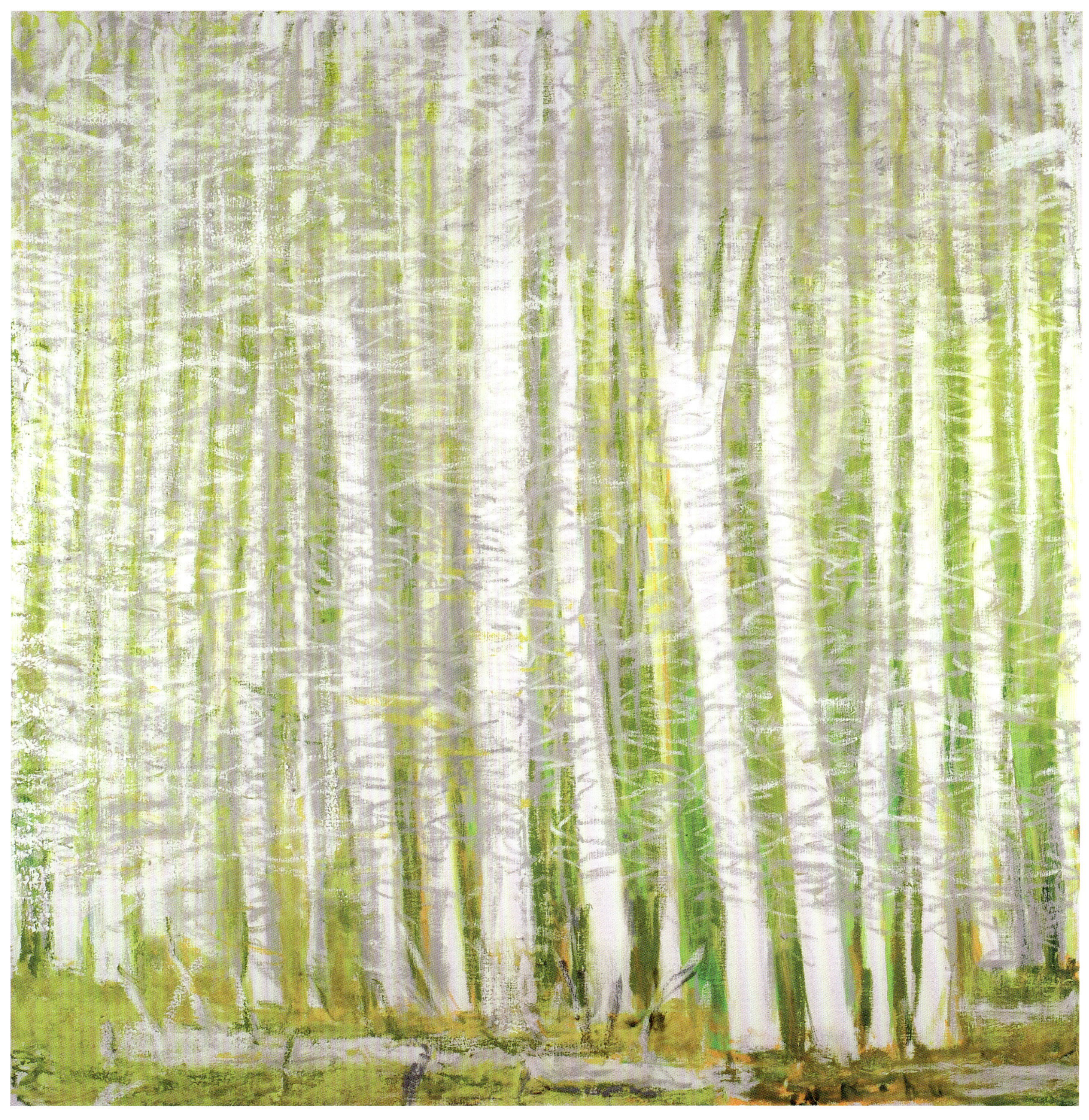

Yellow, White, and Silvery Gray
2015
oil on canvas
52 x 52 inches

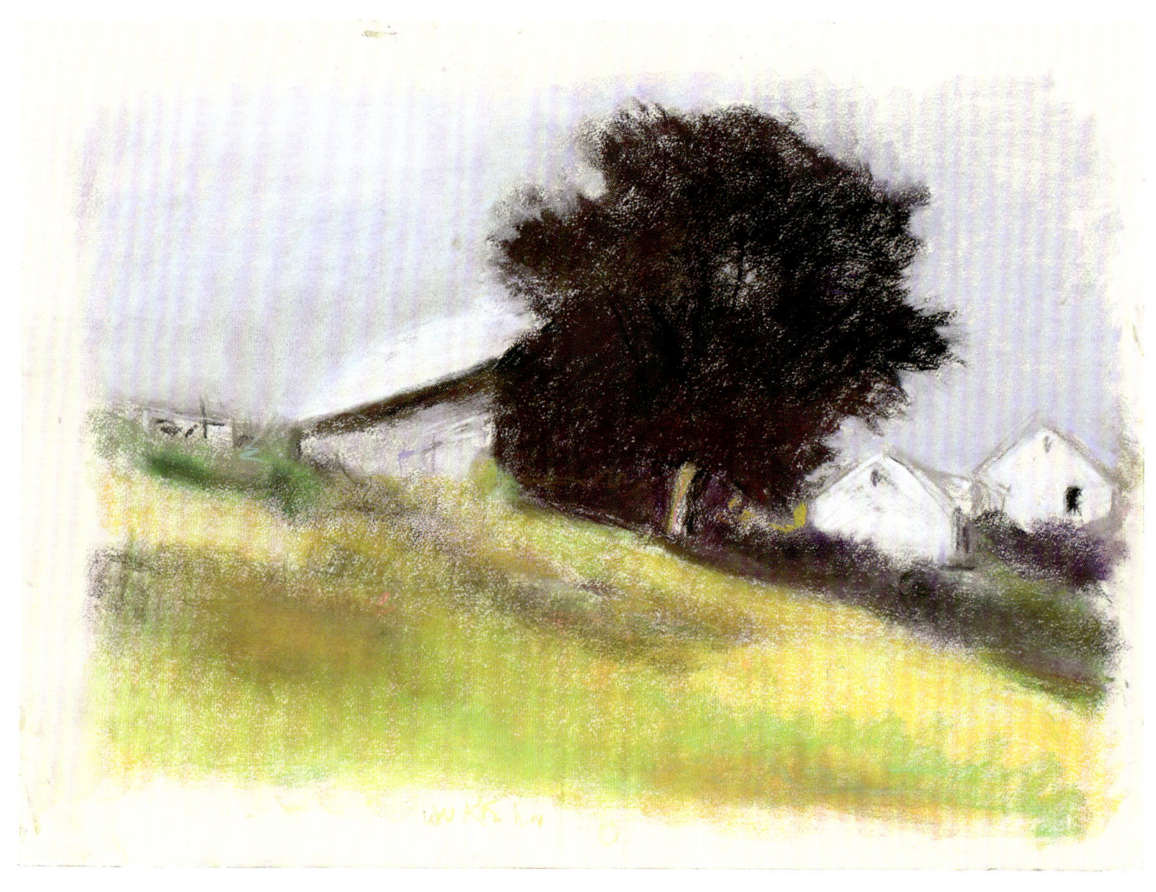

Winchester Farm
2014
pastel on paper
22 x 30 inches

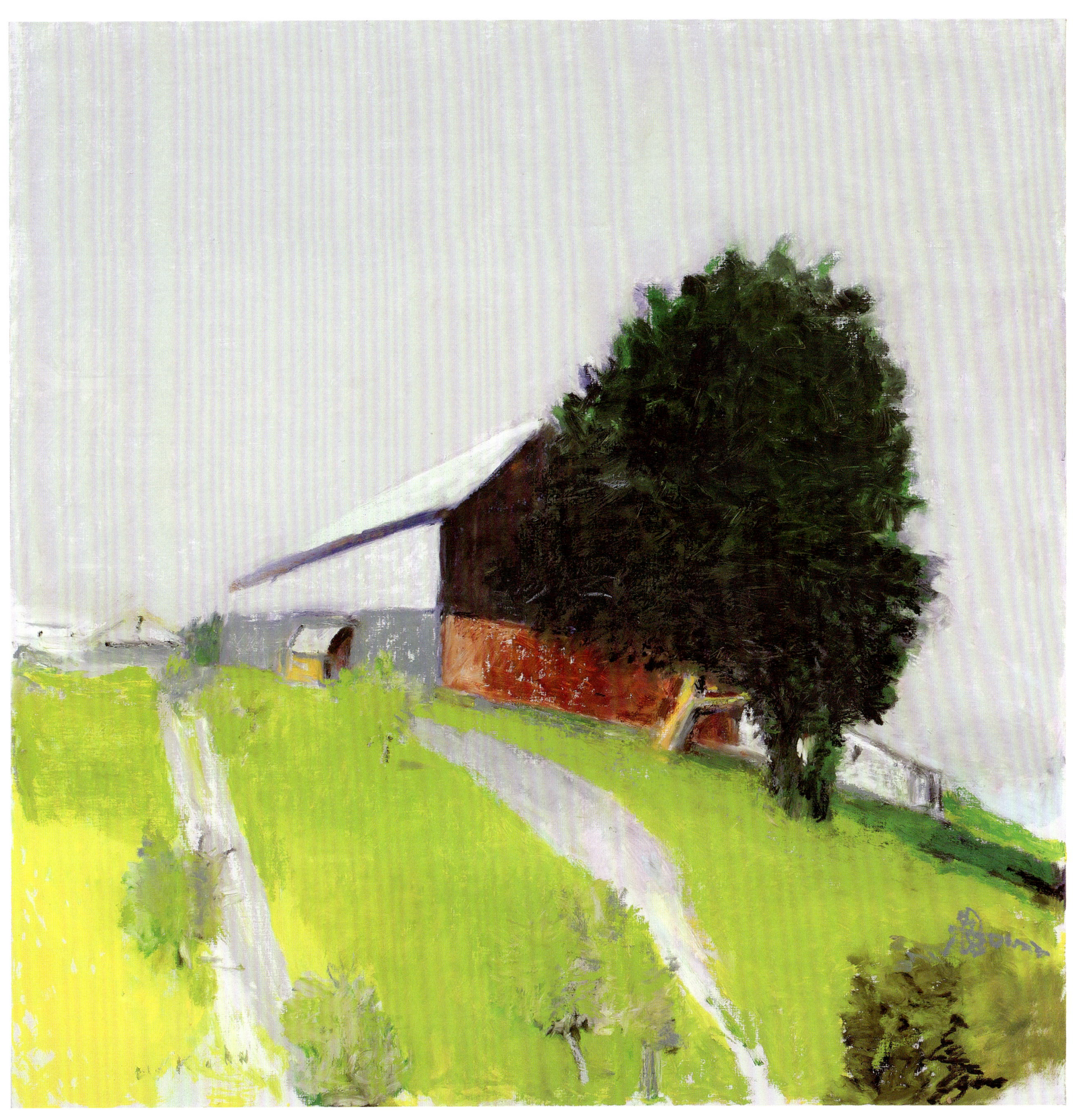

Winchester Barn
2015
oil on canvas
52 x 52 inches

Distant Green
2015
oil on canvas
34 x 52 inches

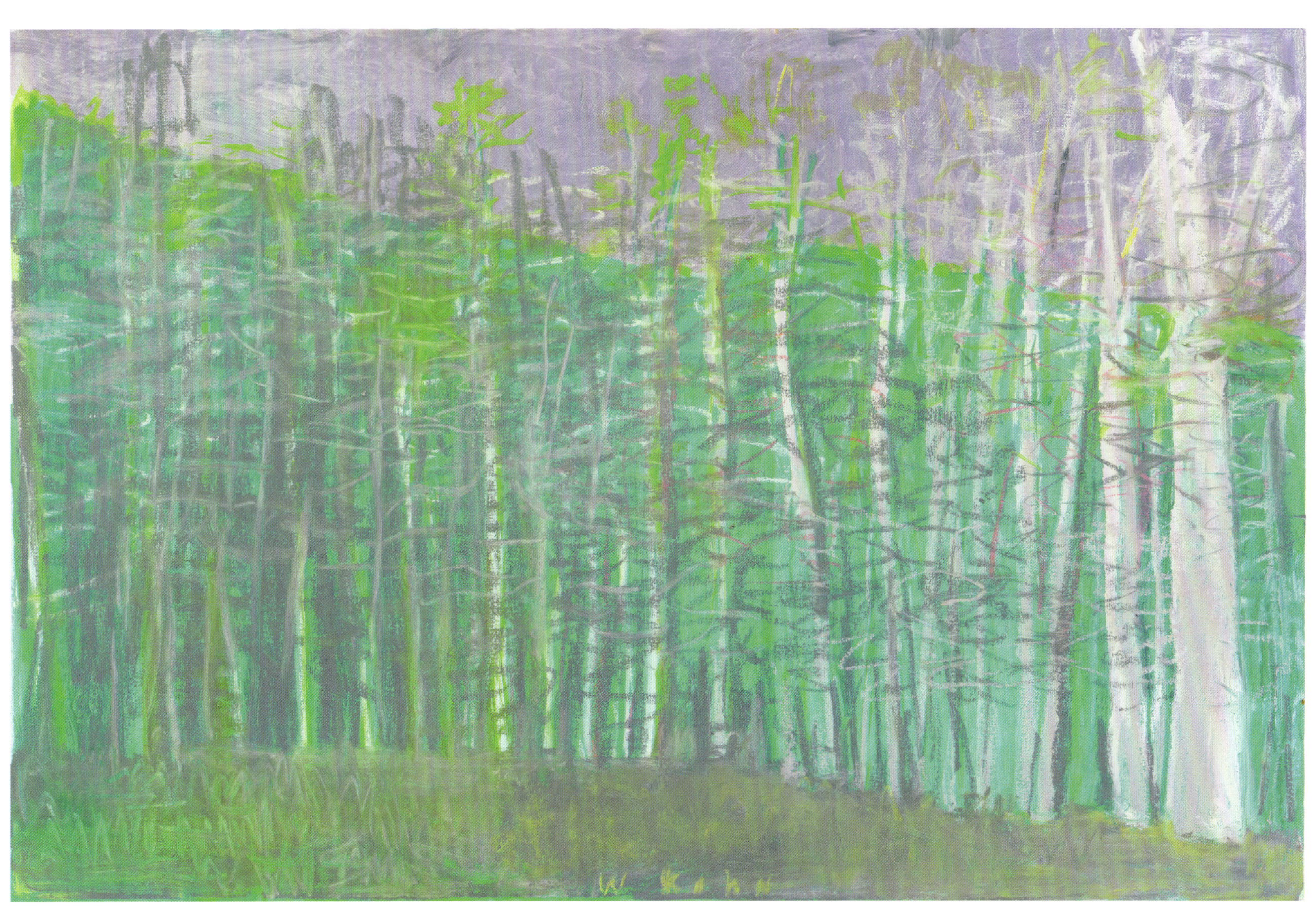

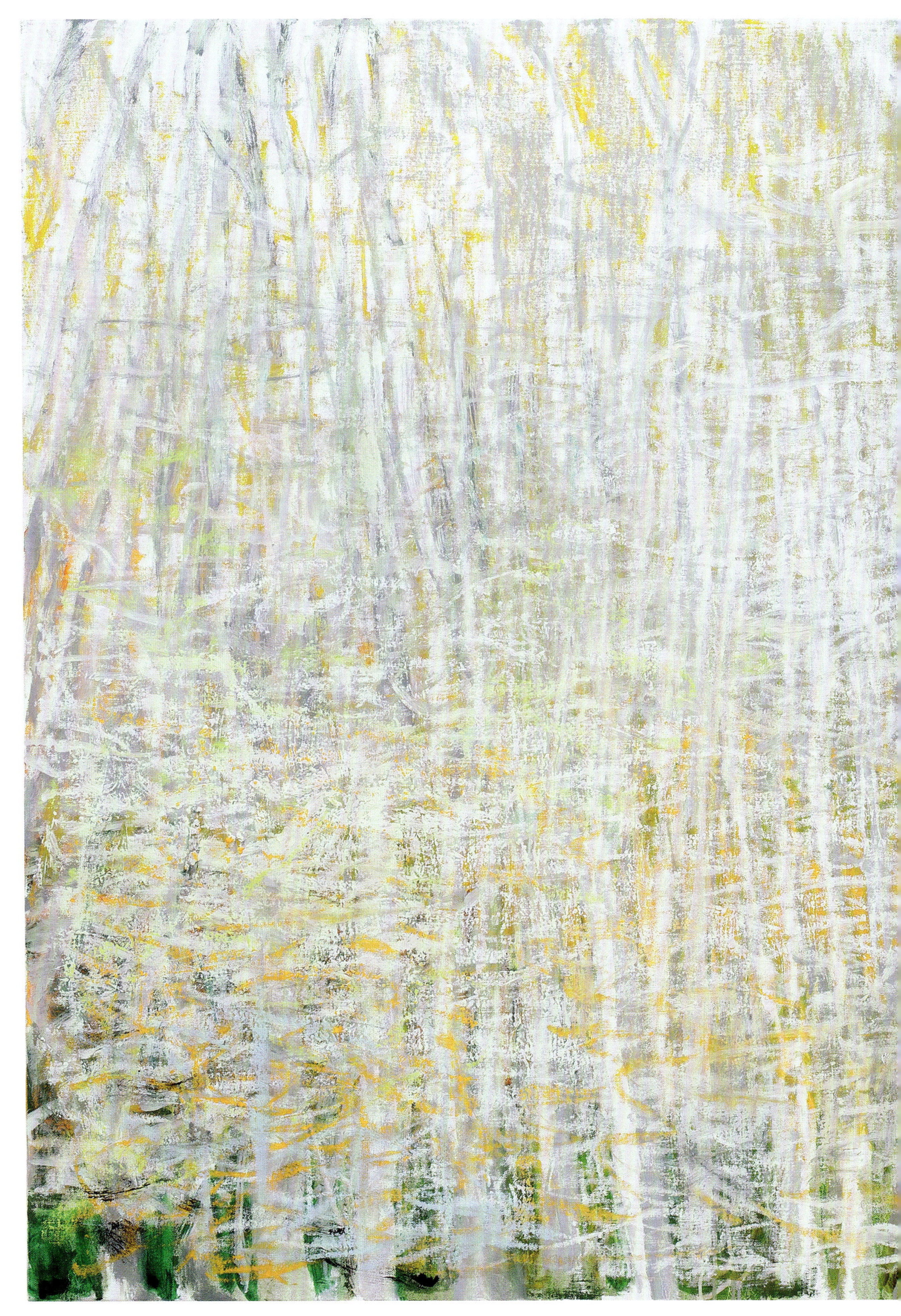

Unusually Untitled
2015
oil on canvas
40 x 68 inches

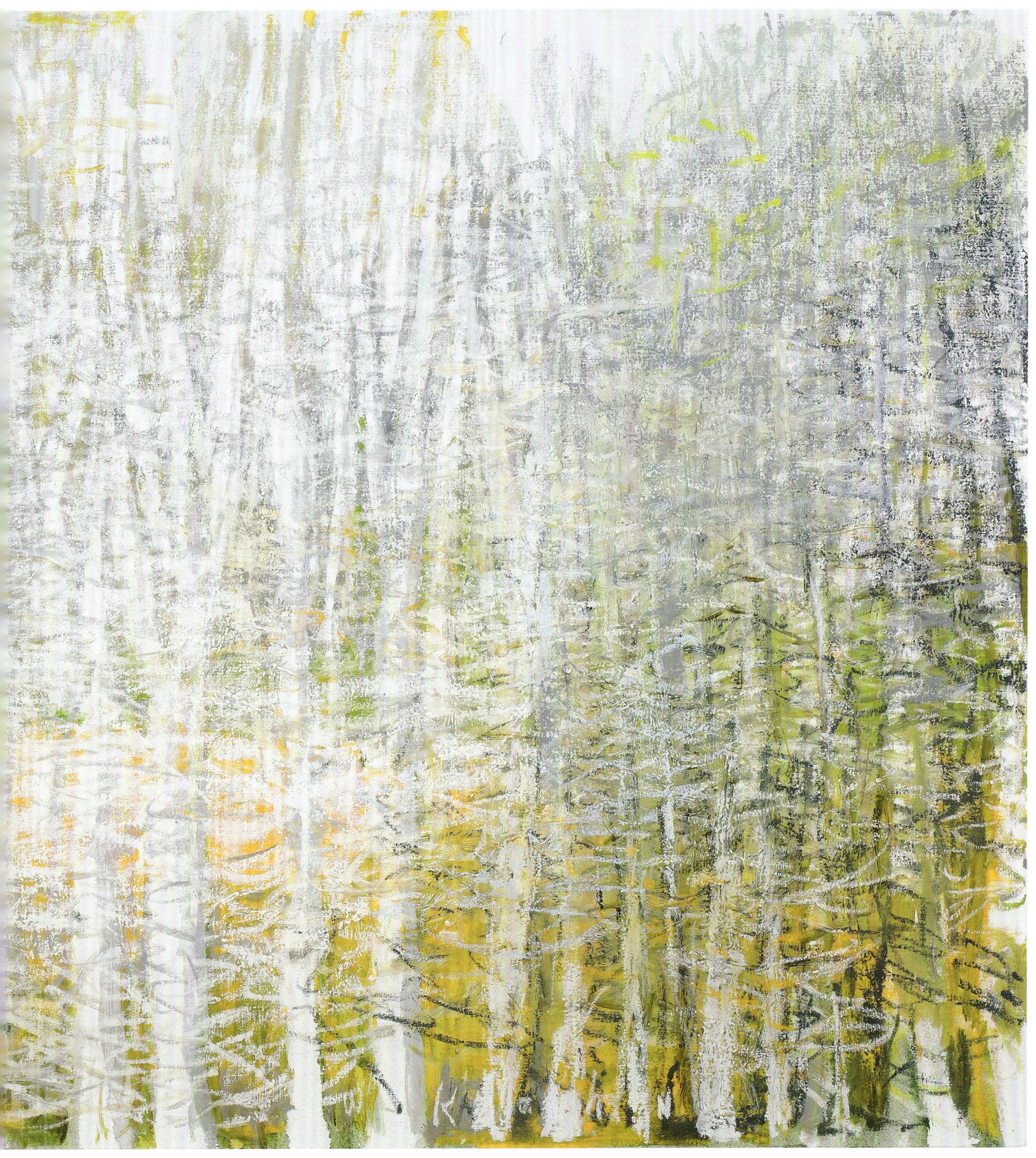

Among Birches
2015
oil on canvas
68 x 68 inches

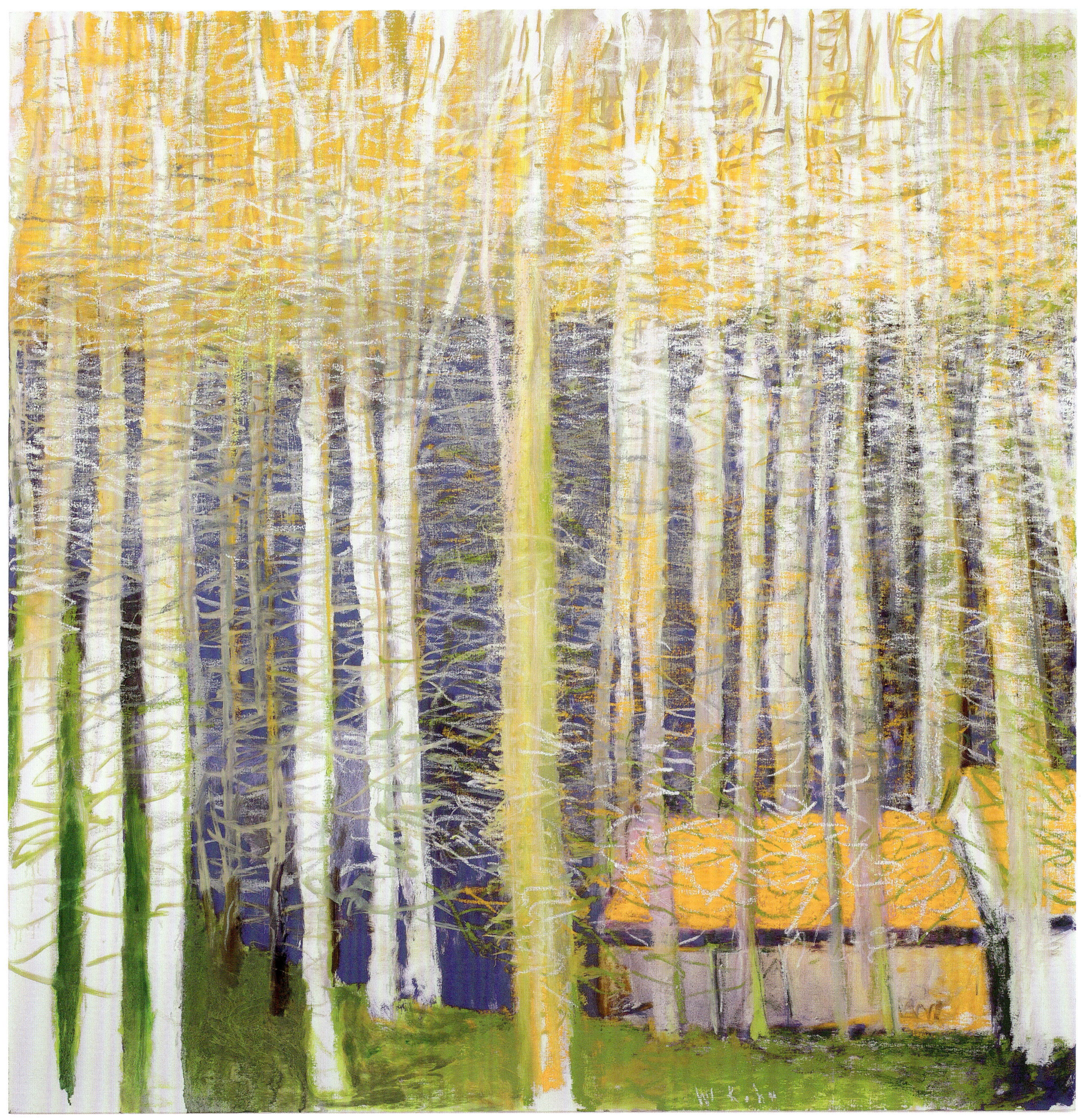

Studio Pond
2016
oil on canvas
52 x 60 inches

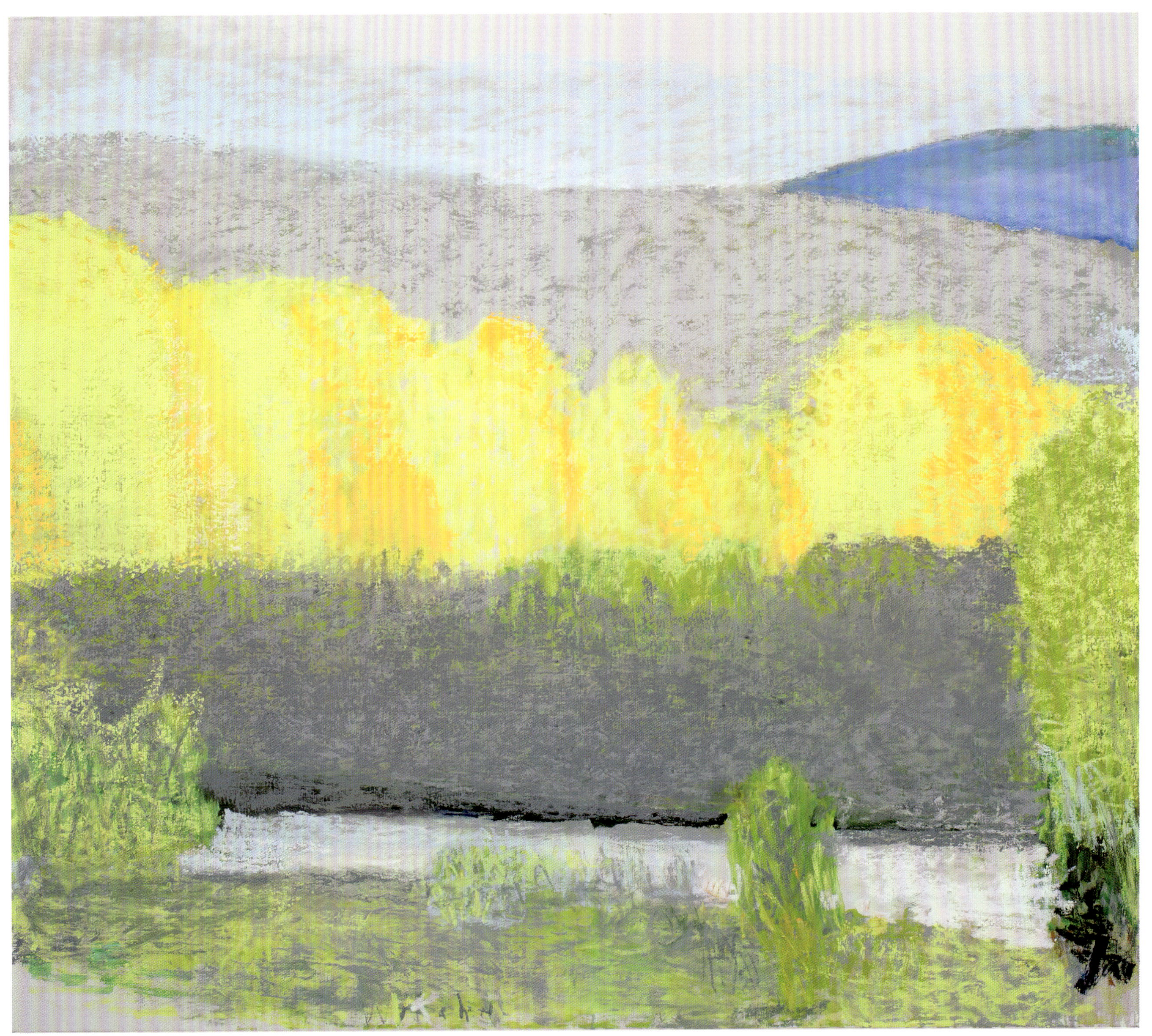

Trees Along the River
2016
oil on canvas
36 x 52 inches

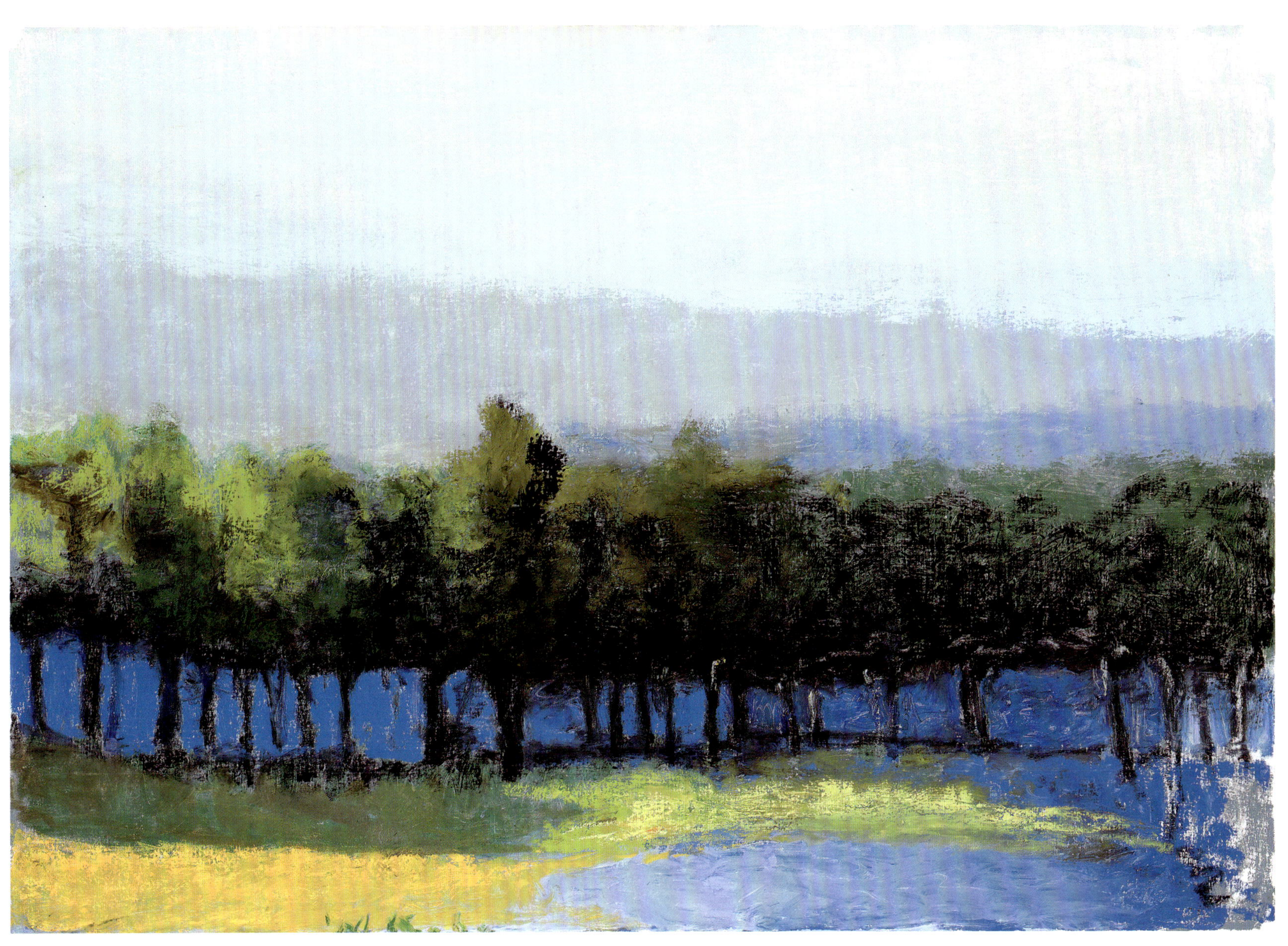

Blue to Yellow Through Green
2016
oil on canvas
52 x 52 inches

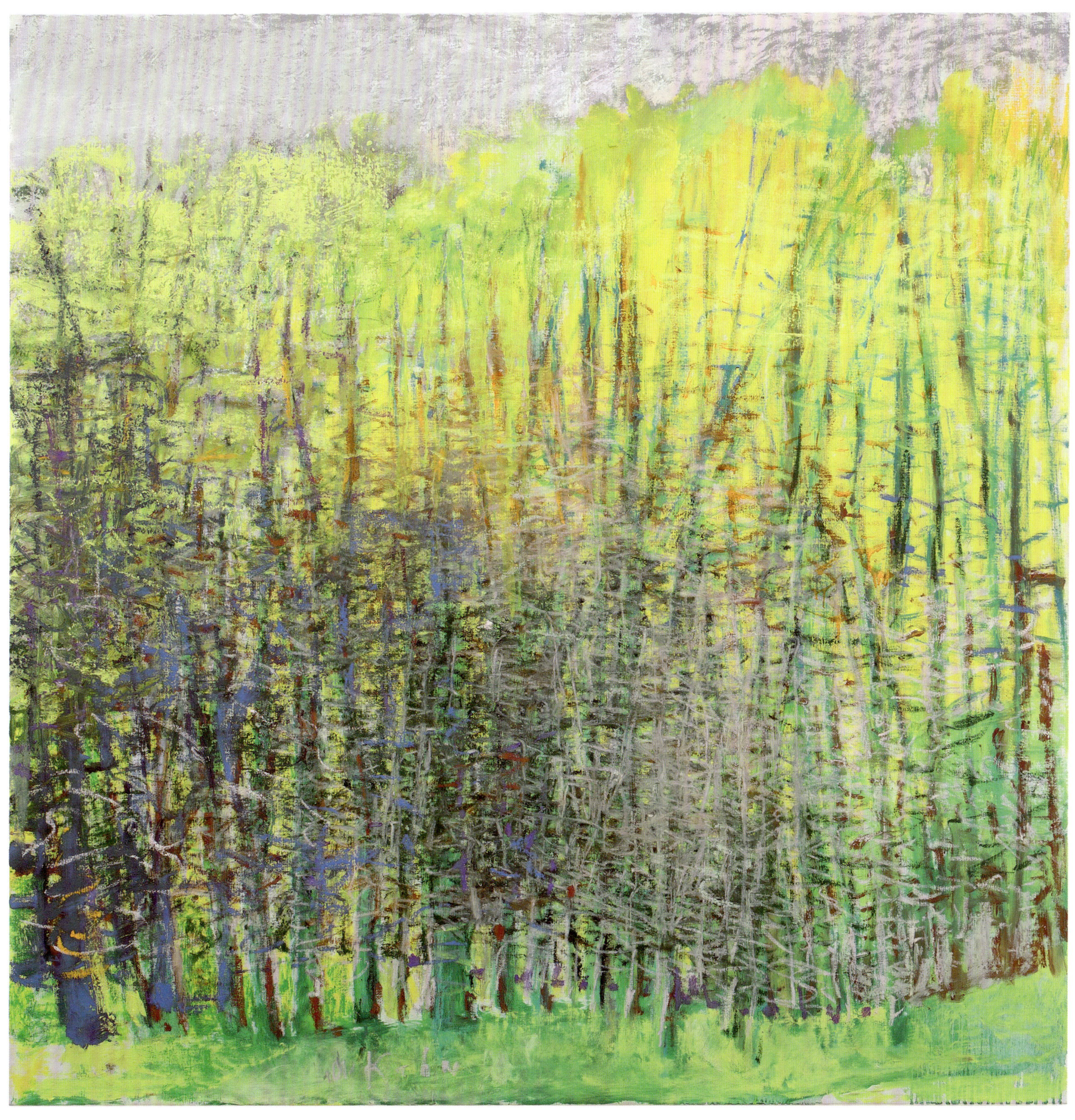

Rows
2016
oil on canvas
52 x 48 inches

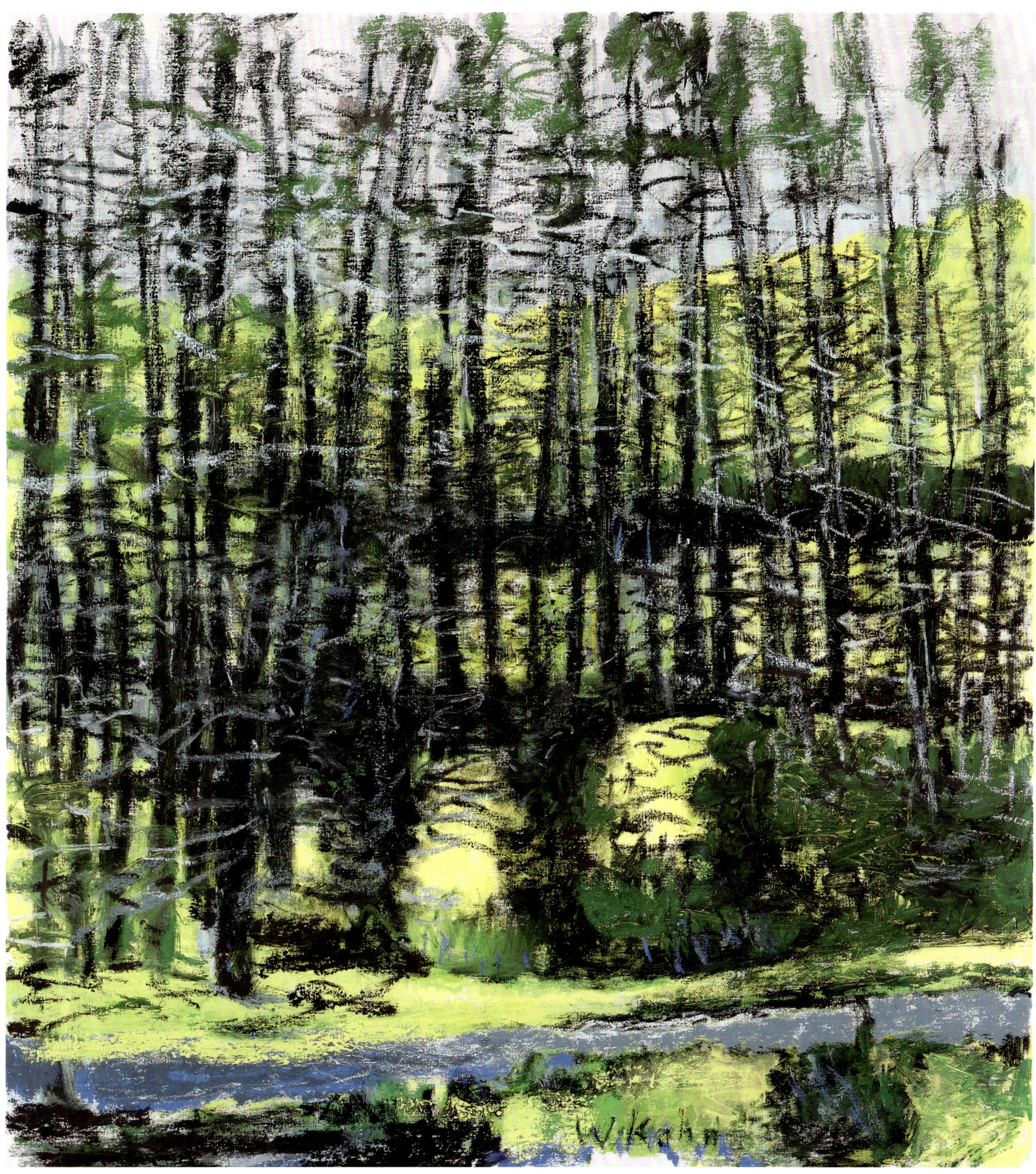
WKahn

High Pink Sky
2016
oil on canvas
52 x 52 inches

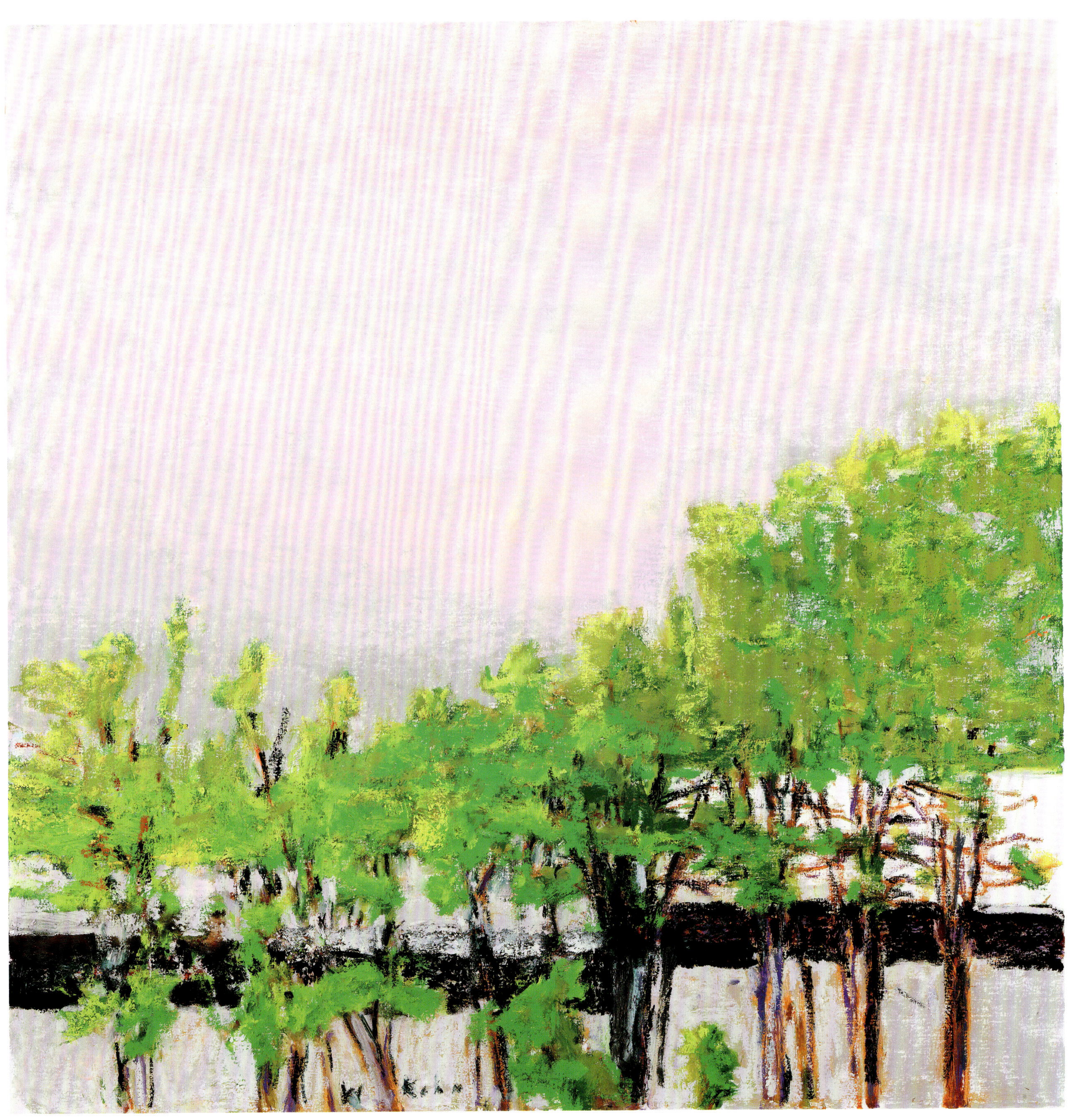

Weight on the Right
2016
oil on canvas
46 x 55¾ inches

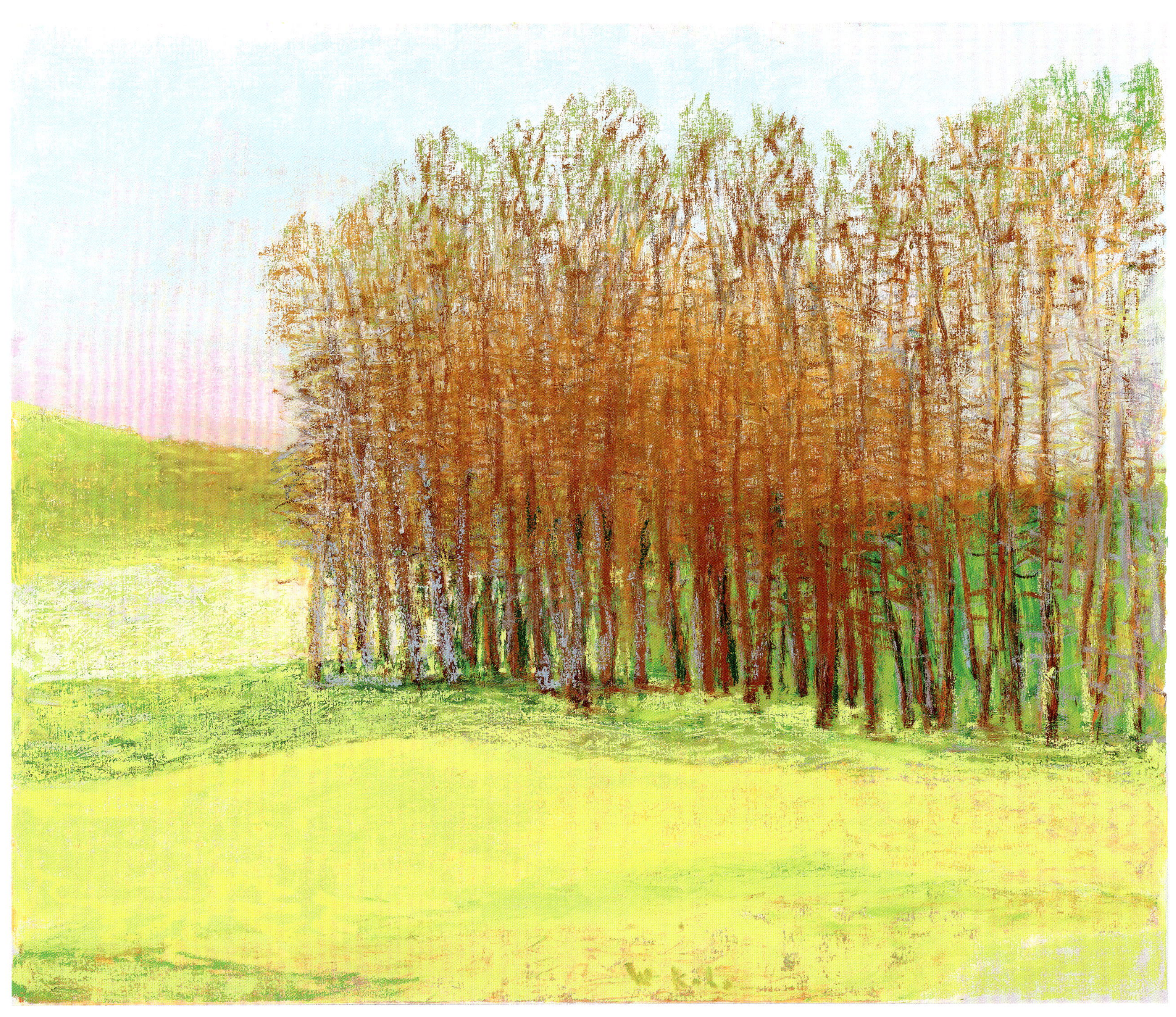

Young Beech Trees,
Large Version
2016
oil on canvas
52 x 52 inches

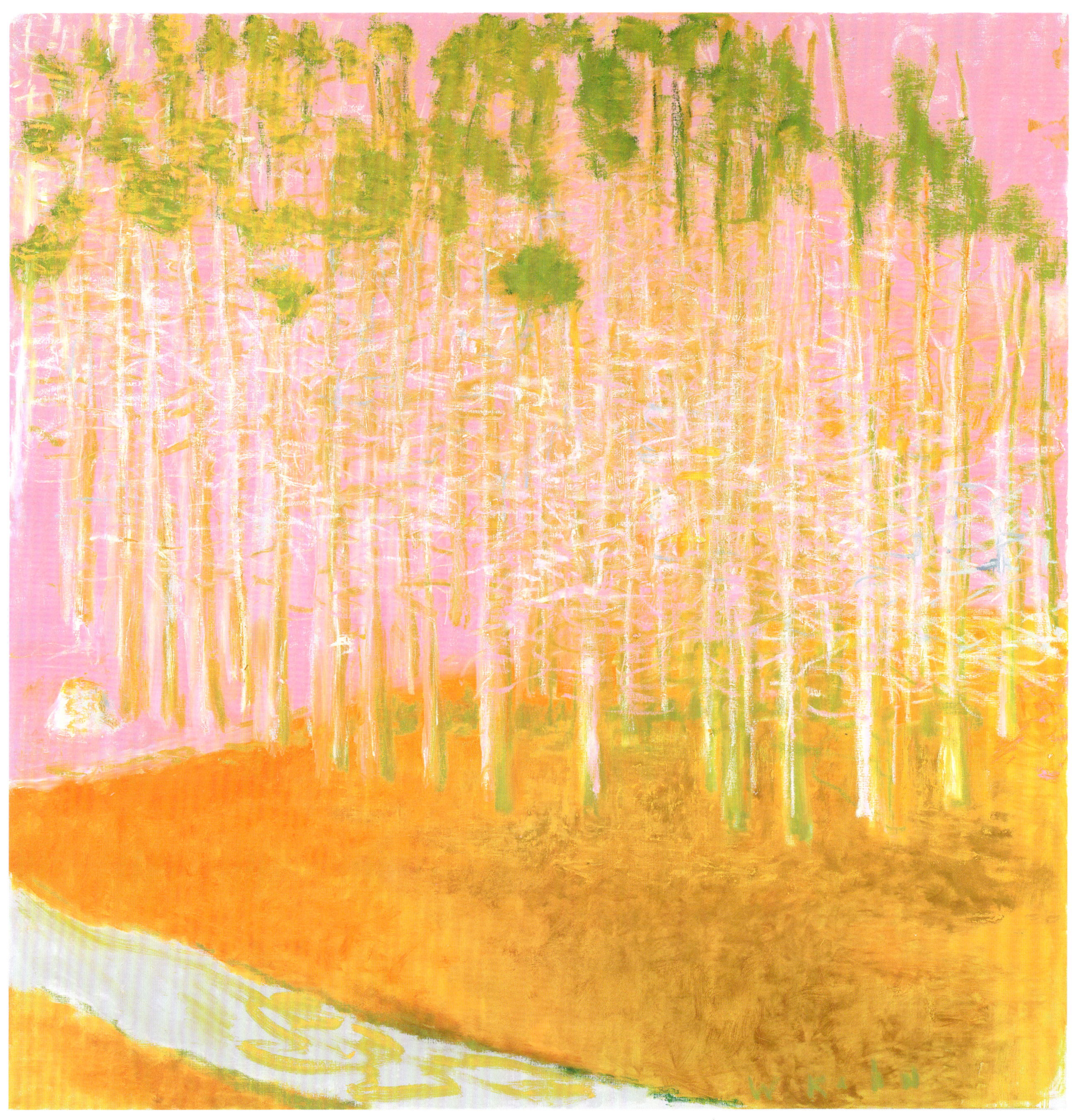

Blue Trees
2016
oil on canvas
52 x 66 inches

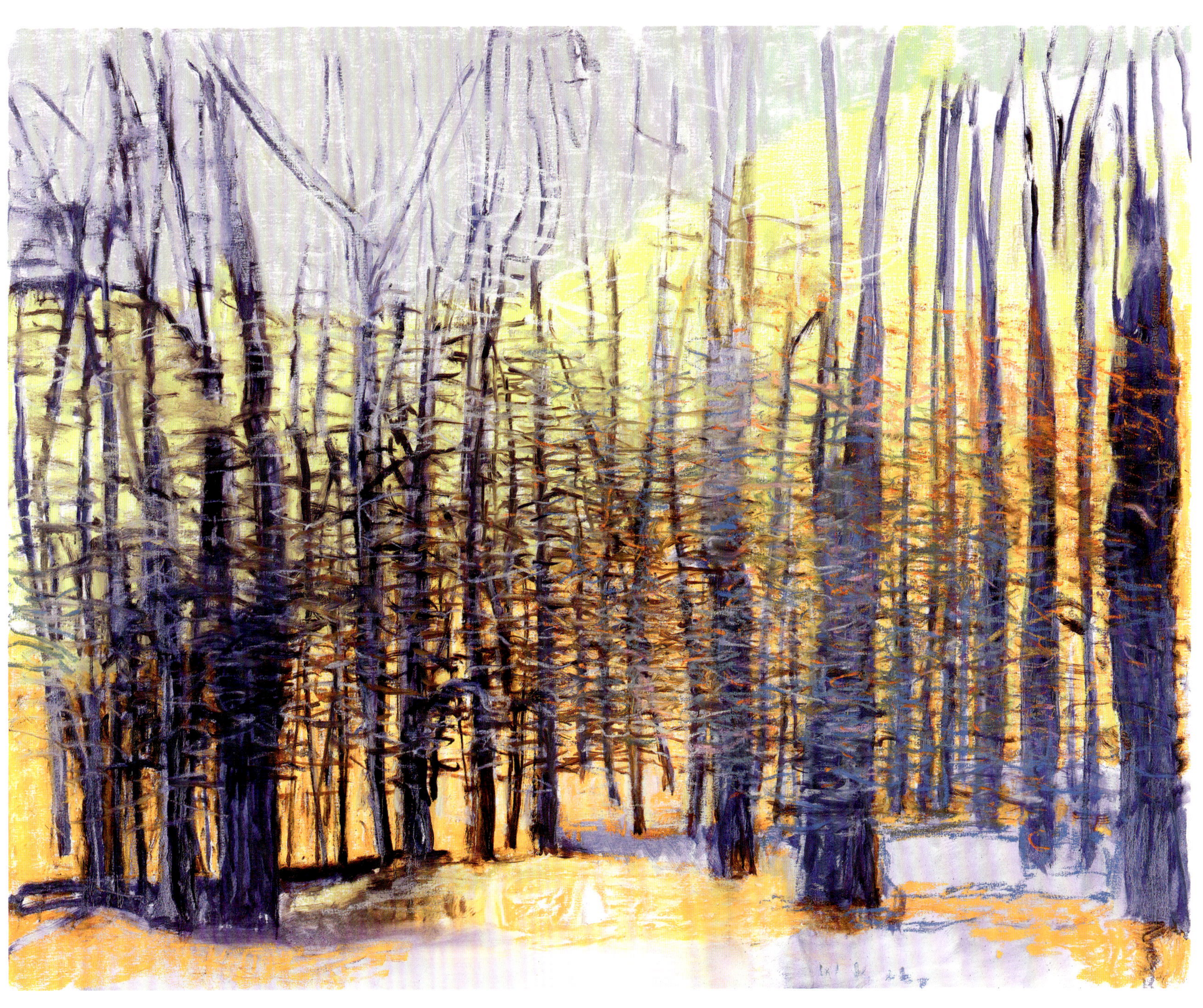

White Giving Way to Blue
2016
oil on canvas
50 x 60 inches

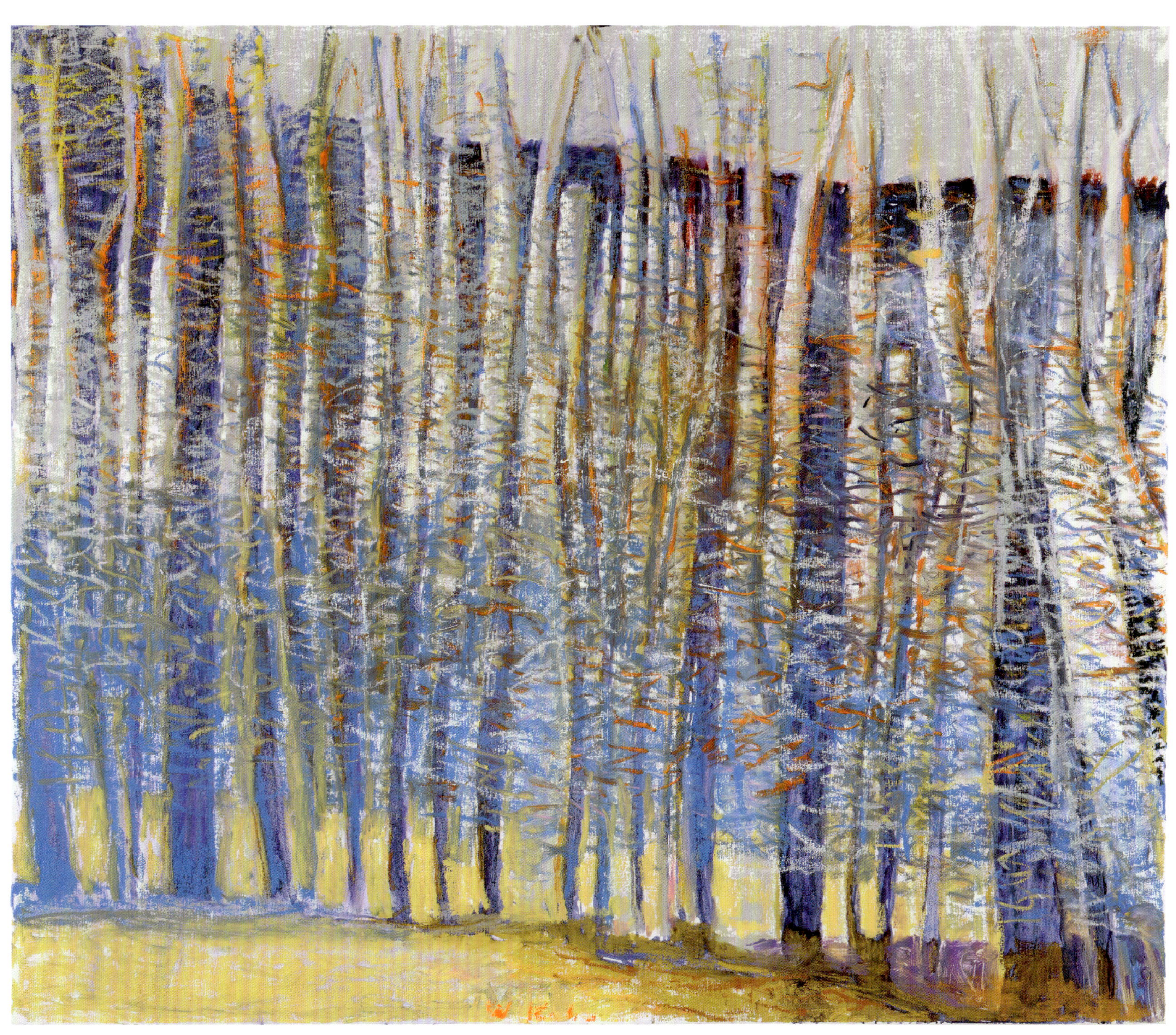

Foggy Morning
2016
oil on canvas
30 x 44 inches

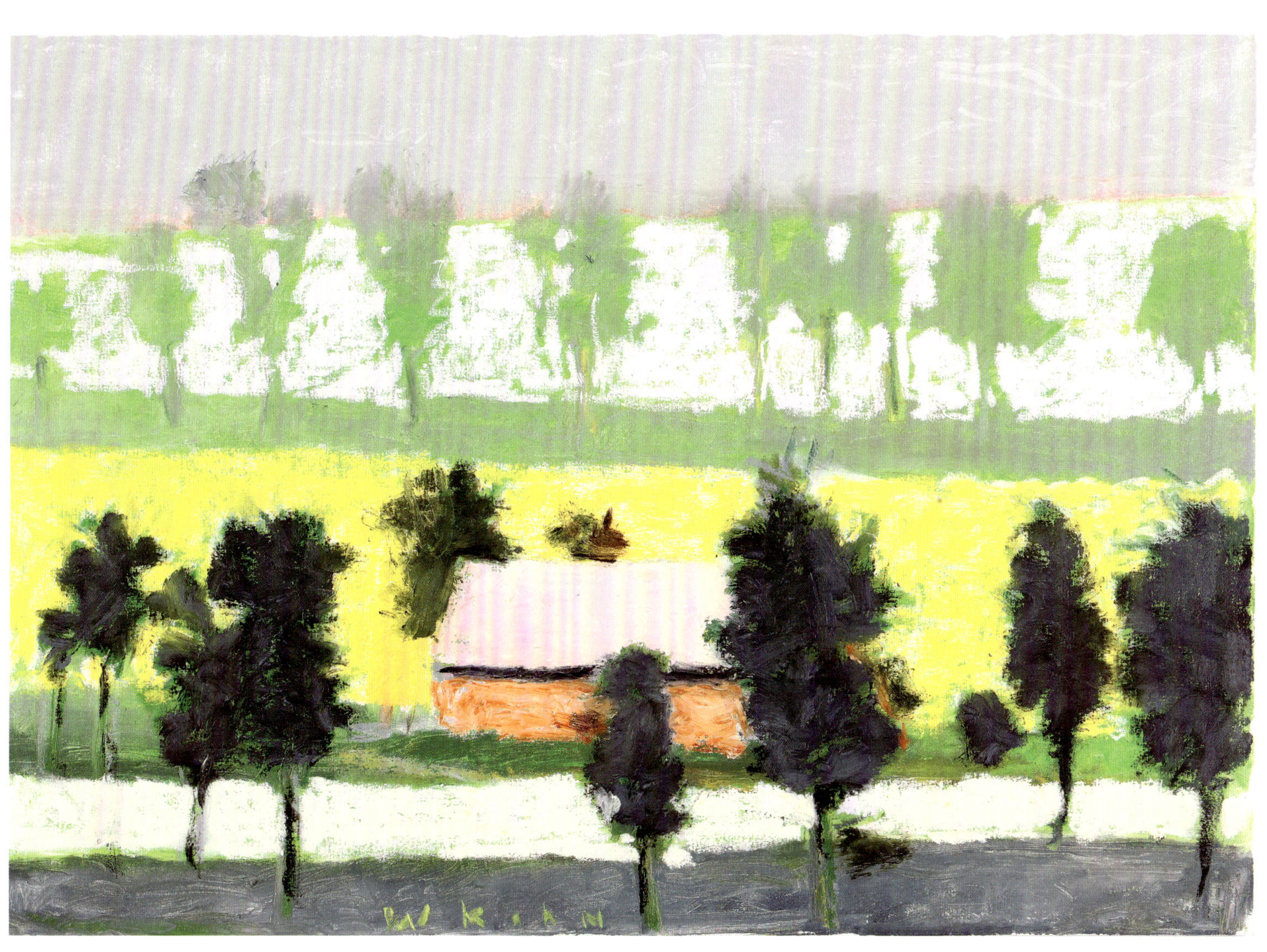

Below a Gray Sky
2016
oil on canvas
40 x 52 inches

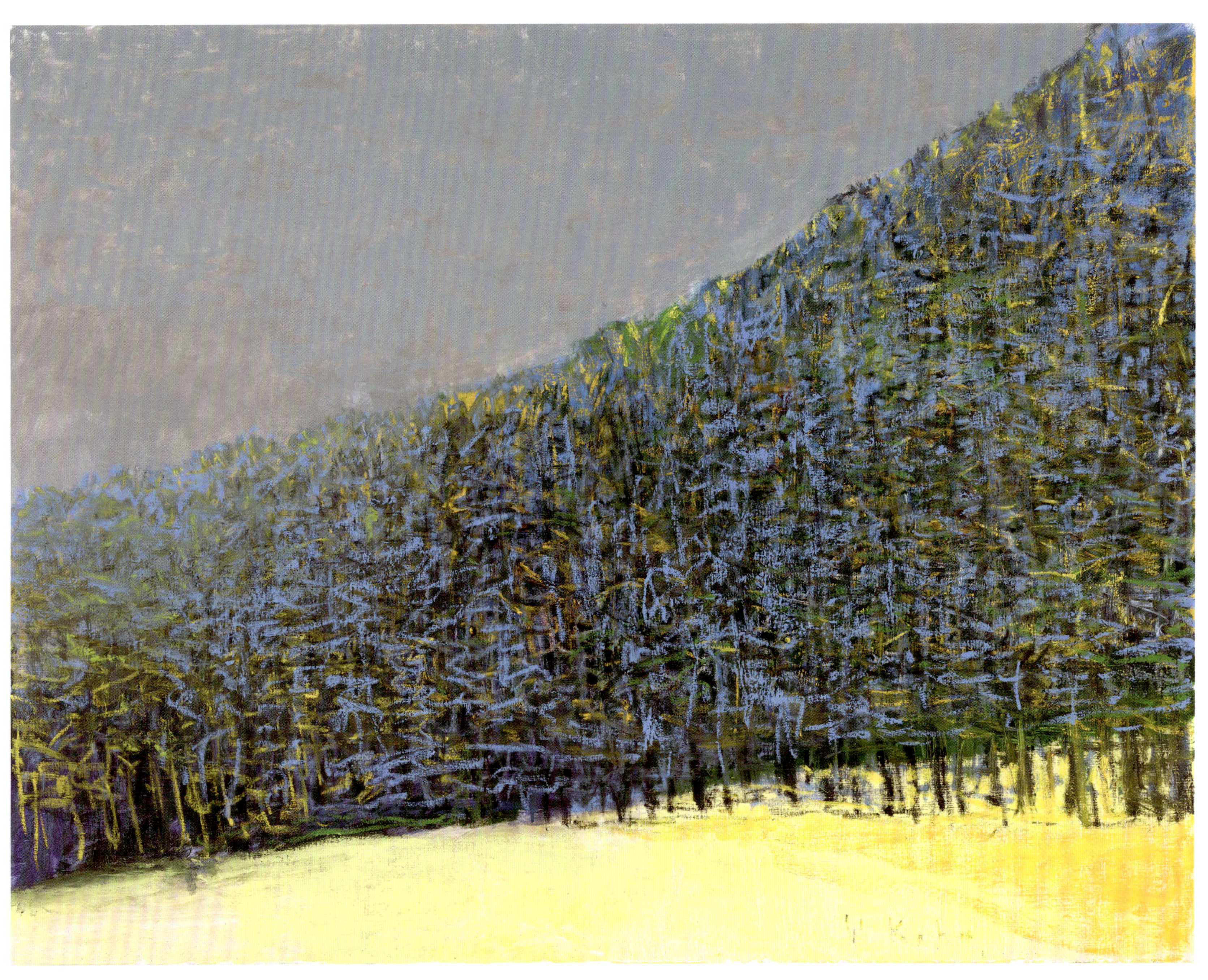

Warm
2016
oil on canvas
50 x 60 inches

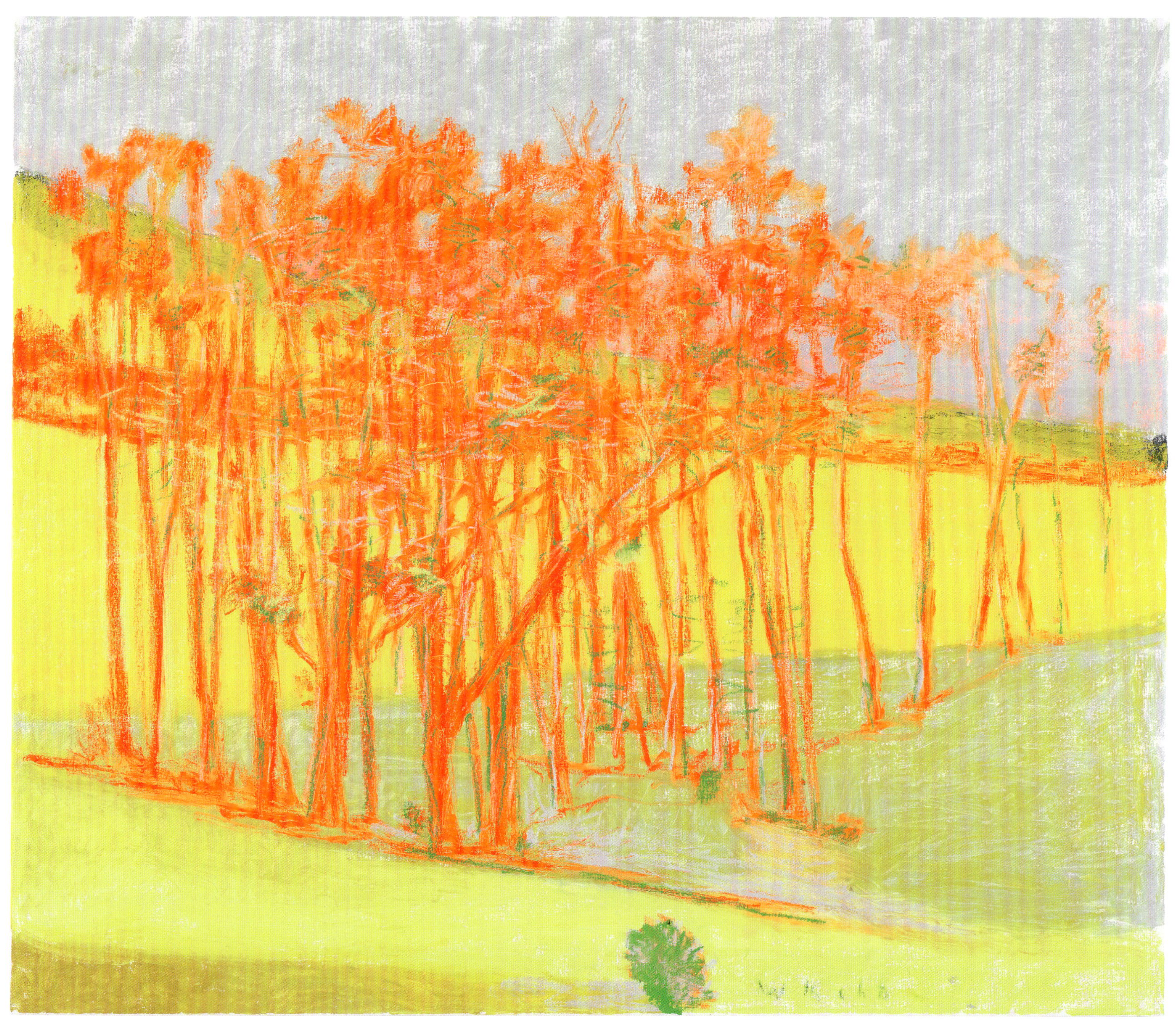

Early Blooming Fruit Tree
(Small Version)
2016
pastel on paper
11 x 11 inches

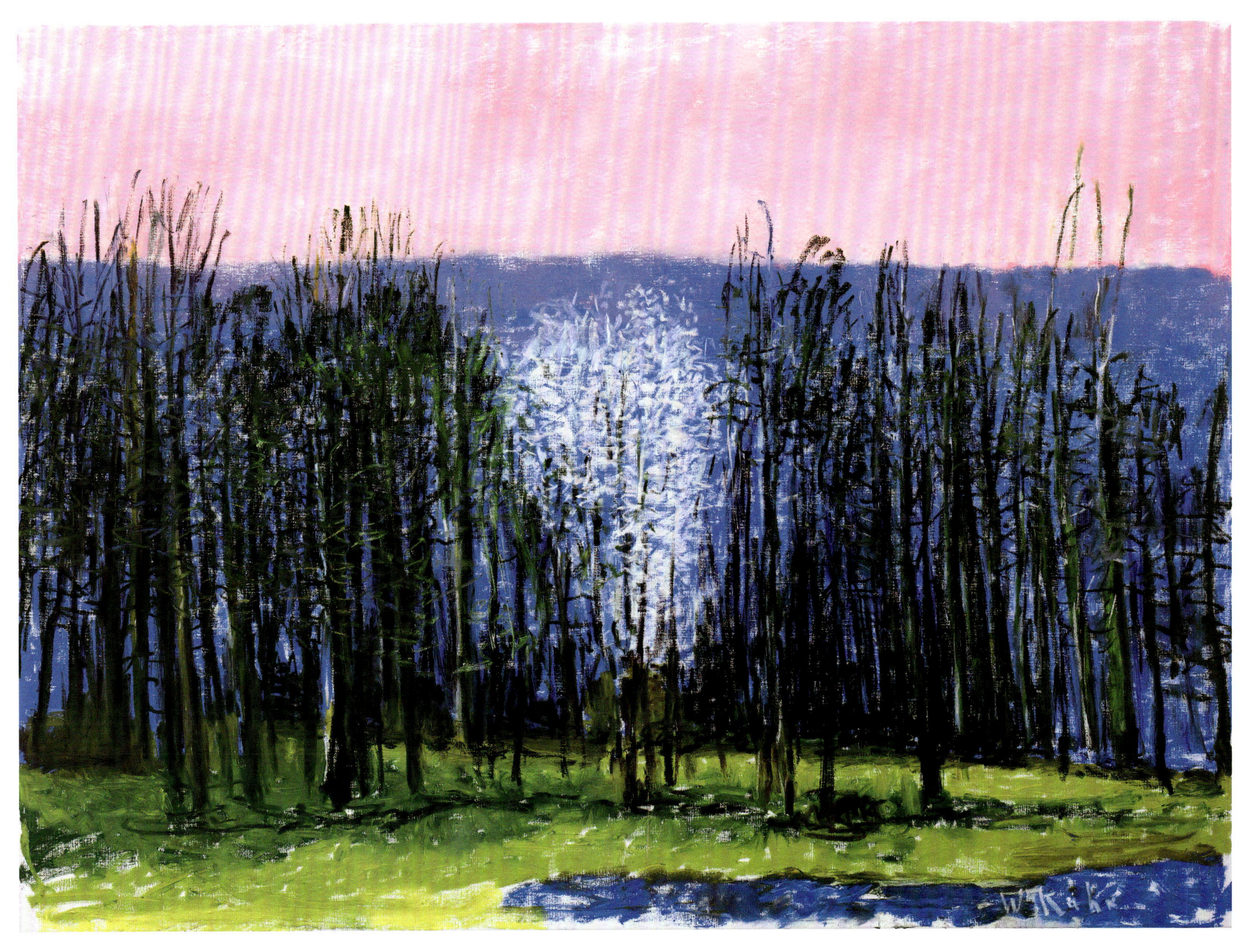

Early Blooming Fruit Tree
2016
oil on canvas
52 x 72 inches

Dense Plantation of Silver
2017
oil on canvas
52 x 52 inches

Blue Below and on the Sides
2017
oil on canvas
52 x 52 inches

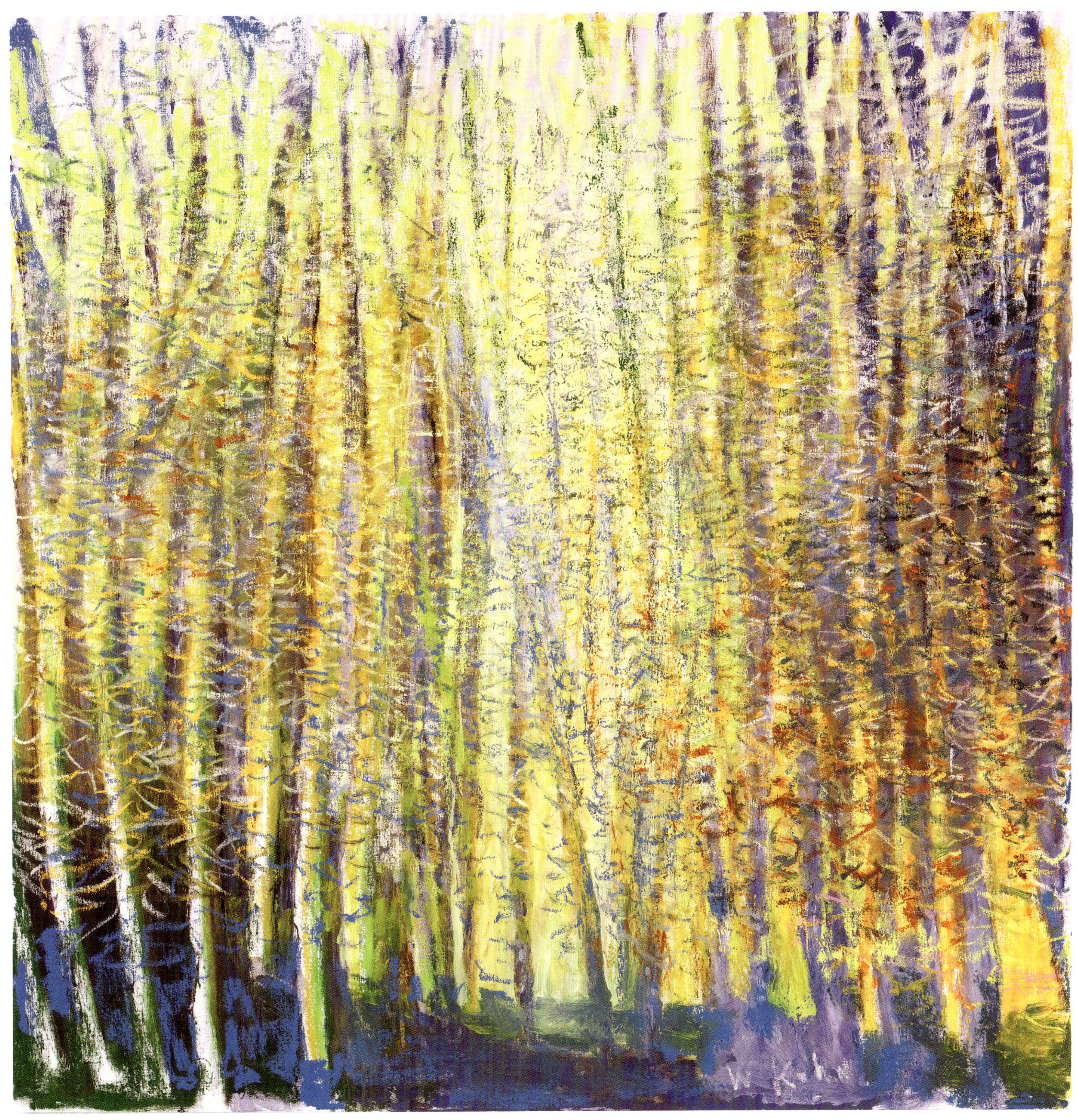

Provence Blue
2017
oil on canvas
52 x 60 inches

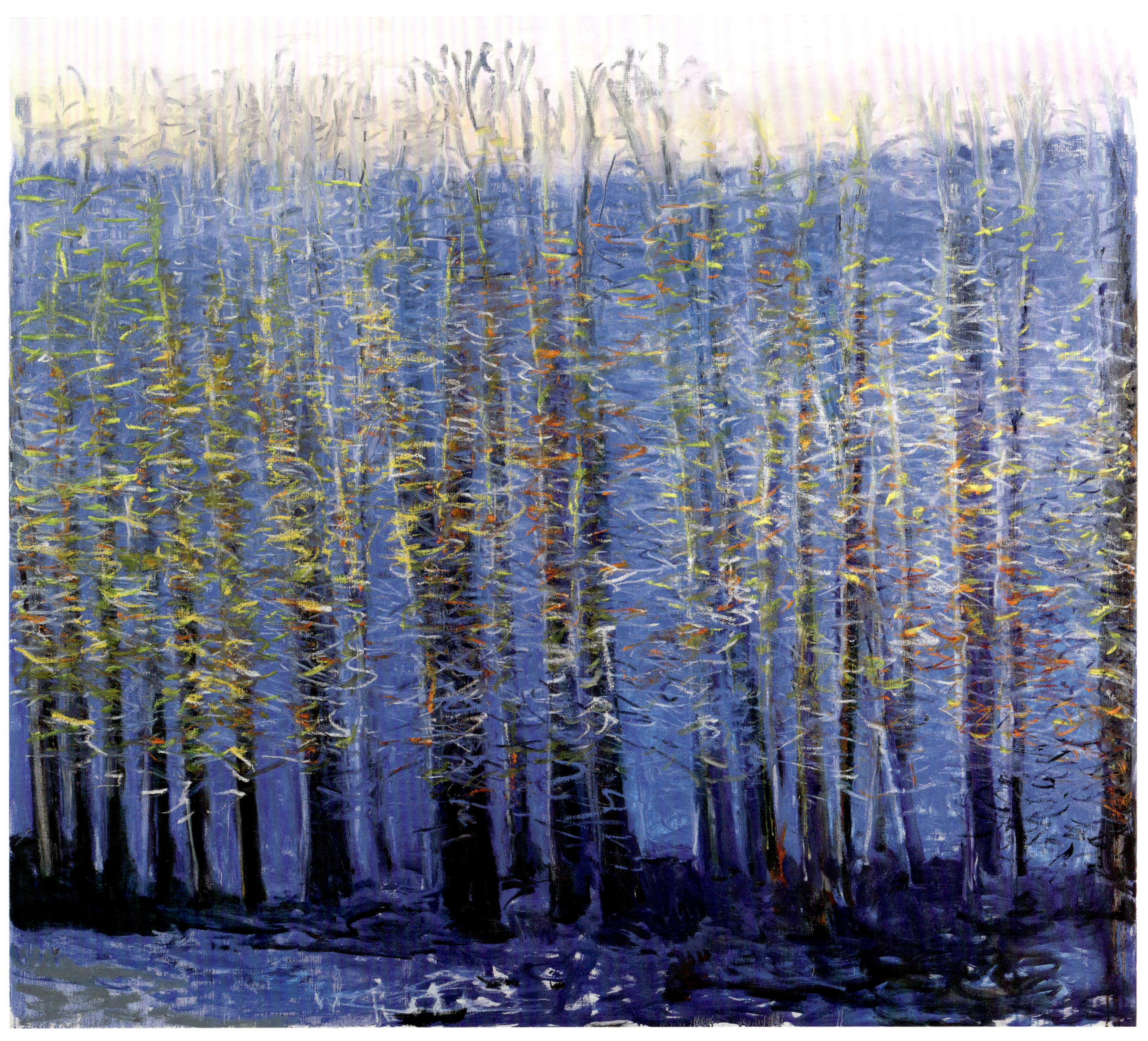

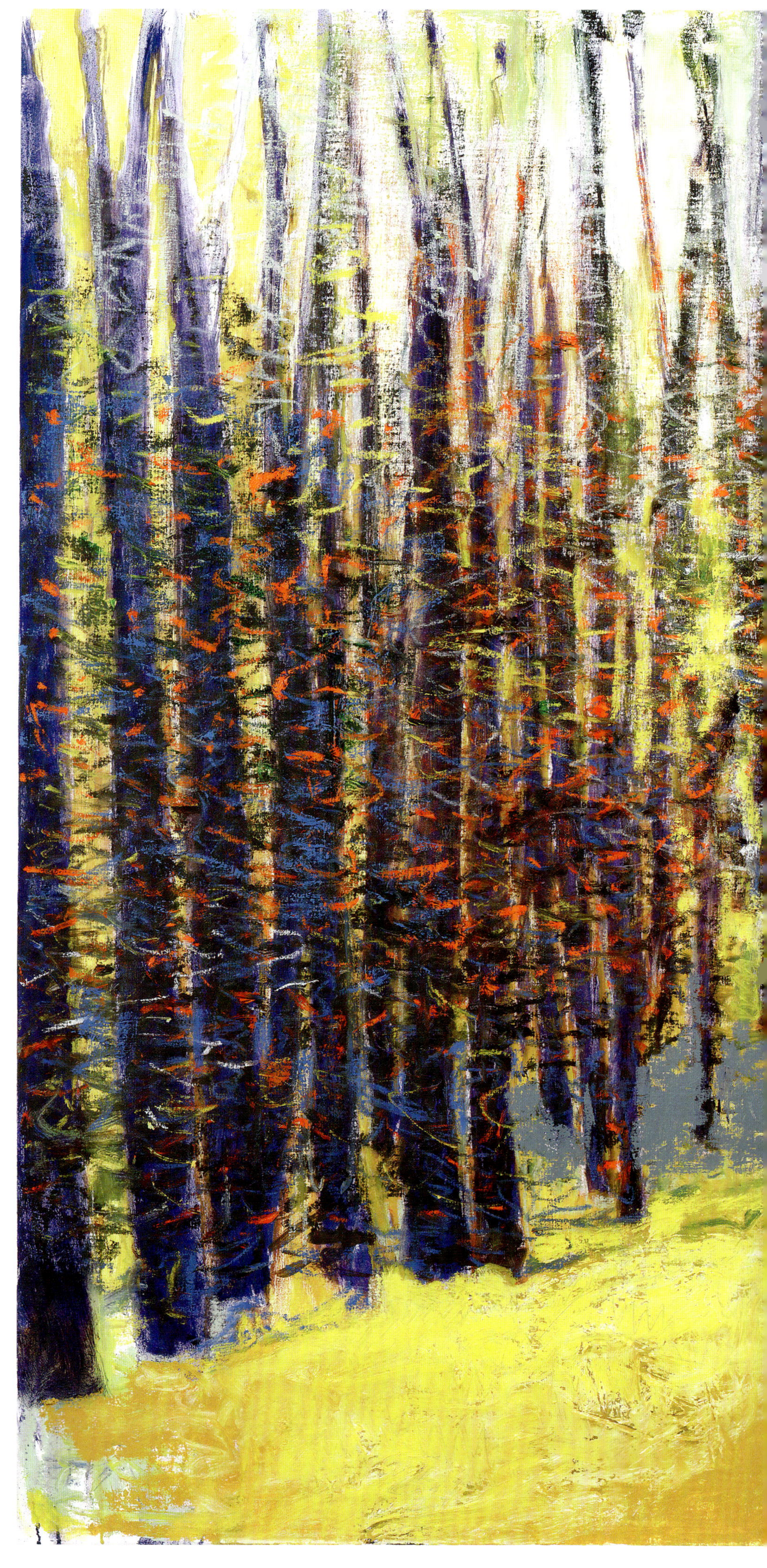

Yellow Overflow
2017
oil on canvas
52 x 72 inches

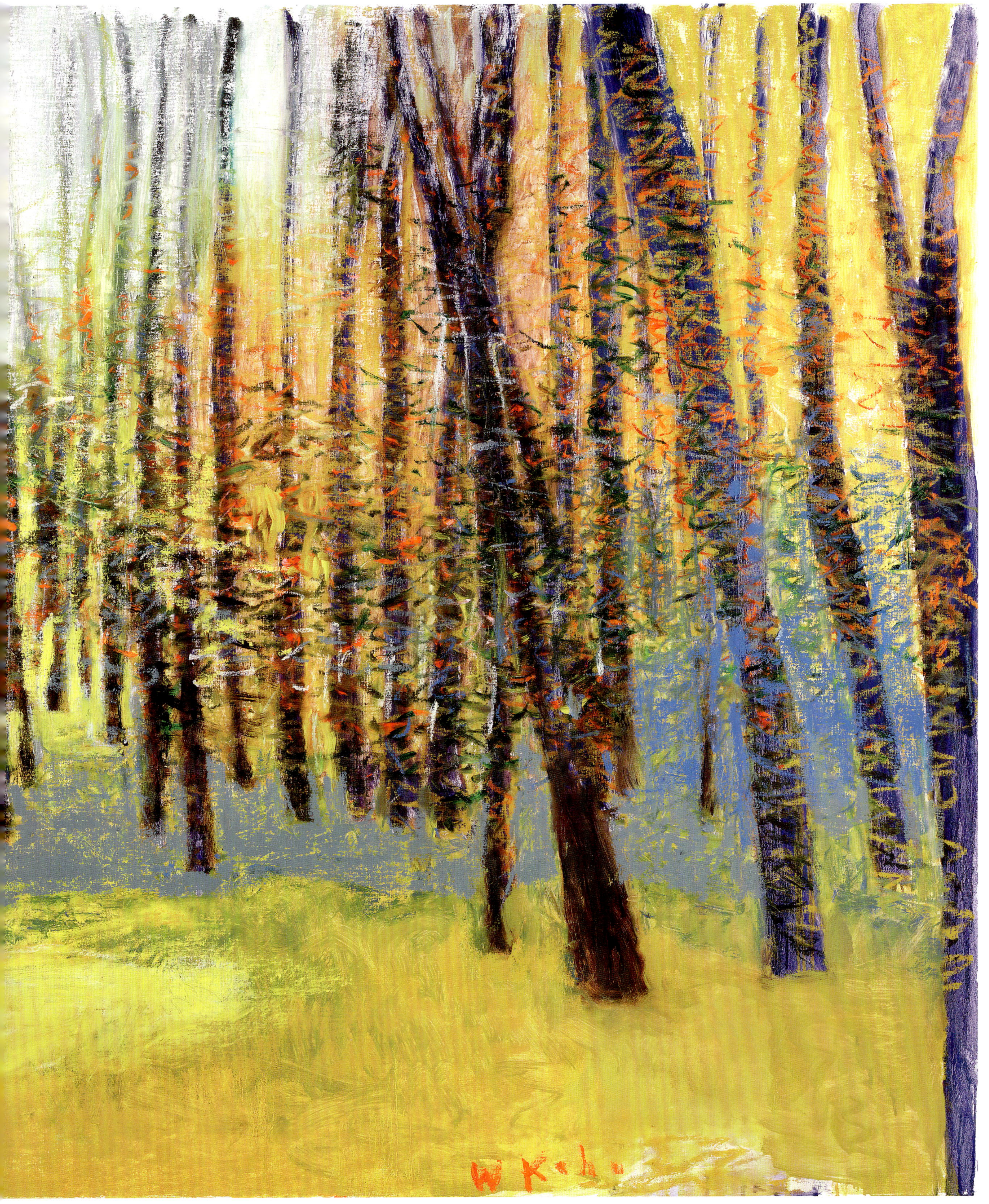

Rose-Colored Sky
2017
oil on canvas
36 x 52 inches

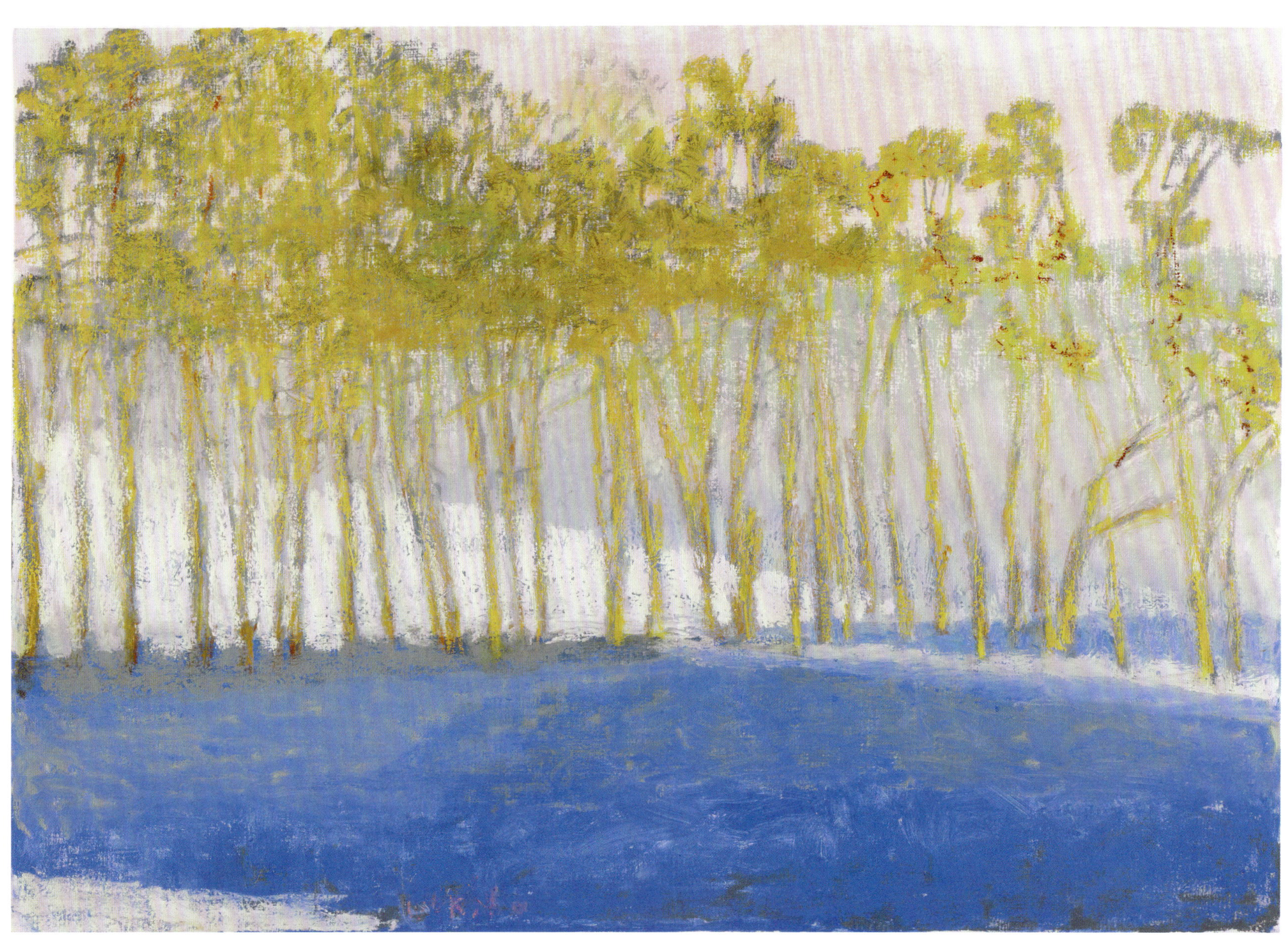

The Interior Light of the Forest
2017
oil on canvas
52 x 66 inches

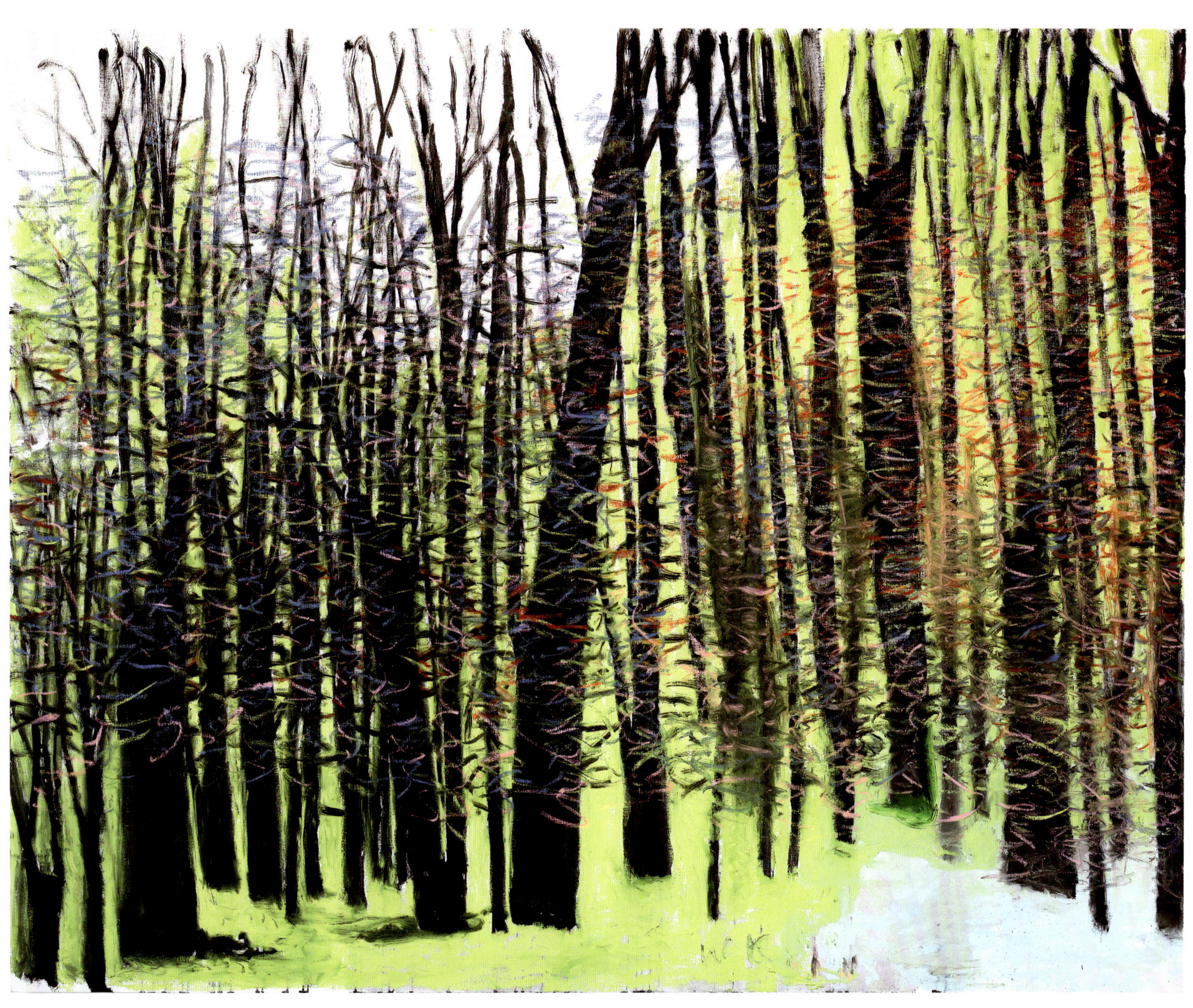

Background Barely Visible
2017
oil on canvas
52 x 72 inches

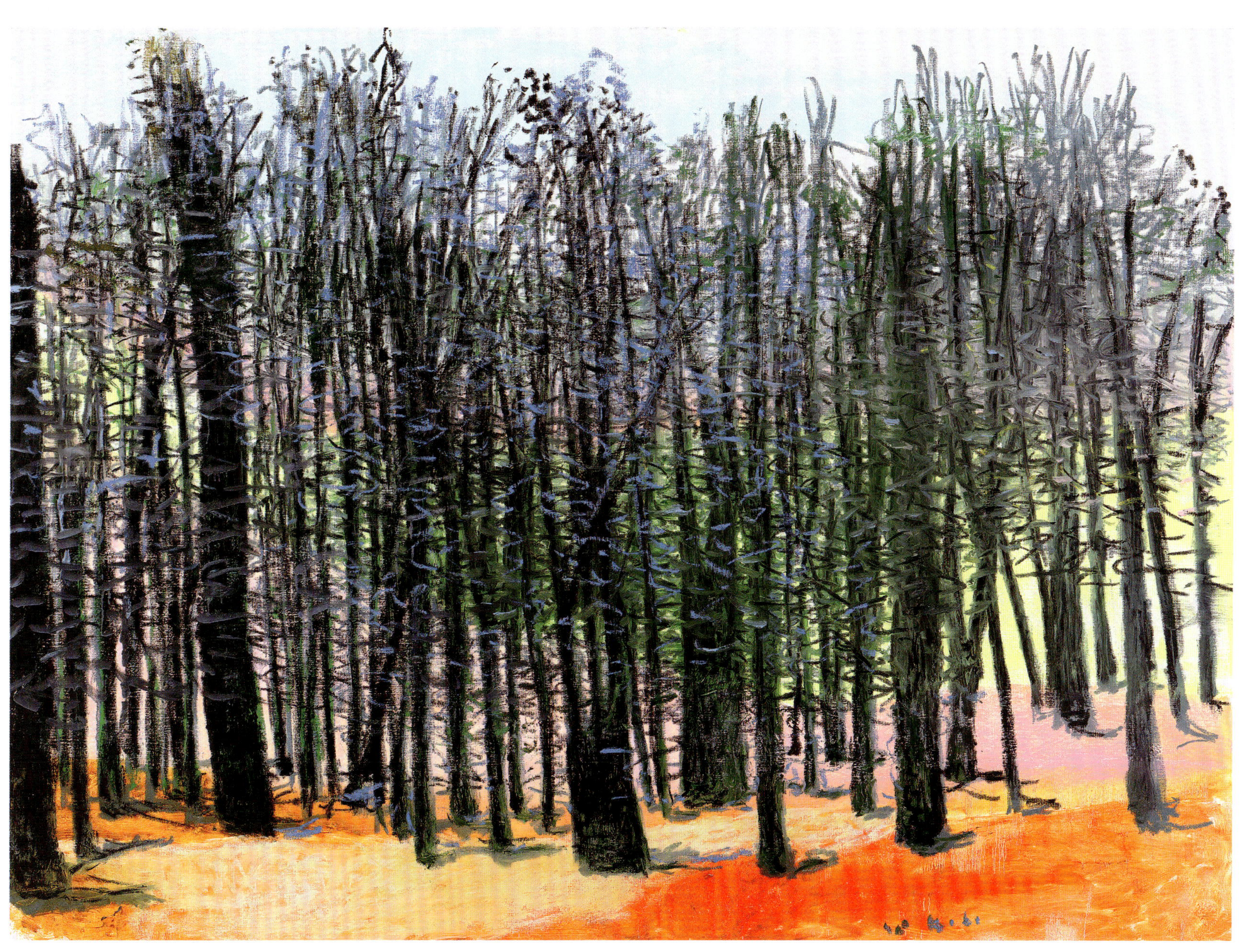

Half Wild Landscape
2017
oil on canvas
52 x 52 inches

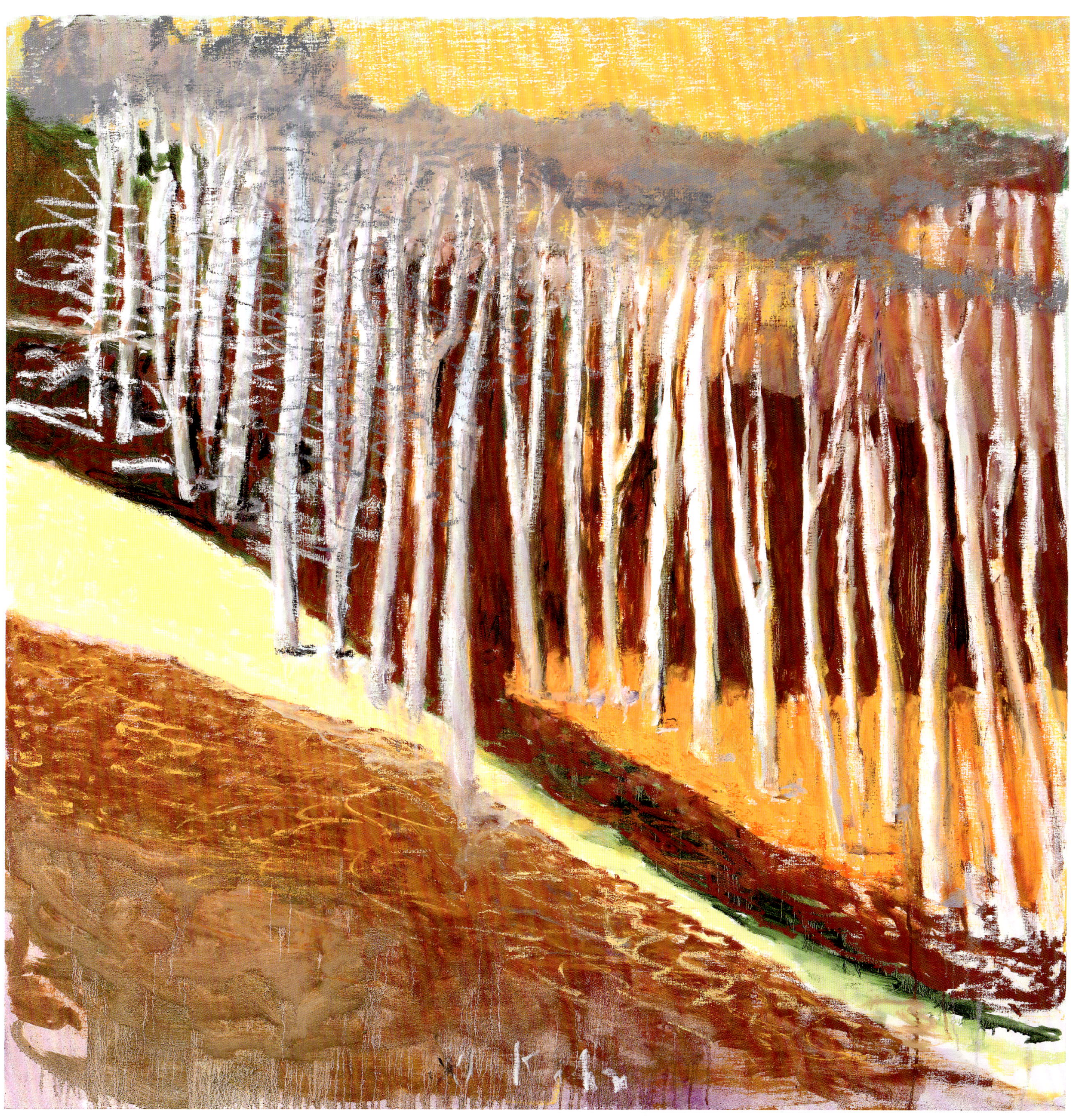

Yellow Square
2018
oil on canvas
36 x 36 inches

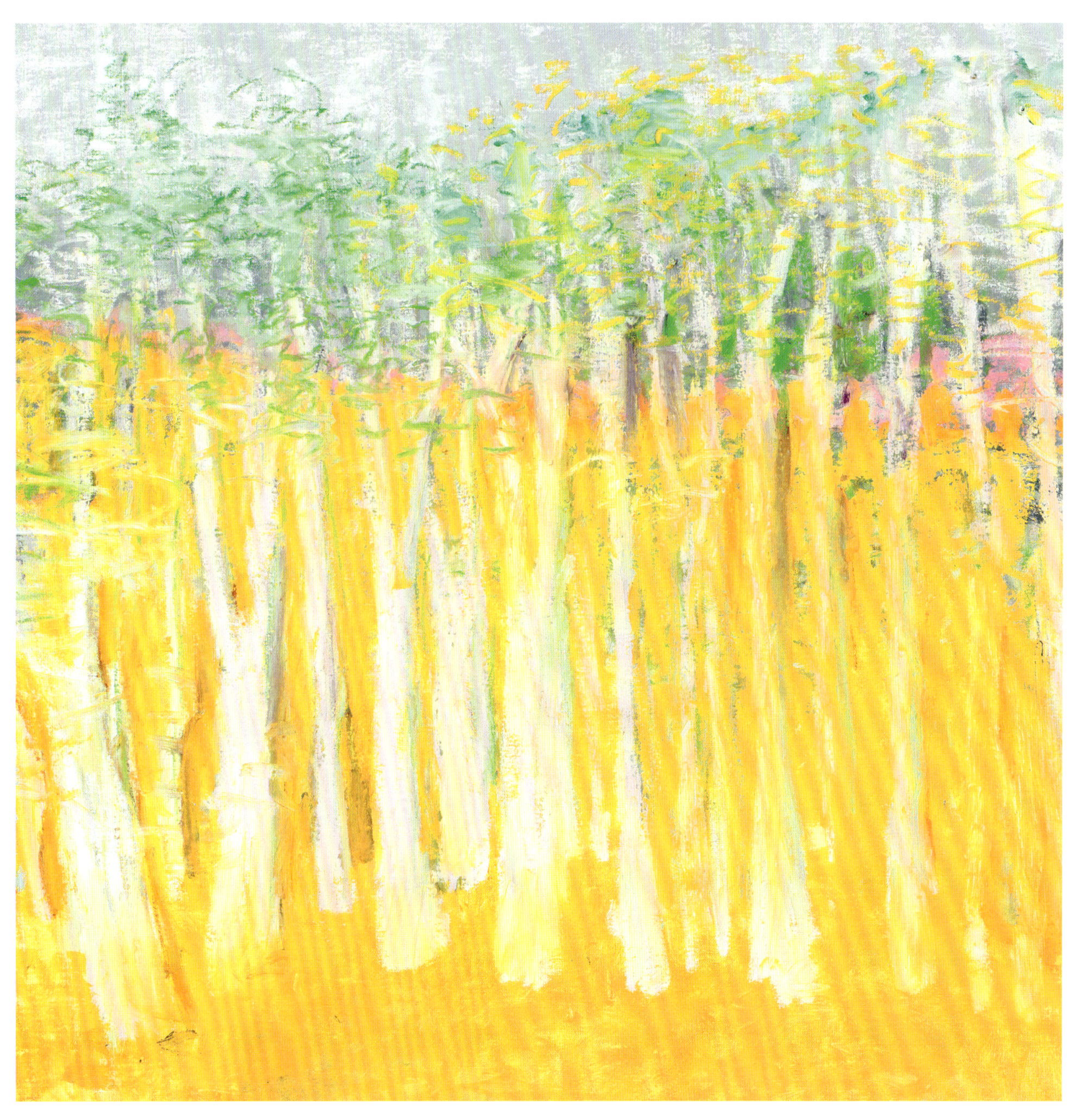

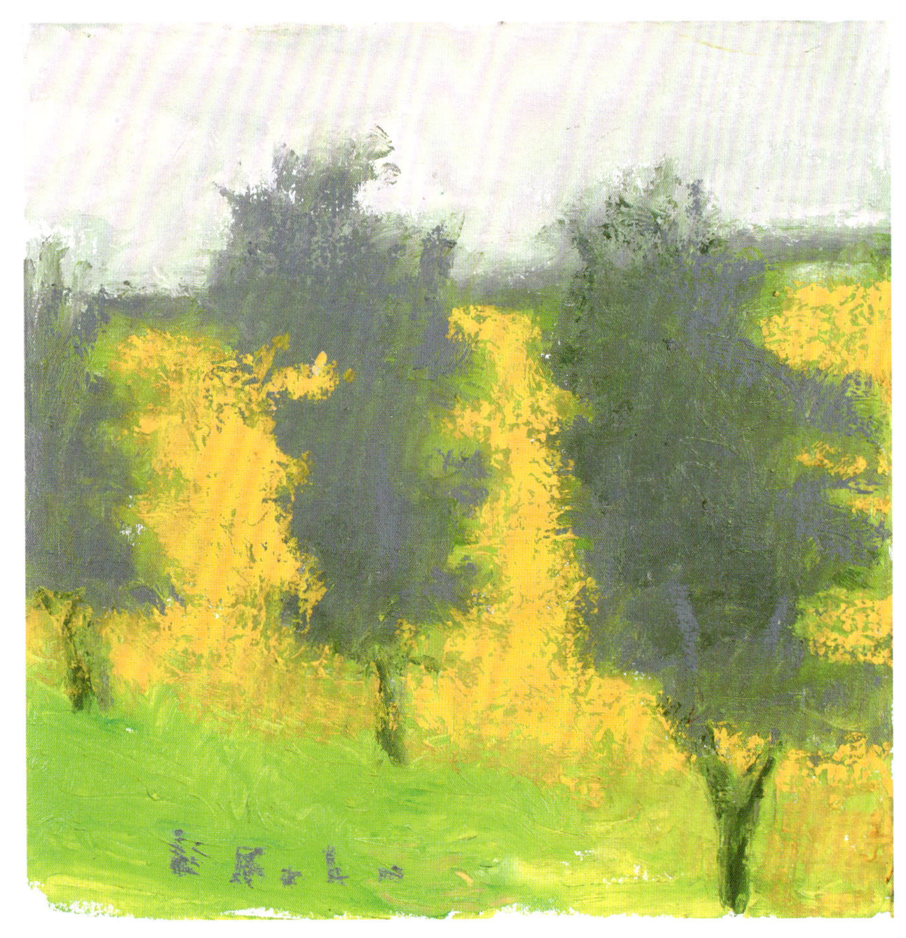

Two and a Half Trees
2018
oil on canvas
16 x 16 inches

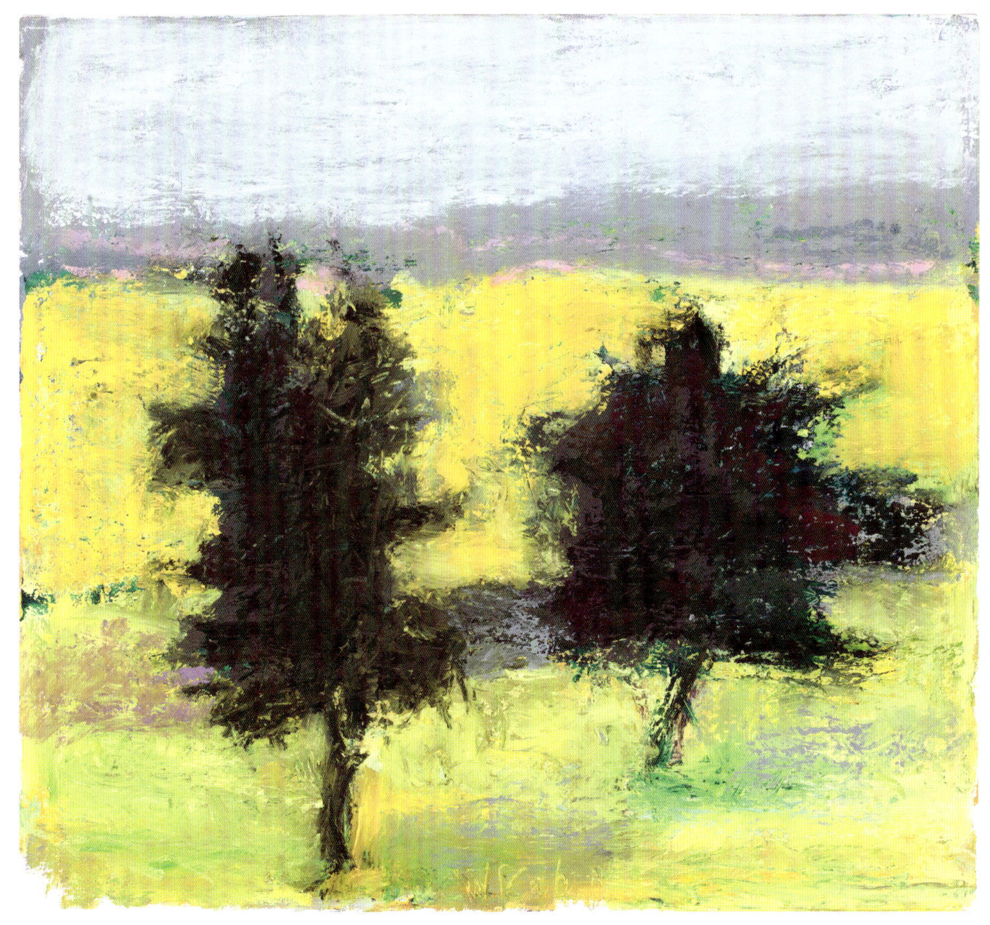

Two Trees, Almost a Square
2018
oil on canvas
18 x 20 inches

Dark Purple Corner
2018
oil on canvas
52 x 60 inches

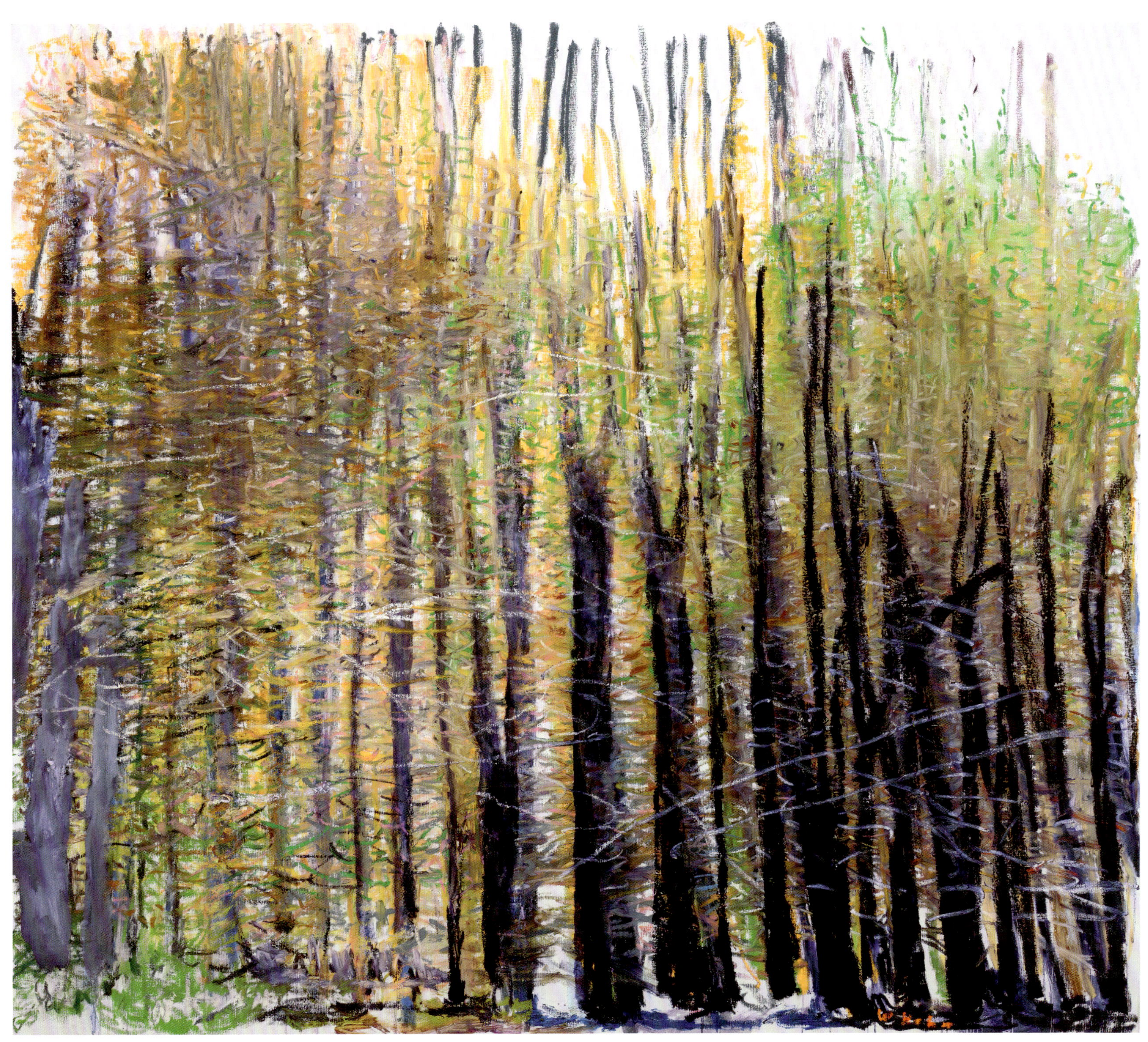

Olive Green
2018
oil on canvas
52 x 52 inches

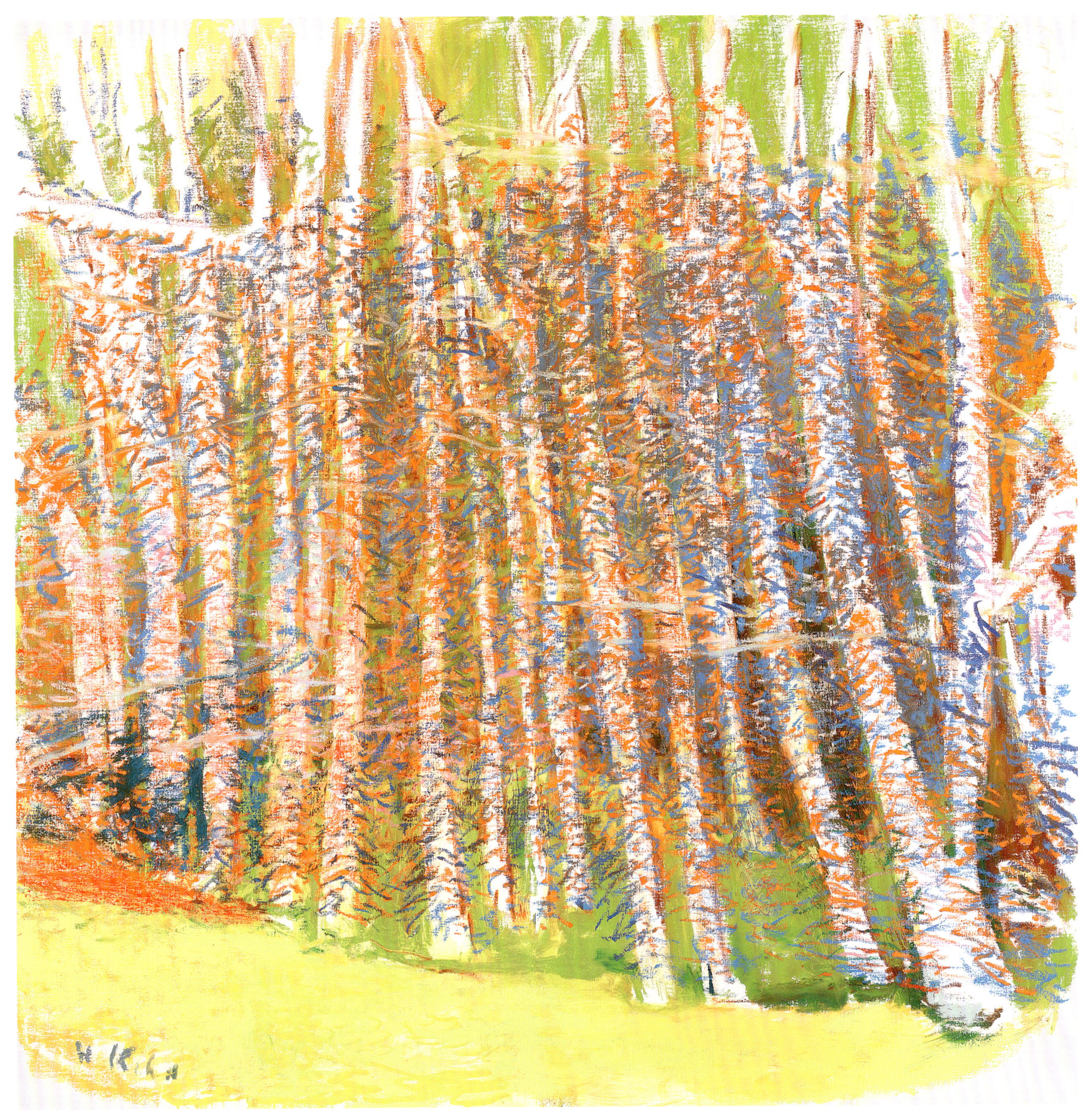

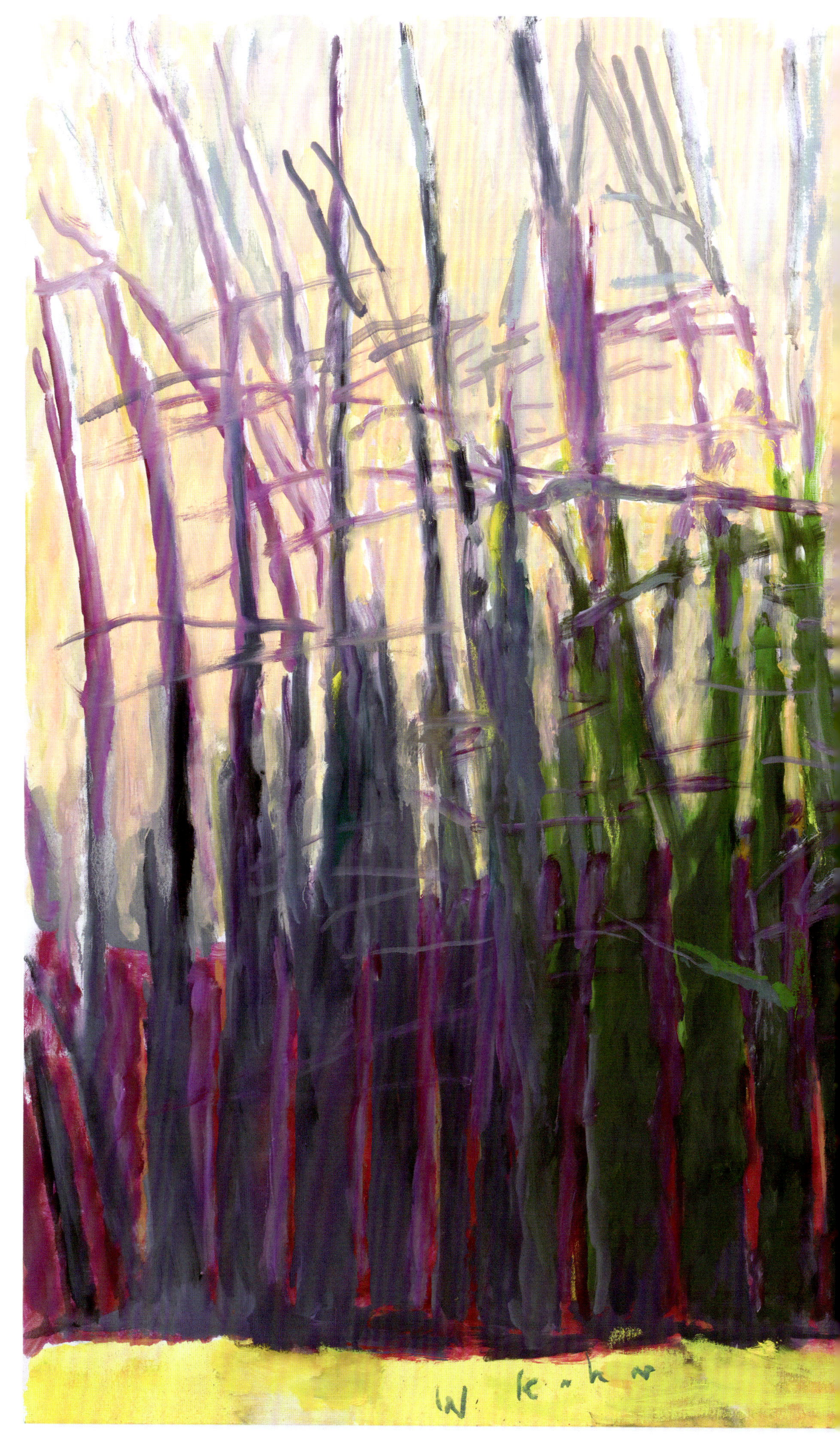

Against a Red Slope
2018
oil on canvas
46 x 68 inches

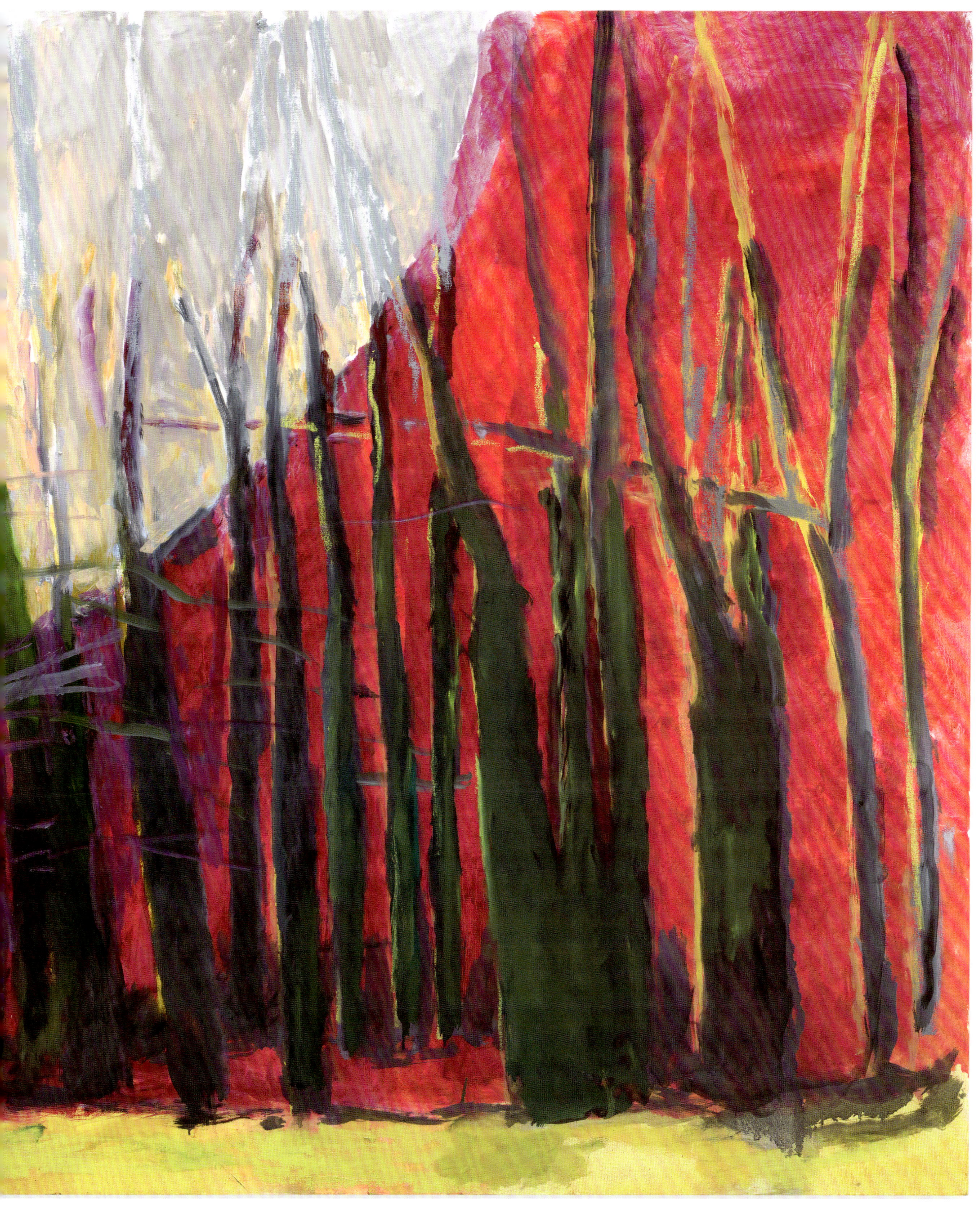

Two Levels of Green,
One of Orange
2018
oil on canvas
52 x 68 inches

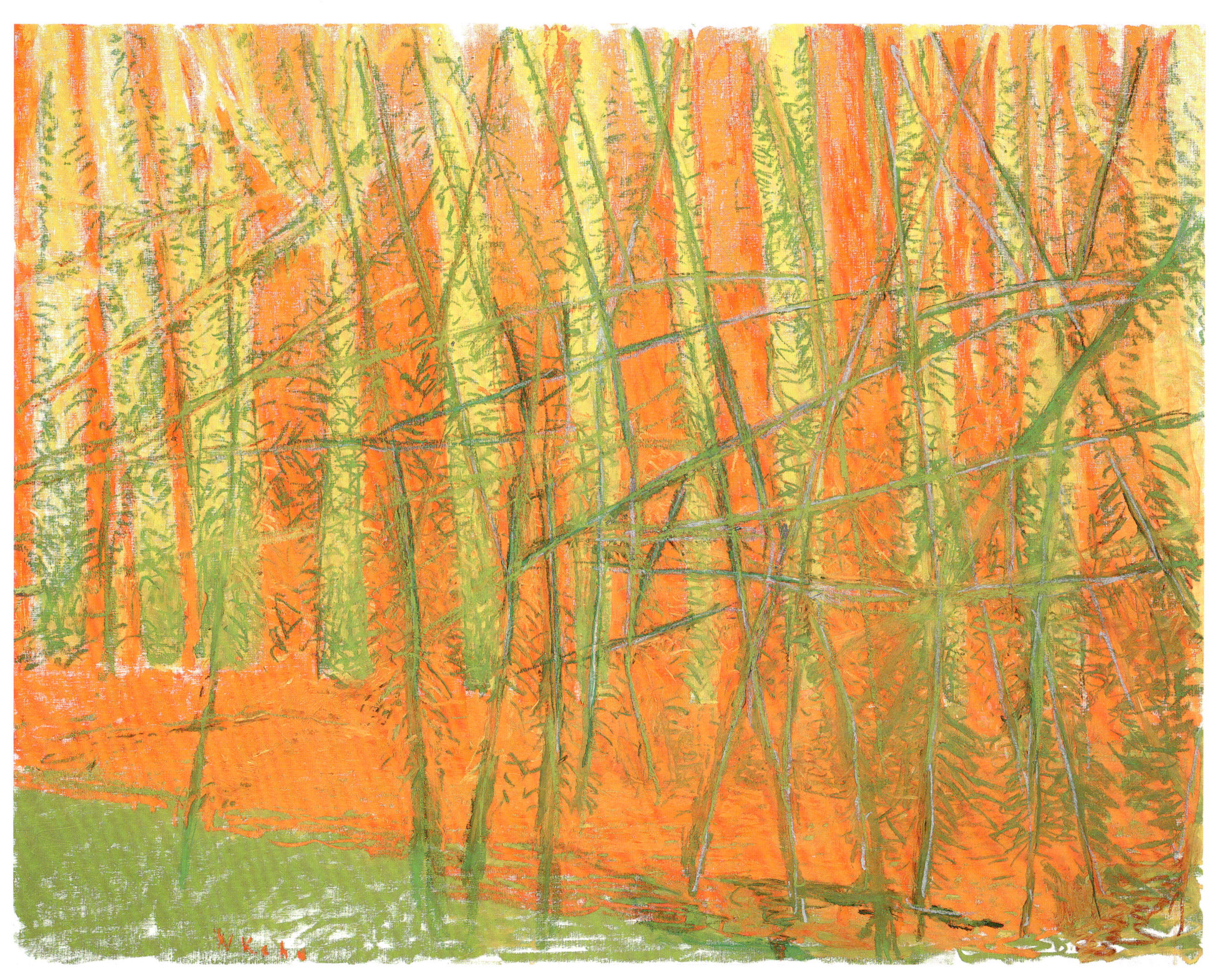

Blue Stage, Orange Wings
2019
oil on canvas
52 x 60 inches

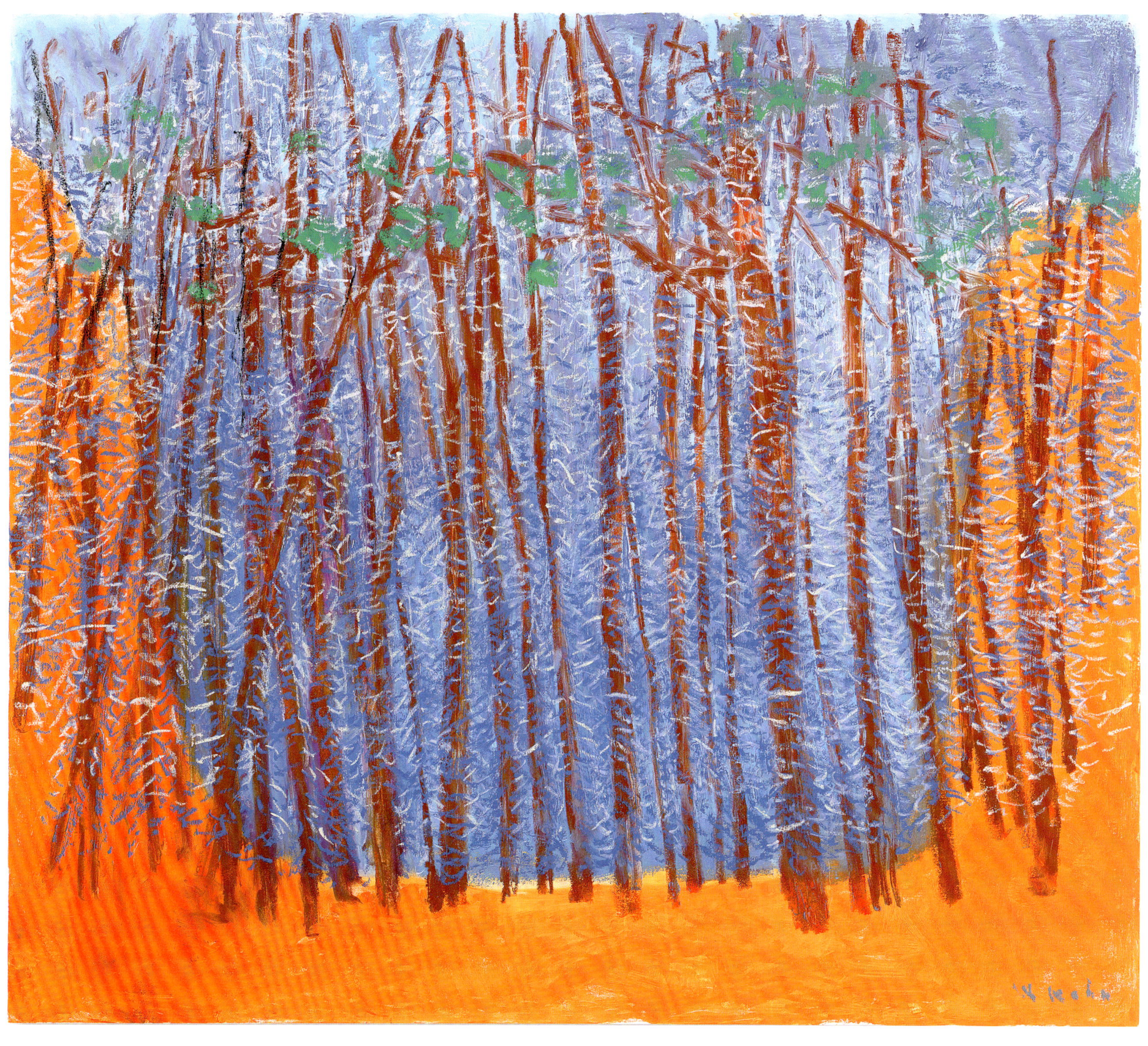

Orange, Barely Blue
2019
oil on canvas
52 x 60 inches

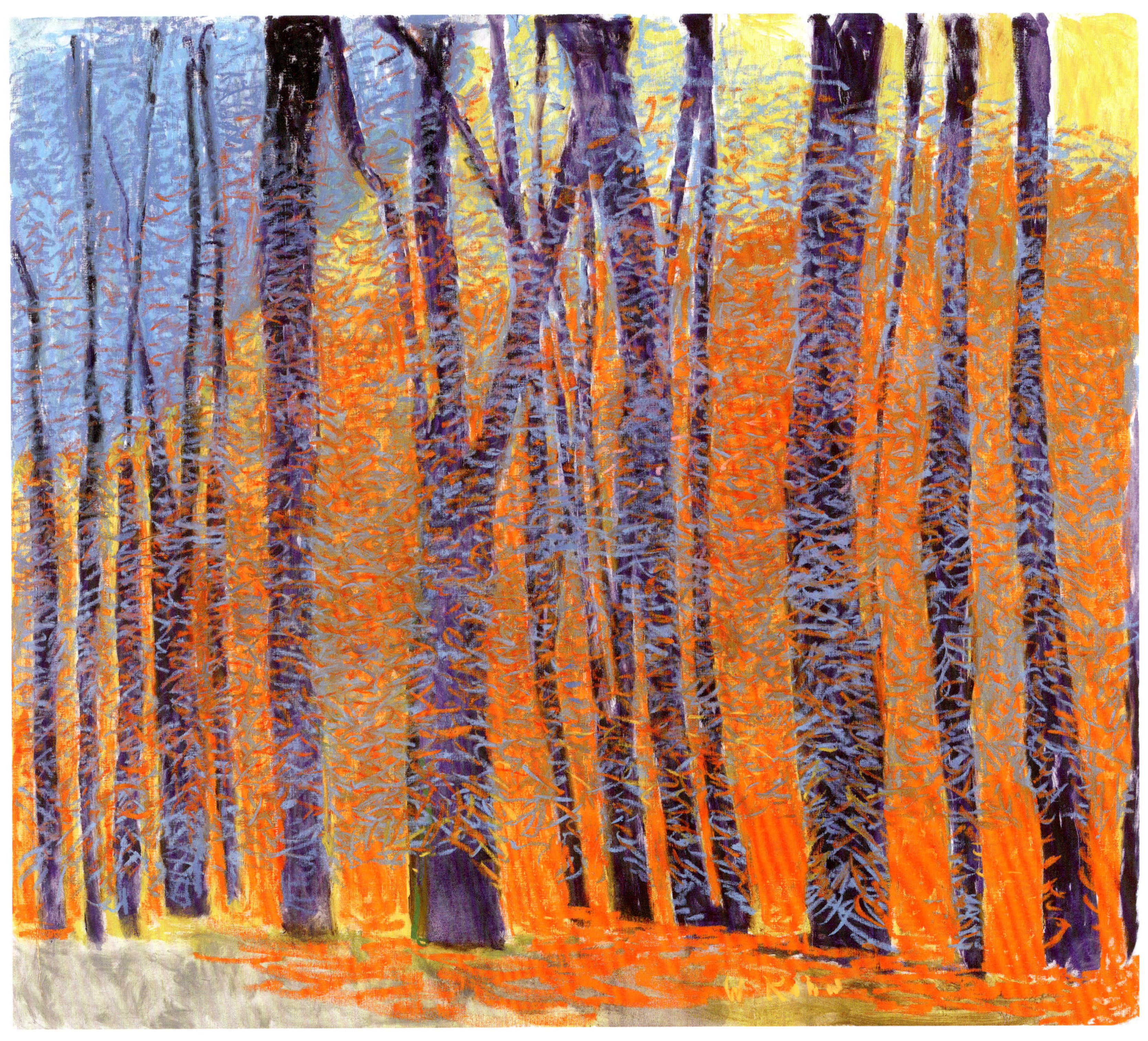

Redwoods
2019
oil on canvas
52 x 52 inches

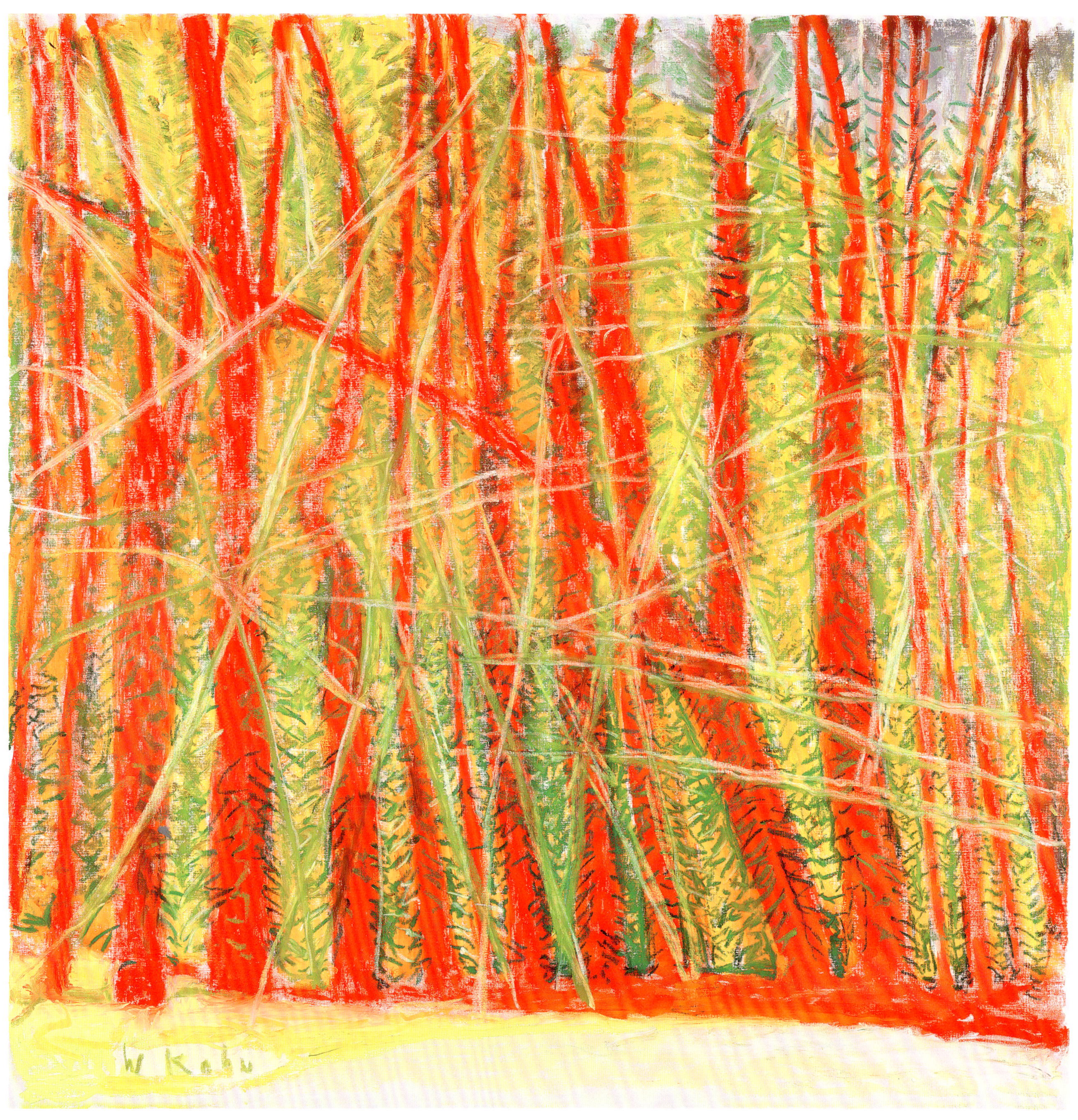
W Kahn

Confetti
2019
oil on canvas
28 x 28 inches

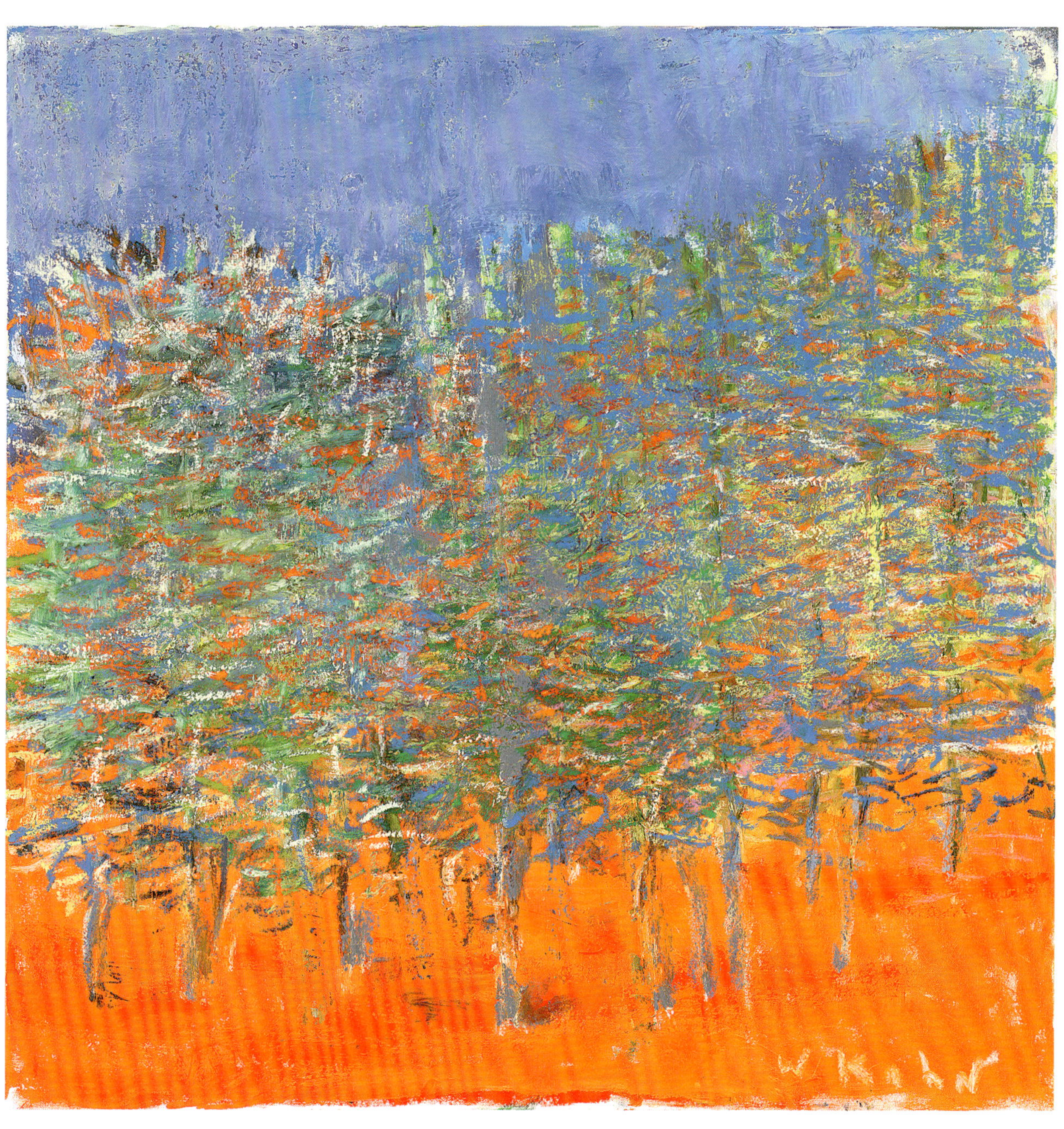

Difficult to Enter
2019
oil on canvas
40 x 52 inches

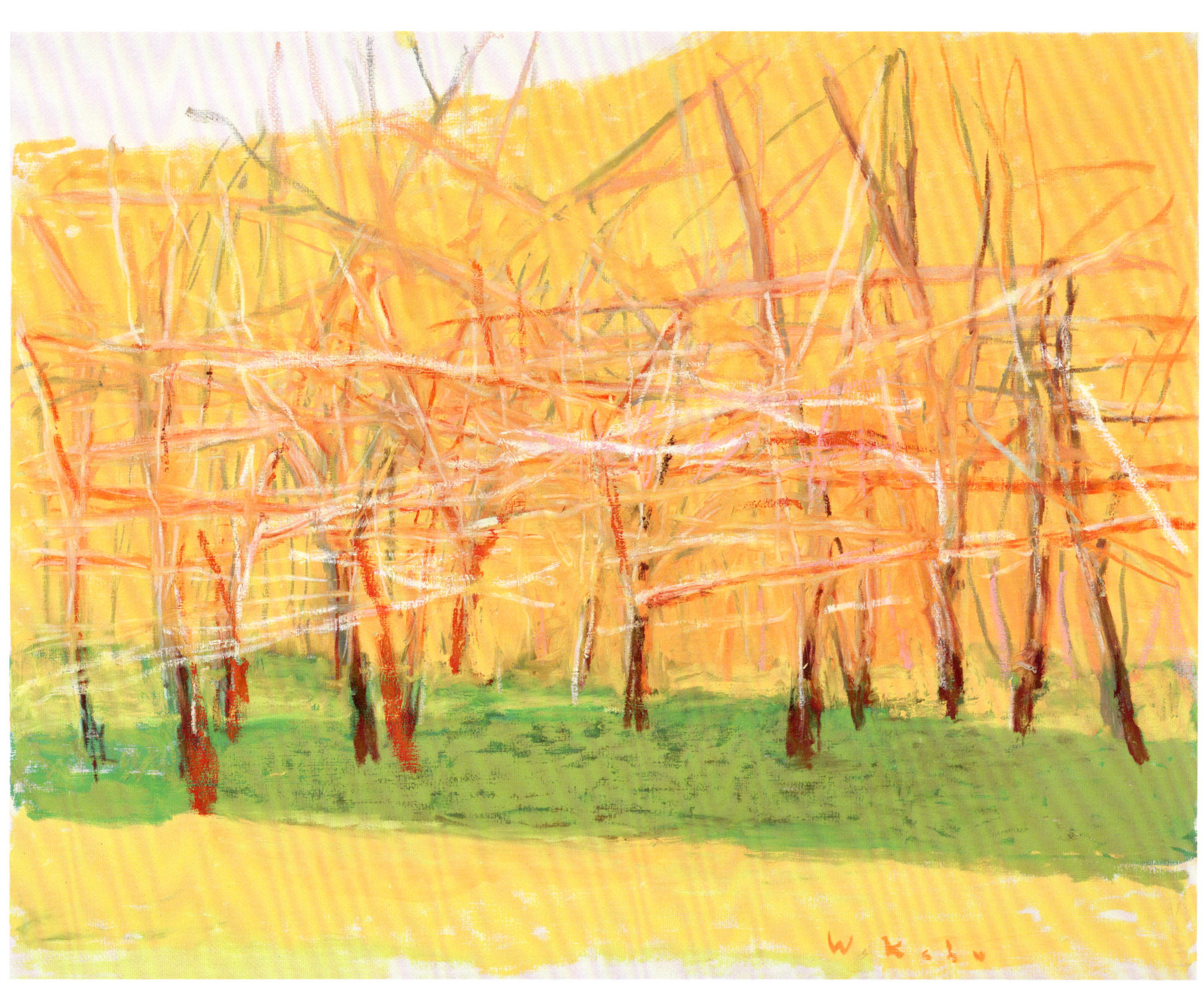

Somber
2020
oil on canvas
40 x 40 inches

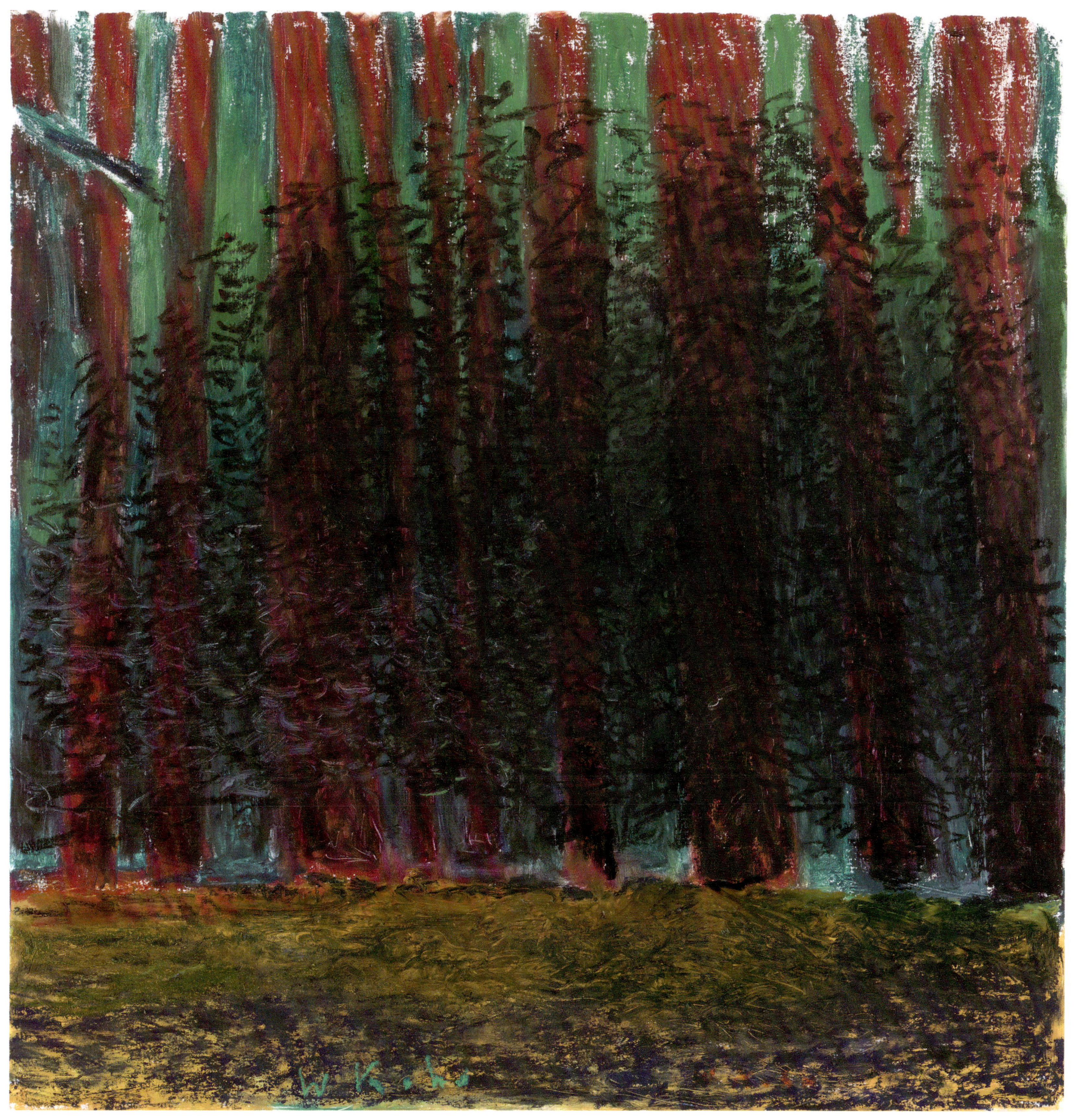

Sycamore (Diana's Favorite)
2020
oil on canvas
52 x 52 inches

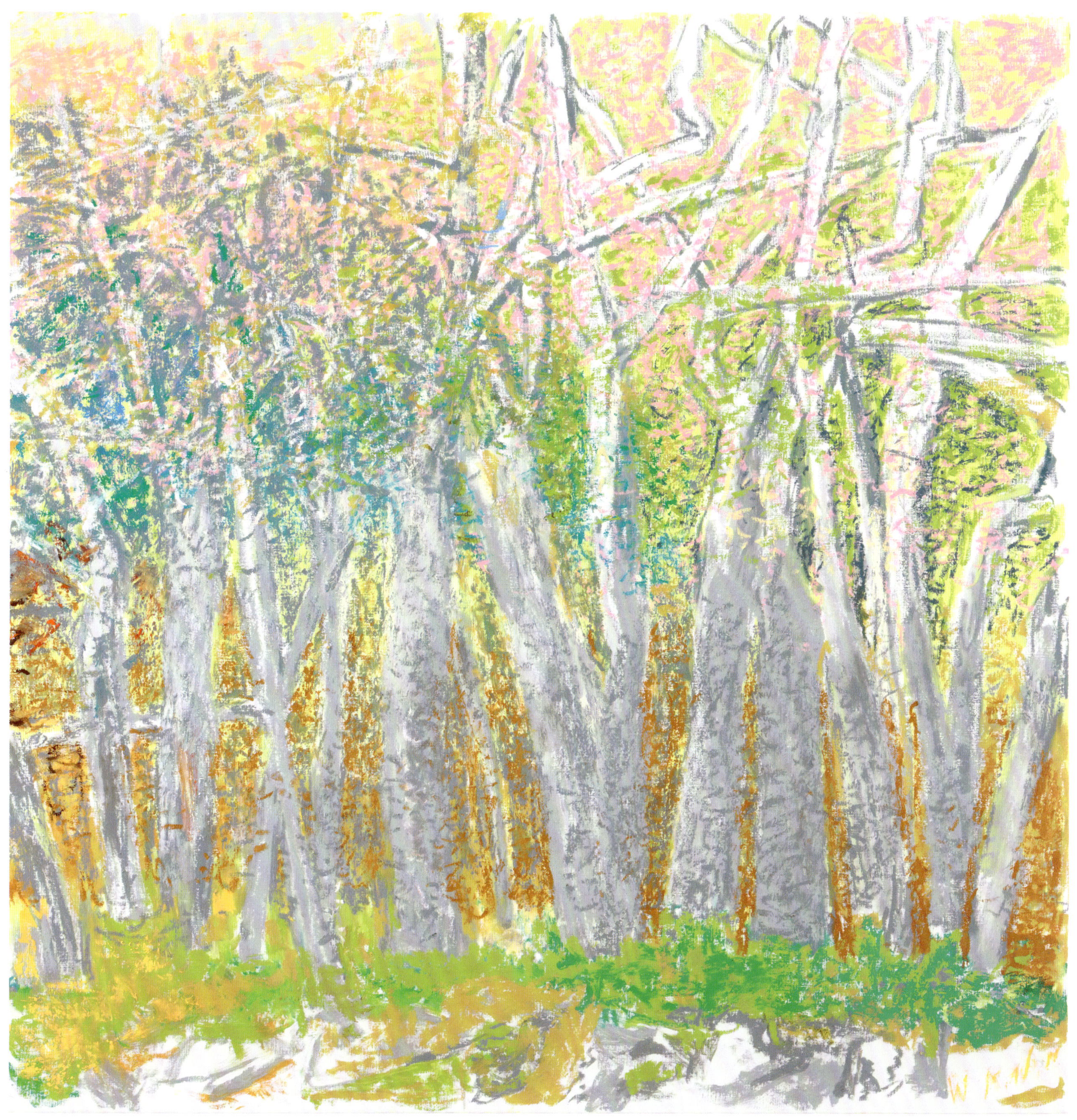

Talking with Wolf Kahn

WILLIAM C. AGEE INTERVIEWS WOLF KAHN IN MAY AND JUNE 2019

Excerpted from conversations between Wolf Kahn, art historians William C. Agee and Sasha Nicholas, and studio manager Diana Urbaska.

AGEE: Wolf, you mentioned that you believe there have been some definite changes just in the last year or two?

KAHN: Yes, I do.

AGEE: Can you talk about that?

KAHN: They talk about painters in their late periods. We have Titian and [Pierre] Bonnard and a few people like that who are really my gods. So, I figured now I'm starting my late period.

AGEE: At ninety-two.

KAHN: Well, it has a lot to do with modern medicine, because I've been in the hospital quite a few times in the last couple of years.

AGEE: Do you think you're now beginning your real late style?

KAHN: Who knows if I'm still alive in another six months and my late style started twenty years ago.

AGEE: But could we say that about you, that you went into a late style?

KAHN: Well, I didn't purposely go into it, but I guess it happens. I noticed that I'm doing things somewhat differently than I did, let's say, ten years ago.

AGEE: Can you describe those?

KAHN: I'm not in a great habit of talking about my own work, but I know that something that happens now that makes me a little worried is that sometimes it becomes easier to finish a painting. That's supposed to be a sign of laziness. But in most cases, it's just as difficult to do these paintings now as it was to do my paintings forty years ago.

URBASKA: You've also adapted your technique with the introduction of the paint sticks. I think that's been a major developmental change in the last ten years.

KAHN: I've been using them more and more—because I have to stay seated, I can't go walking back and forth, and I can't really hold a big palette. I'm not [Claude] Monet, who walked around with a huge palette and big brushes. I have a table full of these paint sticks and I almost build my whole paintings around them.

AGEE: When I last spoke with you, I remember going around the studio and I could always tell you were looking at a painting more than you were listening to me. And it was beautiful. I mean you jumped like an eagle. You saw something in the painting and you would go over and mark something, change something, add something. It was beautiful.

KAHN: Well, I'm feeling as long as the painting is in my studio, it's up for grabs.

URBASKA: It doesn't matter whether it has a frame on it or not.

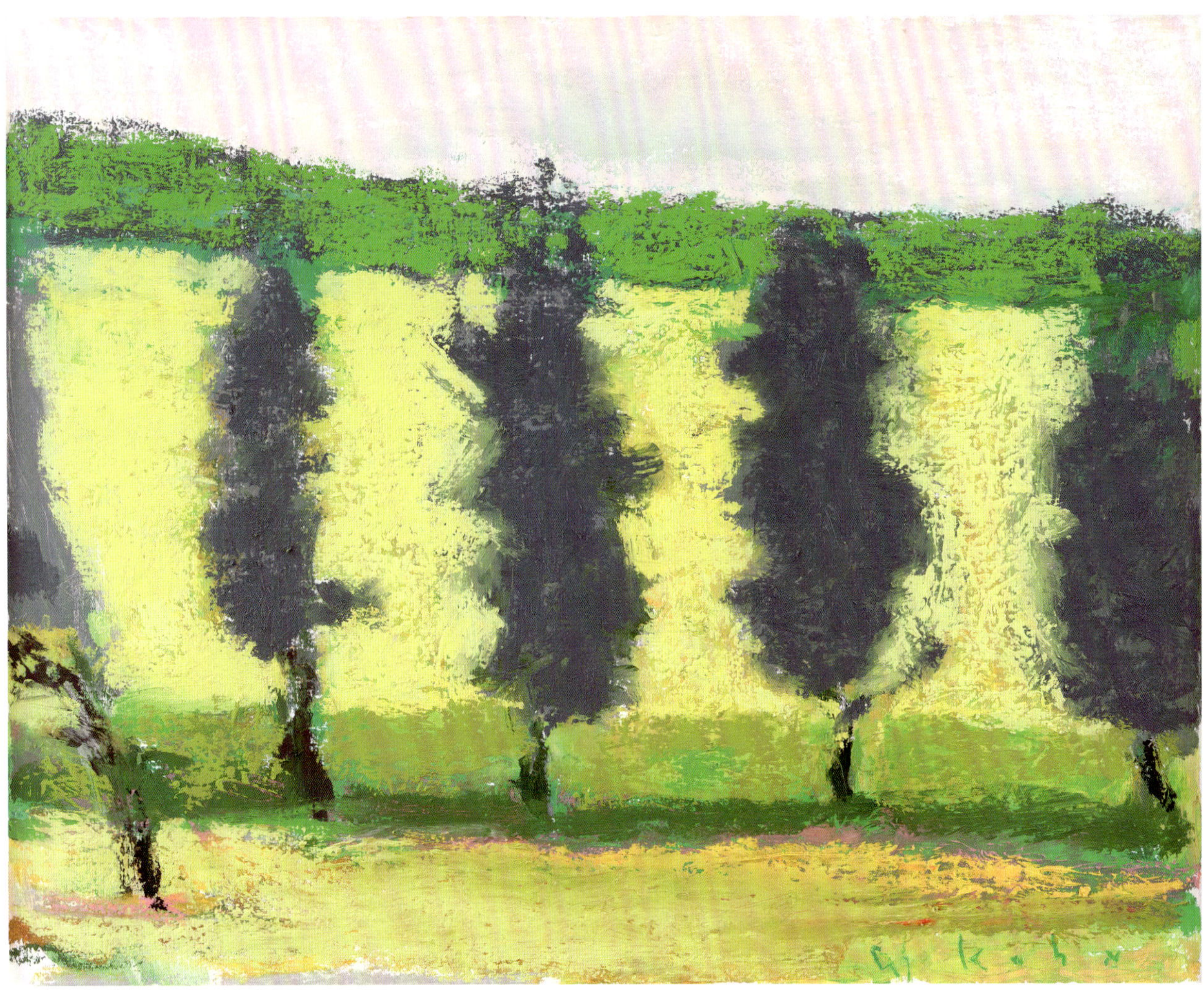

Five Trees in Silhouette
2018
oil on canvas
22 x 28 inches

AGEE: No. Do you think they're getting easier?

KAHN: Well, I mean I have a sense about them that either they work or they don't work. And once they don't work, they don't leave the studio until they do. And the idea of having to struggle and . . . What do they call it when you have to keep struggling?

URBASKA: Suffer?

KAHN: Yes, suffering over one's work, that idea is no longer so central to me.

AGEE: Well, don't you think maybe that after all these years of really first-rate painting your skill is now such that you don't have to?

KAHN: I get bored very easily, so the only way to save yourself from being bored is to do something new, something that you haven't done before, that you feel is a challenge. So, I've been doing that. But even the challenges are less challenging, because after all, after a lifetime of work, there are a few things you carry away that you could call "knowledge."

AGEE: For sure. It seems to me there's more contrast in your colors. The areas seem broader and more clearly marked. They don't seem to fuse as much as they did just a couple of years ago.

KAHN: Well, I don't know. I still have the feeling that a painting really should be just a field of texture. And to mark the areas clearly, of course, that works against it. So, that's one of the things that I try to overcome—the idea of having very clearly marked and designated color areas or drawing areas.

AGEE: A field, yes. Would you say the colors are more intense or brighter? I say the blue and orange over there really seem to pop out.

KAHN: One of my aims is not to make paintings that are like the rest of the paintings. To have each painting be a jumping-off point to something new.

AGEE: Well, this is interesting in this painting. It's almost like you're enclosing this. The trees and the blues not encircling, but framing it.

KAHN: Yes, sometimes, I think of the theater, and you have the wings.

URBASKA: The title is *Blue Stage, Orange Wings.*

AGEE: Like the theater.

KAHN: I've always liked [Nicolas] Poussin, the French painter.

AGEE: Of course.

KAHN: His paintings were all sort of built around two wings of happening—like a sunset, with something happening in the middle, where the light and the texture change is less dense—and I admire that. I wish I could do that regularly. I sometimes start a painting with the idea of having a light center and two darks on either side, and I guess this belongs to that genre. And, of course, one of the things that happens as you work is that you want to be sure the thing doesn't get symmetrical. I mean it should continue to be like life in general, asymmetrical, so that you don't feel you're repeating everything.

AGEE: An artist once said to me, while installing, "Ah, don't worry about it, Bill. Symmetry is overrated."

KAHN: Yes. Well, quote me on that. And of course, one way to control it is through these verticals.

AGEE: The verticals always remind me of Monet and his poplars.

KAHN: Yes, but I don't want to be mentioned in connection with Monet, because everybody does. Because compared to Monet, it's . . . What do they call it? Persona non grata. I mean of course, I love his work, but I don't like to think that I'm that influenced by him. That everybody should right away say, "Oh, Monet"? Which they tend to do. But if they see my work in its totality, it's really not like Monet. There are all kinds of artists I'm very fond of. I love, for example, [Francesco] Guardi, because I lived in Venice, and also Canaletto. They have this idea of trying to retain some sort of nonsymmetrical symmetry.

AGEE: Earlier you said that Albert Pinkham Ryder was a figure you really admired. Can you talk some more about that?

KAHN: I admire Ryder because, first of all, I think he had a genuinely mystical quality about his work. And people sometimes look at my paintings and they say, "Oh, they have a mystical quality," but since I don't purposely put mysticism into my paintings, I kind of say, "Oh, well, let them rave." I don't like to make large claims for my paintings, and I think neither did Ryder. He was a modest painter. There are these two great virtues that I think one should exemplify. One of them is modesty and the other one is generosity.

AGEE: What do you mean by "generosity" in one's work?

KAHN: It means that you have a feeling that you're dipping into a large trough as you paint. You're not just bound by rules, although they come out anyway. I am a faithful [Hans] Hofmann student, and he was a very generous soul. He taught that to those students who would listen—to be generous and to strive for freedom. One thing with painting: you should always try to be transcendent. That's a good word: transcendent. And as soon as you strive for transcendentalism, you right away get out of the ordinary. You're no longer satisfied with just the ordinary, the day to day. I think the day to day is the enemy of good art.

AGEE: You're like Ryder. The idea of just keep pushing, that there's something more you can explore—I mean, that's really a powerful idea.

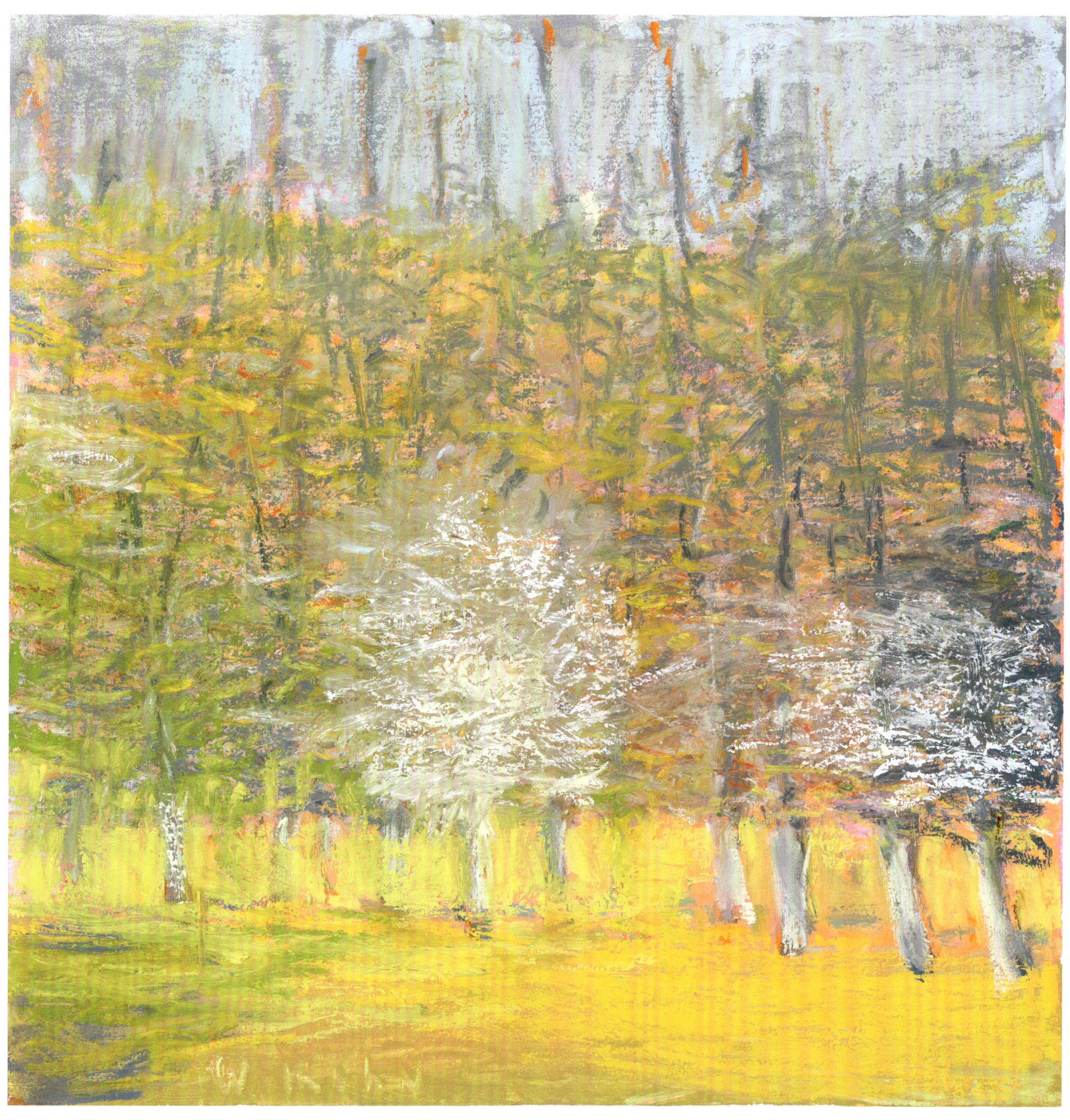

KAHN: My dealer, Miles [McEnery], says he likes best the paintings that were the most difficult for me; he says he likes to see me push. Well, I say, "Gee, that's terrible. You mean I have to work that hard?" Here I am an old man and I still have to work that hard. I can't just lay down on the job.

Inspired by Ryder
2019
oil on canvas
26 x 26 inches

AGEE: So, what other things have changed in your work over the last ten years?

KAHN: I'm really not driving for change—it just happens. And I don't believe in conscious choices that one makes. I believe that things should happen naturally. And they do if you let the idea go that you're driving toward a certain end. You're not. I keep wishing to be surprised by my own work. And sometimes I am, but not always. Like I have a painting, *Five Trees in Silhouette* (see p. 217). See the influence of Ryder? I worked very hard on that painting, especially the spaces between the trees. That's what I like to call "elephant skin." It's so filled with paint. What I wanted to do there is the same thing that I do in a lot of my tree paintings, where the difference between the tree and the background color is interchangeable.

AGEE: The space is as dense as the tree. That certainly would relate to Ryder. It's a beautiful picture.

KAHN: I consider that one of the better paintings that I've made lately. People ask me, "Is your painting about spring or summer or winter?" And I say, "It's about all of those." And this painting is about any place; I'm not trying to think of any single defined place. See, that's one of the things about the barn paintings—each was always about a specific place, and that doesn't lend itself to the way I'm working now.

AGEE: Simple. Is that a fair description of some of the recent work?

KAHN: I'm in favor of it. You might also mention that among contemporary artists, I'm very fond of Agnes Martin. I like her a lot. And not because of the size of it or the spareness of it. Because behind it all you feel a drive toward transcendentalism. Which in my best work I think is also visible. And there's another artist that I like very much: Susan Rothenberg. She has a very nice way of keeping painting alive. Also, she has a feeling of wanting to make a texture. I think I'm subconsciously influenced by her. She has a way of arriving at images rather than starting with them. And I'd like to have that feeling, too.

AGEE: She's a wonderful artist.

AGEE: We started off talking about a question that comes up: Do you have a late style? And I'm thinking, the work has changed and there have been changes, but your fundamental principles have been the same for fifty years.

KAHN: I'm always gnawing on the same bone.

AGEE: And you've also said that every painting leads to something else, to some other issue or problem.

NICHOLAS: If you've been gnawing on the same bone, have you kind of whittled it? Have you distilled what you're doing in some way?

KAHN: Don't want to. You know, distillation is not where I'm at. In fact, what I want to have happen, in my development, is to become less distilled, more fanciful, and less held back. Certainly not stylistic, because style is something that art historians and commentators impose. It's not inherent in the work. *Style* is one of those dirty words. It's a word like *creativity*.

AGEE: I think one of the most telling observations, for me anyway, about your work is that for all these reasons you have made art of the highest standard, and totally original.

KAHN: Well, "totally original"—that's going too far.

AGEE: I don't know of anybody who paints landscapes quite like this. I knew about the importance for you of Hofmann, but then I also found out about your interest in [Mark] Rothko. You said something like "Do Rothko over again, after nature."

KAHN: I like what [Paul] Cézanne said about Poussin, he said that he'd like to paint Poussin over from nature.

AGEE: Cézanne said that? Of course, this stuff goes on and on. I continue to find it interesting that [Jackson] Pollock was important for you, and [Willem] de Kooning, and Rothko.

KAHN: Well, Pollock became important to me quite late. Because I didn't understand what was going on with Pollock until I saw a show of his drawings in the MAXXI, the museum of modern art in Rome. And I could see that he was a direct descendant of Surrealism. And then all of a sudden what he was up to started to make sense. The idea that he liked to paint without any reference to any outside influence except paint itself. He was not a descriptive painter at all.

KAHN: I sometimes say about myself that I try to paint nondescriptive landscape.

AGEE: Nondescriptive landscape. Yes, that's good. One thing that strikes me is that I think a lot's been made of trying to figure out how landscape and abstract art work together. One seems to preclude the other, but for many artists, like Rothko, the abstract work comes out of a landscape format.

KAHN: Hofmann said—this is actually a famous elocution of his—he said, "There is no such thing as figurative painting and abstract painting. There's only stupid painting and intelligent painting."

AGEE: Fairfield Porter said there is not as much difference between abstract and real as we think, because in the abstract there is an overwhelming sense of the real. You were talking about the green line here, and you said, "It was so hard to come by."

KAHN: I don't believe in prior calculation. If I start a painting with the idea that I'm going to go in a certain direction, the painting always takes me in another direction. I certainly never knew that this was going to be a painting with an elephant skin. It's just a record of one's failures. Because doing it right the first time—that doesn't happen.

NICHOLAS: So, it's not something desirable?

KAHN: No, it's not something desirable. It's something that happens in spite of one's best intentions.

AGEE: I have thought maybe that thickness of texture might have been a change in the work, but this may have been just more of a one-shot—

KAHN: Yes, part of the history of the painting.

NICHOLAS: But it wasn't something that you wanted to experiment with?

KAHN: I don't ever want to experiment with anything. It always happens.

NICHOLAS: It's the painting directing you.

KAHN: Yes.

AGEE: You talk about how, as I gather, in almost every painting you run into a rough spot?

KAHN: It's usually the lower left-hand corner. I don't know why.

AGEE: That's great.

KAHN: I had a friend who became quite a well-known painter—Alfred Jensen. Jensen and I were both Hofmann students at the same time. So, I invited Jensen over to see my studio, and he came and he looked at each painting and absolutely unerringly put his finger on this spot that I hadn't resolved, where I was still in trouble. He could do that with each painting.

AGEE: I asked you once that great old question that I remember from Abstract Expressionist dialogues at the club: How do you know when a painting is finished? And you said, "It tells you."

KAHN: [Robert] Motherwell said his painting proceeded by a series of mistakes. And when he got to a mistake that he couldn't correct, then the painting was finished.

AGEE: But what does the painting tell you?

KAHN: What Motherwell said is absolutely true, because when he no longer saw something that needed to be dealt with, the painting was finished. But I disagree with Motherwell insofar as you don't correct paintings—you just allow them to grow.

AGEE: You've talked about looking for a transcendental effect, and I really love that, and I have come over the years to develop a deep spiritual sense. It's not religious, just a one-on-one transcendental connection with some power higher than myself.

KAHN: I feel that when I'm painting, unless I reach that stage where the painting no longer becomes an everyday issue, then I'm on a good track. But I think that's a very unfashionable point of view. I have great respect for what the painting needs.

AGEE: That's the final judge for you, right?

KAHN: Yes.

NICHOLAS: Do you ever just decide, this isn't working, I'm just casting it off? Or do you wrestle with them always until you get to a good place?

KAHN: I wrestle with them, but sometimes I don't get to a good place, but I get somewhere else.

NICHOLAS: A place where you're okay. You continue wrestling.

AGEE: And say to hell with it and throw out the painting?

URBASKA: Rarely, but it's happened.

AGEE: So that becomes the challenge for you, making it worse?

KAHN: Sometimes you have to make it worse in order to make it become better.

AGEE: Do you ever worry about fiddling too much? Do you think sometimes you just ought to let it go?

KAHN: I used to worry about that all the time, but usually if you don't let it go, it's better. It helps the painting.

AGEE: So, you take out a canvas and it's blank. How do you get it started? We've talked about the finish, but how do you get it started?

KAHN: You worry about that moment a lot. And you finally decide, well, I might as well put down something and see what happens. And then pretty soon you've got something going, but the beginning on a bare canvas is a painful moment. A lot of times I do what I've done here: I have a small painting of red and blue, and I decided I'd do another one a little bigger. I think there is such a thing as a painterly space.

AGEE: Painterly space?

KAHN: Yeah, realistic painting, in my mind, means unsuccessful painting. You've got to take it somewhere else.

NICHOLAS: I like the colors on this painting. It's an unexpected group of colors for me.

KAHN: That's a good word, *unexpected*.

AGEE: That's a good point, the color is always unexpected. And you talked about the fact that you like chemical, acidic colors that everyone hates, or no one thinks of, and you make it into something.

KAHN: In my studio you can see the one I'm working on right now, which is in the middle of undergoing changes. It's really at the stage where I don't even know what it's about. I'm trying to determine whether it's worth continuing on that painting.

AGEE: But you always do.

KAHN: Yes. I like to say, "No seamless mending."

AGEE: No seamless mending.

KAHN: They have that saying in a tailor's shop. Then there's another saying: You must always go further than you must go. I use both of those sayings in guiding me to make changes. I start messing around, making little tiny changes, and I know that I'm violating the one that says, "You must always go further than you should go." [Jean] Cocteau said that. As soon as you've started making small changes, you're in trouble. You've got to be able to project strength. Once you get into thinking that you've cut something there and all you have to do is just make a small change here and there, you're no longer projecting strength; instead you're projecting insecurity.

NICHOLAS: I remember reading in one interview where you said something about how a branch looks better when it looks like a brushstroke, and if you start fiddling with it too much—

KAHN: It starts to look too much like a branch. The idea of making a branch look like a branch always means that you're weakening the initial impulse. While if you put it in strongly as a brushstroke, then you're still on your original impulse.

NICHOLAS: Right. I wondered if that was an example of seamless mending. If you start fussing with a detail of a branch or something like that.

KAHN: Well, it's seamless mending, and it has more to do with in general keeping the painting in a state of suspension as long as possible. I think that's what I'm bringing from the Abstract Expressionists. Because they have that idea. Trying to drive toward a finished painting is the wrong way to go about it. What you try to do is keep the strength of the initial impulse. I'm sure I've painted my way past good stages in a painting many times. But you see, the whole idea is not to go toward a finish. Avoid thinking of going toward a finish. What you want to do is to take the painting on its own terms and then allow it to speak to you in such a way that you haven't driven toward some kind of finish.

NICHOLAS: When a viewer comes in, and looks at a finished painting, is it important to you that they're seeing the process?

KAHN: You can't control that. What you do is you just hope. You hope that people see the painting the way you want them to, but you can't control that.

AGEE: You said that you like to push the painting toward the point where you may get yourself in trouble, but it retains its strength. What did you say? The strength, drama . . .

KAHN: Austerity?

AGEE: And austerity. Now, I don't feel these are austere paintings. That color, the richness.

KAHN: I'm not driving toward strength and austerity. You just hope they come about. I mean a lot of the stuff you just hope that it works for you rather than against you. I don't want it to have even the smallest aspect of being an illustration. That's one thing that Hofmann taught. One of the things I really try to do is to make a nondescriptive landscape.

AGEE: You do start from some memory of what you've seen though, right?

KAHN: Sometimes. See this one here? Totally without a memory of something that I've seen. Just a painting that arrived at a certain point and then I drove it toward conclusion. Get the painting to arrive at a certain point. That's a mysterious process. You just keep on worrying about the picture until it tells you what it wants to be. That's also the Abstract Expressionist point of view. I am a formalist artist. That means that you're primarily interested in structure rather than in description. That's me, being a formalist, but at the same time, I like to draw. I do like to describe. I'm constantly fighting against taking that too far.

NICHOLAS: Here, this one you call *Difficult to Enter (Small Version)* (see fig. 9). Here, it's about how our eyes play off the trees and the space between them. Here, it's much denser.

KAHN: One of my titles is *Dense and Transparent* (see p. 224). I think you want both going on at the same time. It's a paradox. In successful paintings, that's what happens. One thing I kept having to work on is to keep this density, and at the same time, be transparent enough that the tree could exist within that context.

AGEE: It's a balancing act.

KAHN: I like to think of the painting very much having its own life and slowly allowing its needs to be felt. I'm

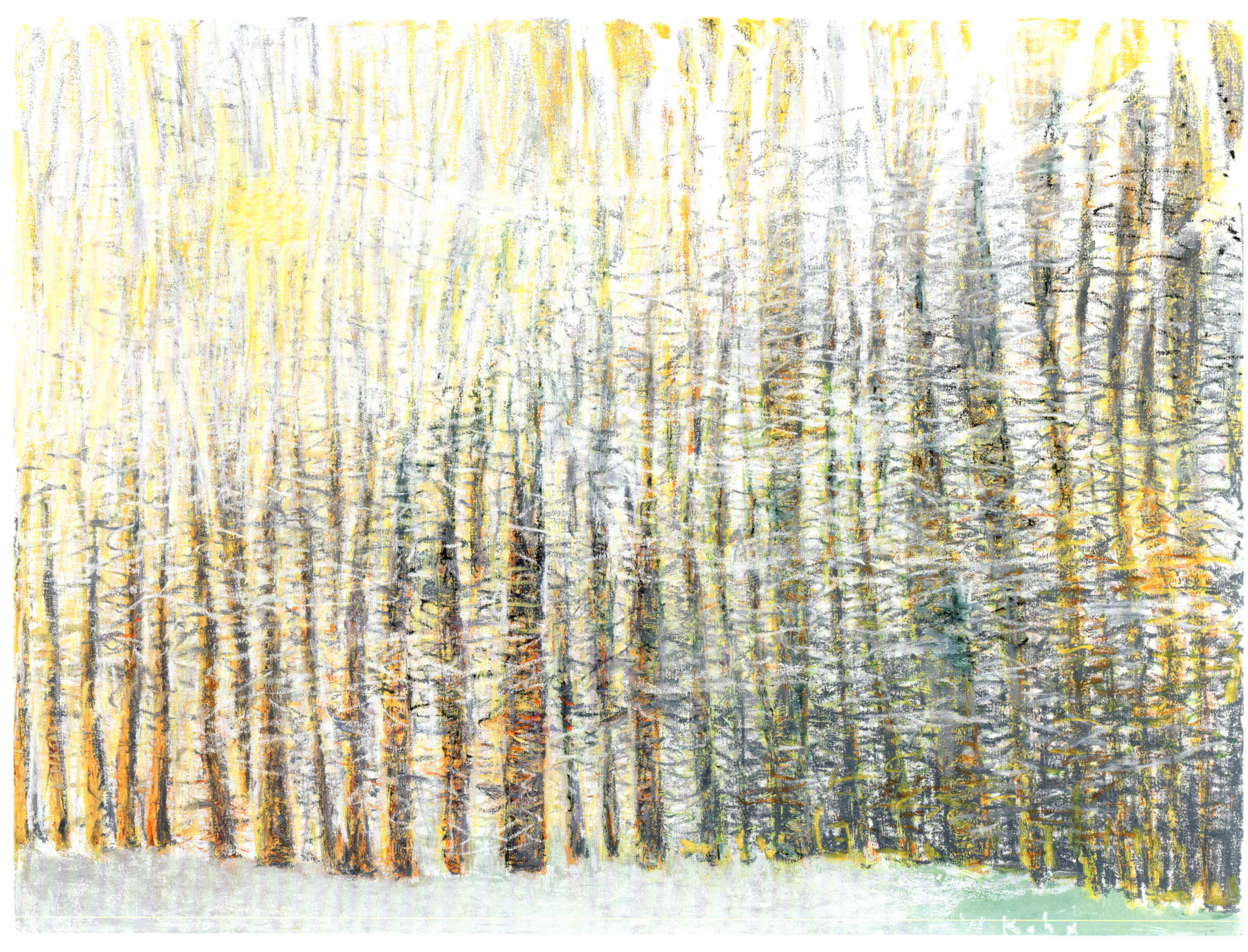

Dense and Transparent
2016
oil on canvas
52 x 72 inches

trying to make paintings that are severe and austere. I like that word, *austere*. I've been accused, I think unjustly, of making easy paintings.

AGEE: Don't listen to those people, Wolf. Anybody who uses color is always accused of being too easy, too decorative, because people don't understand color. That goes back to [Henri] Matisse, at least. Probably echoed against the Impressionists, too, but especially Matisse.

KAHN: That's right. I think Matisse was brilliant with color and also austere. The overall feeling of the painting was not to be a pleaser. I feel like I'm doing things that are going to destroy the initial impulse of a painting altogether. That doesn't make me unhappy. The painting deserves to be punished.

NICHOLAS: The unruly painting.

KAHN: Yes.

NICHOLAS: Well, maybe it's an adventure.

AGEE: I think that's a good analogy. I think you always see a painting as a new adventure, right? I mean, it's something new to pursue.

KAHN: The word *new* doesn't mean much to me. No. Ezra Pound said you should always go for the new. That's not my sense of the struggle at all.

AGEE: Well, new also means that you set to yourself certain problems and challenges a long, long time ago and you're still in pursuit of that. If it was something always new for you, you would have had thirty late styles, but you haven't really.

KAHN: No, I mean that's also one of the things I look at as an ongoing process. That seems to me it's been quite healthy because I've been developing things that have been innate in the work that I've been doing since the time I was in art school. I've never had to change from being abstract or representational, or trying to paint landscapes and painting nudes. Those problems didn't exist for me. I've got plenty of other problems.

AGEE: One thing that we haven't talked about is the intense light in your pictures.

KAHN: That again is something that happens by itself.

AGEE: Sure, but color is light in one sense, right?

KAHN: More blackish color, too.

AGEE: There is an interesting history of black, right? It was banished from the Impressionist palette, but there was a German color theorist who in about 1915 said, "No, black can be a primary." Matisse was one of the first to pick up on it.

KAHN: Well, Matisse was the only one of the Fauves who was able to use black. I mean, he thought of it as a color.

AGEE: There is, of course, that whole history of black and white in painting. It's color. It's just another color.

NICHOLAS: You've talked about wanting to achieve a danger point in color.

KAHN: Yes, the danger point is when the painting starts to lack austerity.

NICHOLAS: That's the danger point.

KAHN: Yes. When it's no longer a painting that has inherent austerity.

AGEE: You've said before that color is the only thing that distinguishes painting from—

KAHN: All other modes or media. Hofmann used to say that painting is 80 percent color.

NICHOLAS: If color is 80 percent, what's the other 20 percent?

KAHN: I would say descriptive substructure of some kind.

AGEE: I mentioned the row of vertical trees used by Monet, [Piet] Mondrian, and others.

KAHN: It's a good way to organize. It's a good way to organize one's structure.

AGEE: It gives you a way to start. Then, one thing after another. That's what the American flag is—stripes, one thing after another.

NICHOLAS: Right. Mondrian's grids came out of trees, right?

AGEE: Sure. Exactly.

NICHOLAS: What are the things that you think people don't know about your work that they need to know?

KAHN: I'm really not involved in nature when it comes down to it. I'm a non-naturalist landscape painter. I just think that landscape is a tradition that's always going to be around. Nobody can make it go away.

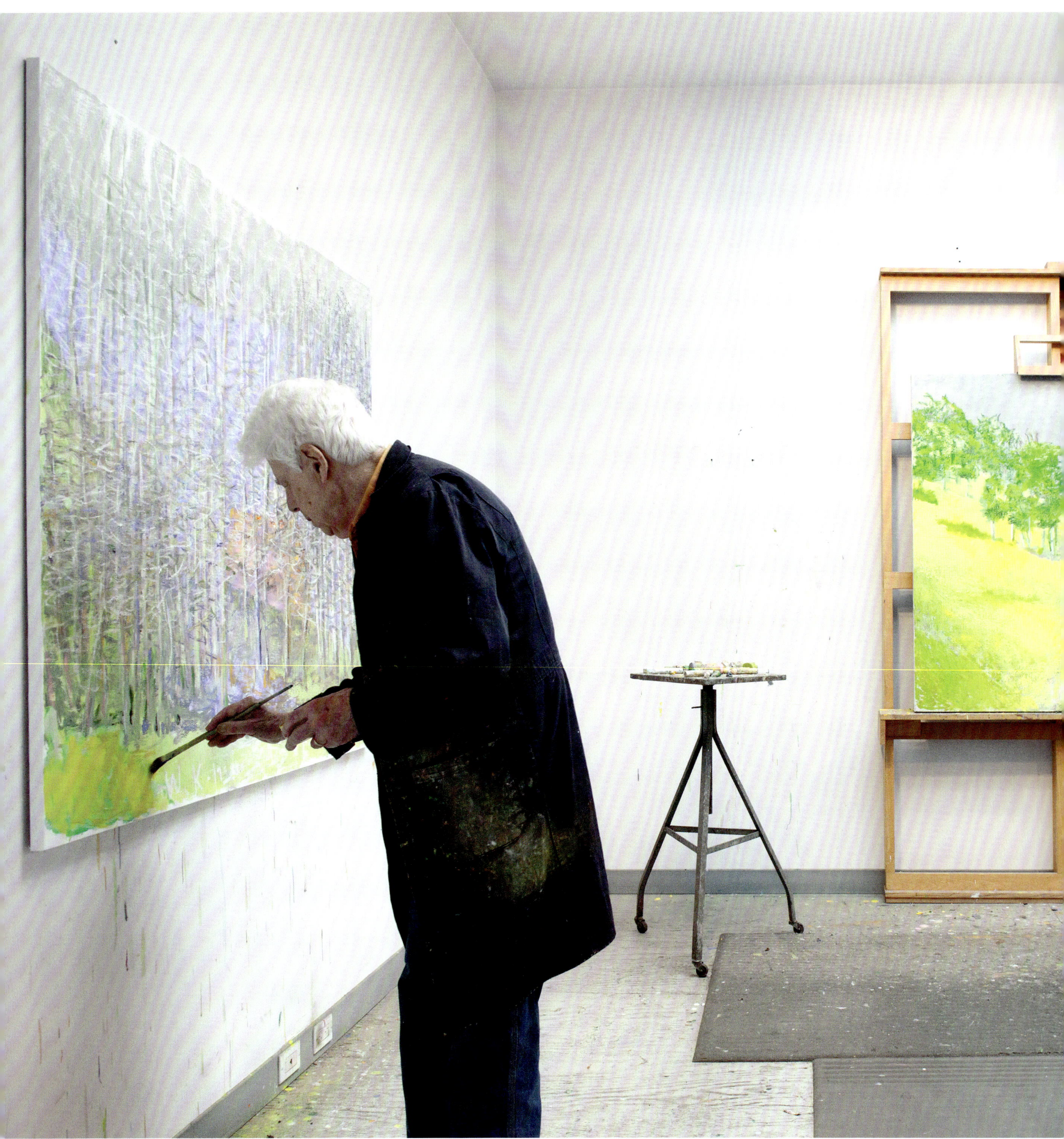

Wolf Kahn in his New York studio, 2015

CHRONOLOGY

1927

Hans Wolfgang Kahn is born on October 4 in Stuttgart, Germany, the fourth child of Nellie Budge and Emil Kahn. His father is conductor of the Stuttgart Philharmonic and the South German Radio Symphony Orchestra. Shortly after Kahn's birth, his mother leaves the family. In 1930, Emil Kahn marries Ellen Beck, a young singer who does not wish to raise a toddler, so Kahn is sent to live with his paternal grandmother, Anna Kahn. Kahn's mother dies in Berlin in 1932.

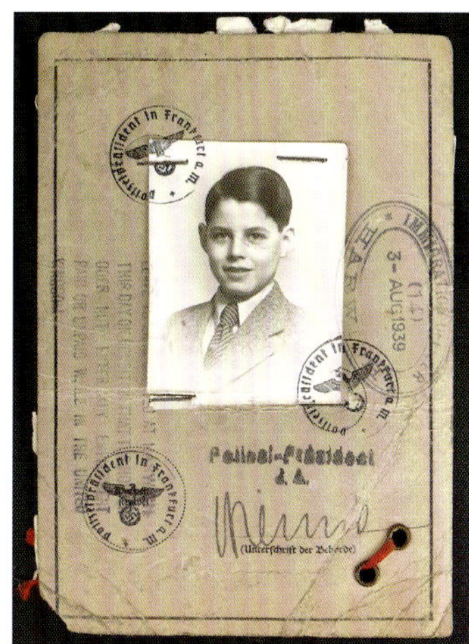

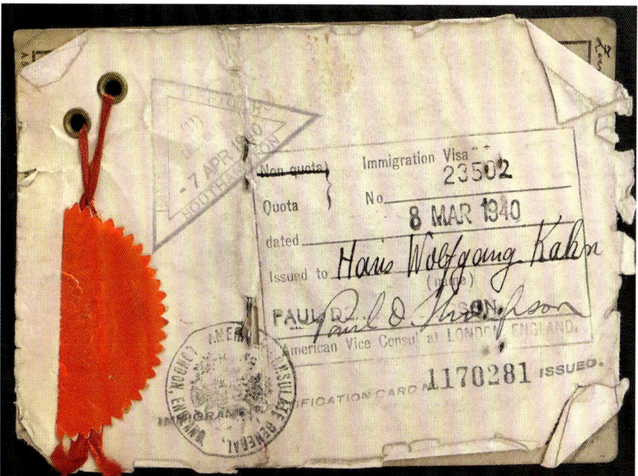

Wolf Kahn's refugee transport documents, 1939 and 1940

Kahn, though separated from his father, brothers, and sister, enjoys childhood with a doting grandmother, her maid, and an English governess. He also spends time with his equally devoted maternal grandparents, Siegfried and Ella Budge. He is raised in privilege, surrounded by antiques and the family's art collection. Kahn's early interest in art is encouraged, and he enjoys using his art to make people laugh, drawing caricatures, as well as military and athletic subjects.

1937

Kahn's father, having lost his appointment to the Stuttgart Philharmonic in 1933 when Hitler came to power, takes Kahn's stepmother, two brothers, and sister to live in the United States. Because finances are uncertain, Wolf Kahn remains in Germany with his grandmother. He attends Philanthropin, the gymnasium (secondary school) of the Frankfurt Jewish community, for two years. When he is ten years old, Kahn begins private art lessons with Fräulein von Joeden.

1939

Two months before the outbreak of World War II, Kahn, age eleven, is sent to Cambridge, England, on a children's refugee transport. He stays with two host families over the next year and attends Cambridge and County High School for Boys.

Kahn's three grandparents are sent to the Theresienstadt concentration camp, and he never sees them again. There are no records of how or when they died. The only objects from either household to survive are Kahn's drawings, which are gathered by his grandmother's maid and sent to Kahn's father after the war ends.

1940

Kahn joins his family in Upper Montclair, New Jersey, where his father teaches at Montclair State Teachers College. After leaving Europe, Emil and Ellen Kahn divorce, and Kahn's seventeen-year-old sister runs the household, cooking for five and acting as a surrogate mother to her younger brother. Kahn attends the Experimental Laboratory School of Montclair State Teachers College and other New Jersey schools.

1943

Kahn and his family move to New York City and live on Riverside Drive at 102nd Street. He attends the High School of Music and Art, graduating with the class of 1945. Among Kahn's classmates are Allan Kaprow and Rachel Rosenthal, both of whom later become avant-garde artists. Kahn spends long hours sketching animals at the Central Park Zoo and the Museum of Natural History.

1945

Kahn enlists in the United States Navy and attends radio school. He is stationed in Chicago, in Del Monte, California, and at the Anacostia Naval Research Laboratory in Washington, D.C.

1946

Kahn is discharged from the Navy and takes classes at the New School for Social Research in New York City, studying with the painter Stuart Davis and the printmaker Hans Jelinek.

1947

At age nineteen, Kahn enters the Hans Hofmann School of Fine Arts, located at 52 West Eighth Street in New York and in Provincetown, Massachusetts. Among fellow students are Jane Freilicher, Paul Georges, Robert Goodnough, Allan Kaprow, Jan Müller, Larry Rivers, Leatrice Rose, and Richard Stankiewicz. With the aid of the G.I.

Bill, Kahn remains with Hofmann for eighteen months as Hofmann's studio assistant and the school monitor. He is included in *New Provincetown '47* at the Jacques Seligmann Gallery in New York, an exhibition of work by students in Hofmann's summer classes, curated by critic Clement Greenberg.

1948

Kahn attends lectures on modern art by Meyer Schapiro at Columbia University and the New School for Social Research. During this time, he develops a lasting friendship with painter Larry Rivers.

1949

Kahn enrolls at the University of Chicago on the last of his G.I. Bill benefits and receives a bachelor of arts degree. He takes classes with the American philosopher Kenneth Burke.

1950

Kahn travels across the country, working odd jobs, including harvesting peas at a Shoshone Indian reservation on the border of Oregon and Idaho and toiling at a logging camp in Deadwood, Oregon. He is offered a scholarship to continue studying humanities at the University of Chicago, but he turns it down.

1951

Kahn returns to New York and teaches arts and crafts to children and teenagers in city settlement houses for two years. He takes a loft at 813 Broadway, near the corner of Twelfth Street, which he keeps until 1995. With Miles Forst, John Grillo, Lester Johnson, Jan Müller, and Felix Pasilis (most of whom are former Hofmann students), Kahn organizes the *813 Broadway Exhibition*. Out of this exhibition comes the artists' cooperative Hansa Gallery, located at 70 East Twelfth Street. Meyer Schapiro buys a drawing from Kahn, which leads to a lifelong friendship.

1952

Kahn travels to Baton Rouge, Louisiana, where his brother Peter is teaching art at Louisiana State University. Remaining there for six months, he paints rodeo encampments and levees. He exhibits paintings in the Hansa Gallery group exhibition.

1953

At age twenty-six, Kahn has his first one-man exhibition of expressionist landscapes, still lifes, and portraits at the Hansa Gallery. It is reviewed in *Art News* by painter and critic Fairfield Porter, who writes, "The excellence of this first exhibition . . . comes as no surprise." The critic Dore Ashton writes an article on Kahn's life and work for *Pen and Brush*. Kahn spends the summer painting in Provincetown, living alone in a shack on Race Point. He is included in the *Second Annual Exhibition of Painting and Sculpture* at the Stable Gallery in New York.

1954

Kahn develops a close and lasting friendship with the painter Elaine de Kooning. The poet and critic Frank O'Hara includes Kahn in his essay "Nature and New Painting."

1955

Kahn's second one-man exhibition at the Hansa Gallery, which has moved to 210 Central Park South, is well received by the critics. He meets the painter Willem de Kooning, who, having seen Kahn's exhibition, gives him encouragement. They maintain a friendship. Kahn lives and paints for six months in Tepoztlán, Mexico. His work from this period is shown at Galería Antonio Souza in Mexico City the following year. He develops a lasting friendship with Fairfield Porter. His drawings are used to illustrate Peter Viereck's poem "Some Refrains at the Charles River" in *Art News Annual*.

1956

Kahn has his first one-man exhibition at Grace Borgenicht Gallery in New York; he exhibits regularly at Grace Borgenicht until the gallery closes in 1995. The critic Thomas B. Hess includes Kahn in "U.S. Painting: Some Recent Directions" in *Art News Annual*. Kahn's work is selected for the *Fifth Annual Exhibition of Painting and Sculpture* at the Stable Gallery. Meyer Schapiro notes Kahn's work in his essay "The Younger American Painters of Today" in *The Listener*.

At a meeting of the Artists' Club, Kahn meets Emily Mason, a beautiful young painter who is the daughter of the artist Alice Trumbull Mason. They spend the summer in Provincetown, absorbed in their work and each other. Kahn recalls this summer as one of the happiest of his life. His paintings change, and he begins what he calls "my love affair with Bonnard," influenced by Pierre Bonnard's taste for vibrant color and luminosity. Kahn is also greatly impressed by the dignity and self-assurance of another artist he meets that summer, Milton Avery.

1957

Kahn travels to Venice to join Emily Mason, who is there on a Fulbright scholarship. They marry in Venice and remain in Italy for two years. A joint exhibition of their work is shown at the Galleria d'Arte San Giorgio in Venice. Kahn is included in *The New York School: Second Generation* at the Jewish Museum in New York as well as the *Annual Exhibition* at the Whitney Museum of American Art. The Museum of Modern Art acquires his work for its permanent collection.

1958

Kahn and Mason live and paint in Spoleto, Italy. There, Kahn meets the painters Louis Finkelstein and Gretna Campbell, with whom he maintains lifelong friendships. Kahn's work is included in group exhibitions in Spoleto and Rome.

Kahn and Mason return to New York at the end of the year, and a one-man exhibition of his Italian paintings is shown at Grace Borgenicht Gallery. He is included again in the *Annual Exhibition* at the Whitney Museum of American Art, which acquires his Italian painting *Large Olive Grove* for its permanent collection.

1959

Kahn spends the summer on Martha's Vineyard, Massachusetts, and starts a new series of sailboat paintings. He exhibits in the *145th Annual Exhibition* at the Pennsylvania Academy of the Fine Arts in Philadelphia and has a one-man exhibition of his work at Union College in Schenectady, New York. In September, Kahn and Mason's first child, Cecily, is born.

1960

While a visiting professor at the University of California, Berkeley, Kahn develops friendships with painters Elmer Bischoff, Richard Diebenkorn, Nathan Oliveira, and Wayne Thiebaud, and the art historian James Ackerman. He has a one-man exhibition at the university. His work is included in *Young America 1960: Thirty American Painters Under Thirty-Six* at the Whitney Museum of American Art. Kahn declines an offer of a full-time position at the university and returns to New York.

1961

Kahn joins the faculty of Cooper Union in New York as an adjunct professor of art, a part-time position he holds until 1977. He spends the summer in Stonington, Maine, and is included in the *Annual Exhibition* at the Whitney Museum of American Art.

1962

He teaches at the Haystack Mountain School of Crafts in Deer Isle, Maine, where he remains for the summer. During that time he visits Fairfield Porter on Great Spruce Head Island, Maine. He is included in *Forty Artists Under Forty* at the Whitney Museum of American Art. He receives a Fulbright scholarship to Italy. There, he takes a studio and apartment in Milan for the winter and summers in Viterbo, near Rome. He meets and becomes friends with the conceptual artist Lucio Pozzi. He meets the painter Pat Adams, with whom he maintains a lifelong friendship.

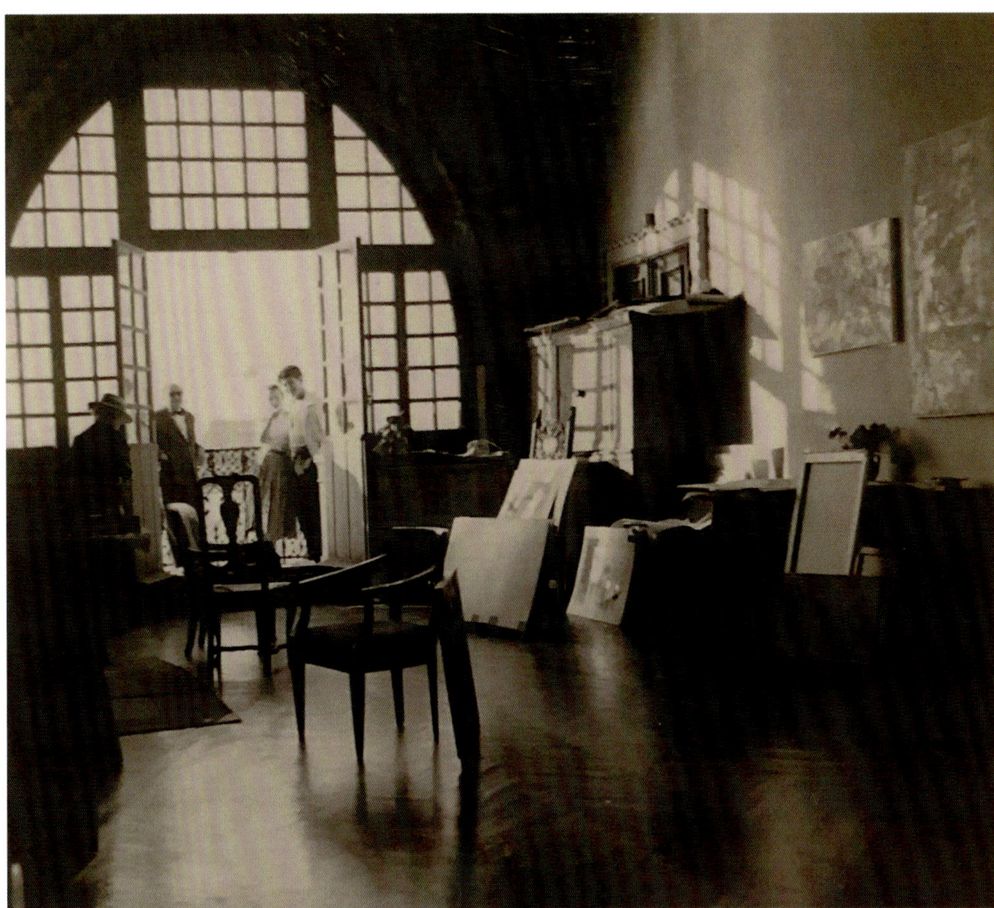

Wolf Kahn and Emily Mason in their Venice studio, 1957

1963

A one-man exhibition is staged at the Kansas City Art Institute.

1964

Kahn moves to Rome, where he has a studio in the Prati neighborhood, not far from the Piazza del Popolo. While Kahn and Mason are in Rome, their daughter Melany is born.

1965

Kahn's family returns to New York in early spring to find the city loft laws have changed and they can no longer live at their 813 Broadway Studio. After some scrambling, the family is offered a walk-up on Fifteenth Street. Kahn and his family spend time on Martha's Vineyard.

1966

Kahn is awarded a Guggenheim Fellowship. He is commissioned to do portraits for the Jewish Theological Seminary in New York in 1966, 1967, and 1968.

1967

Kahn summers in Deer Isle, Maine.

1968

Guided by a friend, the painter Frank Stout, Kahn buys a farm in West Brattleboro, Vermont, where he summers from that point on. Kahn exhibits at the National Academy Museum in New York.

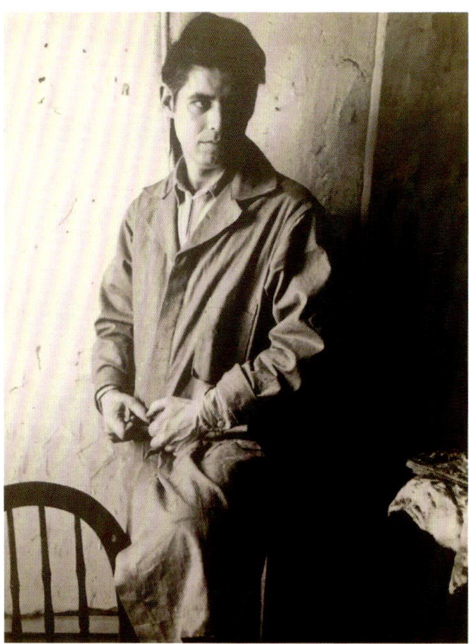

Wolf Kahn in his studio, circa 1960

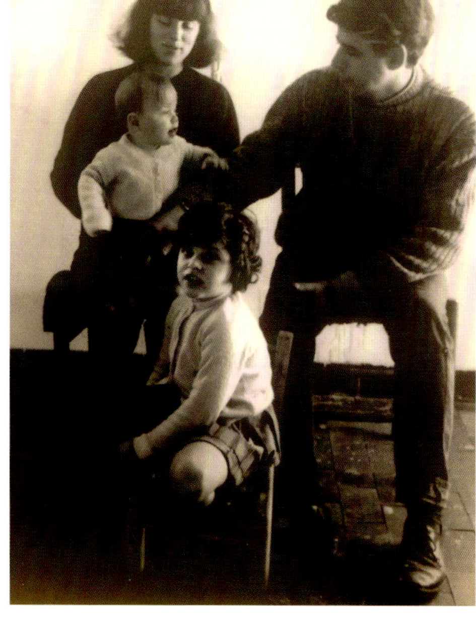

Wolf Kahn and Emily Mason with their daughters, Cecily and Melany, 1965

1970

Kahn executes a commission to paint Litchfield Plantation in Pawleys Island, South Carolina.

1972

Kahn has one-man exhibitions at the University of Nebraska and the Chrysler Museum of Art in Norfolk, Virginia.

1973

Kahn travels with his family to Kenya, and then to Italy. He returns to Vermont to spend the rest of the summer painting the landscape. Kahn delivers a lecture, "On the Hofmann School," at the College Art Association convention in New York and gives a talk titled "On Being an Art Student" at the New York Studio School of Drawing, Painting and Sculpture.

1974

Kahn spends part of the summer painting in Corrèze, France.

1975

As guest lecturer, Kahn speaks on the life and work of the painter Jan Müller, a fellow Hofmann student, at the Alliance of Figurative Artists, a weekly artist-run forum to discuss topics and issues related to the figure in contemporary painting and sculpture.

1977

Kahn is included in *Artists' Postcards* at the Drawing Center in New York.

1979

Kahn accepts the position of chairman of the College Art Association committee to award the organization's Distinguished Teaching of Art Award, which is presented to his friend Louis Finkelstein. Kahn receives the Arts and Letters Award from the American Academy of Arts and Letters in New York. He is included in both *Hans Hofmann as Teacher: His Students' Drawings* and an exhibition of recent acquisitions at the Metropolitan Museum of Art in New York.

1980

Kahn is elected a member of the National Academy of Design and a member of the board of the College Art Association. He exhibits regularly at the National Academy annuals.

1981

Wolf Kahn: Ten Years of Landscape Painting opens at the Arts Club of Chicago.

1982

Kahn's essay "Hans Hofmann's Good Example" is published in the spring issue of *Art Journal.*

1983

Kahn is invited to lecture on Hans Hofmann at the New York Studio School of Drawing, Painting and Sculpture. His essay "Milton Avery's Good Example" is published in the spring issue of *Art Journal. Wolf Kahn: Landscapes* opens at the San Diego Museum of Art and travels to four museums nationwide.

1984

Kahn is elected to the American Academy and Institute of Arts and Letters. He delivers a lecture at the School of the Art Institute of Chicago entitled "You Don't Have to Be Ignorant to Dislike New York Painting." He is selected for the advisory committee of the Vermont Studio School (now the Vermont Studio Center). He is also an artist-in-residence for one term at Dartmouth College in Hanover, New Hampshire.

1985

Kahn is commissioned by AT&T to create five large paintings entitled *The Four Seasons* for its employees' lounge.

1986

Kahn's daughter Cecily, a painter, marries David Kapp, an urban landscape painter, in May.

1987

Kahn is the commencement speaker for the graduating class of the Maine College of Art.

1988

Kahn's first grandchild, Millie Kapp, is born in March. He delivers a lecture

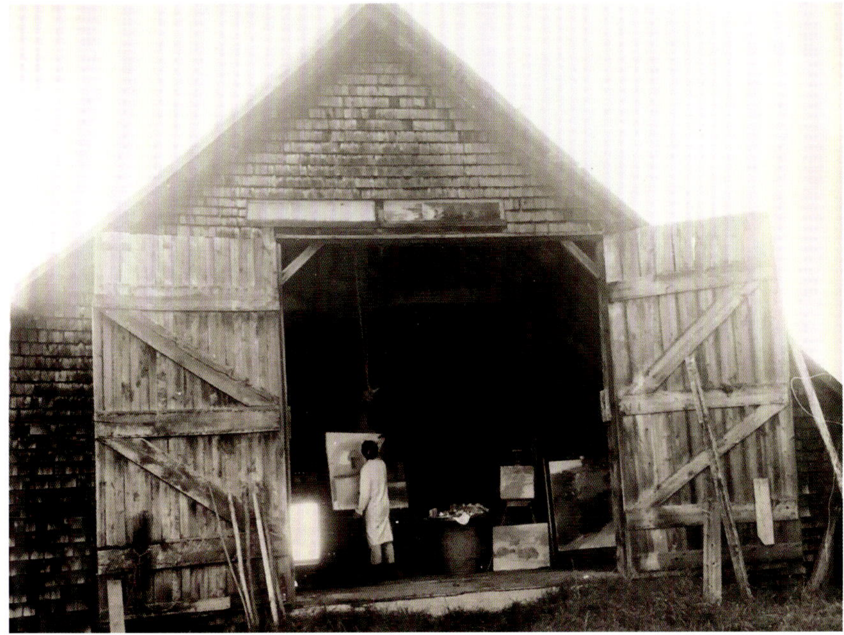

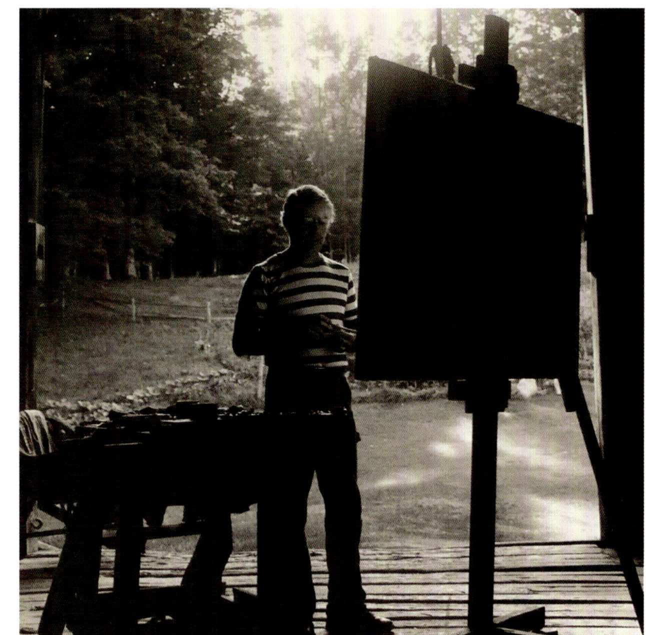

Wolf Kahn at his Vermont studio, 1975 and 1982

at the Arthur M. Sackler Museum, Harvard University, entitled "Traditional Concerns in an Untraditional Era."

1989

Kahn gives the commencement speech at the Pennsylvania Academy of the Fine Arts. He becomes a trustee of the Vermont Studio Center and travels to Venice.

1990

His second grandchild, Arthur Kapp, is born in February. *Art in America* publishes Kahn's essay "Hofmann's Mixed Messages." *Wolf Kahn: Landscapes as Radiance* opens at NSU Art Museum in Fort Lauderdale, Florida.

1991

Kahn is awarded the Benjamin Altman Landscape Prize by the National Academy of Design.

1992

Kahn travels to Zihuatanejo, Mexico, to make pastels of sunsets over the Pacific Ocean. Kahn's article addressing formal aesthetic values shared with young conceptual sculptors, entitled "Connecting Incongruities," is published in *Art in America.* The *Wolf Kahn: Exploring Monotypes* traveling exhibition opens and circulates for three years. He designs a first day of issue postage stamp for the United Nations philatelic collection.

1993

Kahn cruises on the Nile River in Egypt. When he returns to the United States, he is artist-in-residence at Yosemite National Park in California. Once back East, he travels downriver by boat to paint the landscape along the Connecticut River, then exhibits the resulting works at the Lyman Allyn Art Museum in New London, Connecticut. He receives the 1993 American Artist Achievement Award in pastels. He is appointed to the New York City Art Commission and named vice president for art at the American Academy and Institute of Arts and Letters.

1994

Kahn travels to Hawaii. He is commissioned by the Atlantic Golf Club in Bridgehampton, New York, to paint a large picture for the clubhouse.

1995

Kahn moves his New York studio from 813 Broadway to the third floor of 217 West Twenty-First Street.

1996

A traveling exhibition, *Wolf Kahn: A Dialogue between Traditional and Abstract Art*, opens at the Boca Raton Museum of Art in Florida. He delivers the eulogy for Meyer Schapiro at the American Academy of Arts and Letters. He also completes a color etching commissioned by the American Academy for its 100th anniversary celebration. The monograph *Wolf Kahn*, by Justin Spring, is published by Harry N. Abrams.

1997

As one of the founding members of the Hansa Gallery, Kahn is included in the commemorative exhibition at Zabriskie Gallery entitled *The Hansa Gallery (1952–1959) Revisited*. He is also included in *A Tribute to Grace Borgenicht Gallery,* recognizing his dealer of forty-one years, which is organized by DC Moore Gallery in New York. Kahn gives a donation to the Vermont Studio Center, and the Wolf Kahn Studio Building is named after him. *All in a Family* at the New Britain Museum of American Art in New Britain, Connecticut, includes the paintings of Kahn; his wife, Emily Mason; his mother-in-law, Alice Trumbull Mason;

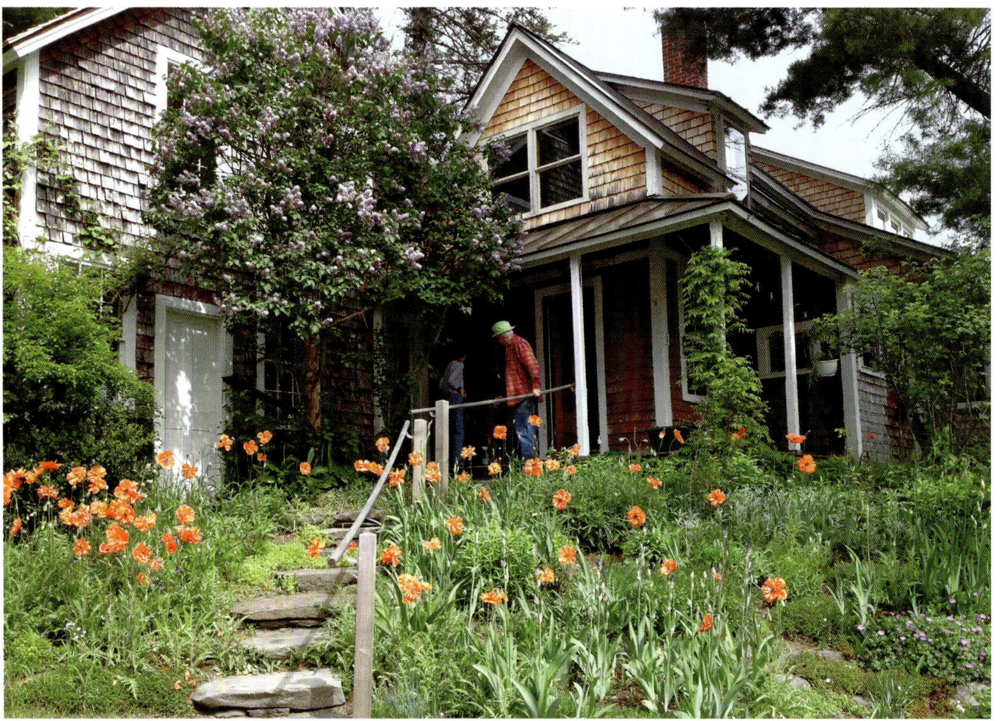

Wolf Kahn and Emily Mason outside their Vermont farmhouse, 2013

his daughter Cecily Kahn; his son-in-law David Kapp; and his brother Peter Kahn.

1998

The Vermont Arts Council presents Wolf Kahn with the Walter Cerf Medal for Outstanding Achievement in the Arts. The Morris Museum of Art in Augusta, Georgia, commissions Kahn to paint in the South. *Wolf Kahn: Southern Landscapes* opens at the Morris Museum of Art, where Kahn also delivers a lecture entitled "Seven Good Reasons Not to Paint the Landscape." As a guest lecturer at the New York Studio School of Drawing, Painting and Sculpture, Kahn speaks on "Intention, Control, and Spontaneity in the Making of Painting." He gives a plenary lecture on "Artists' Inspiration" at the annual meeting of the American Psychiatric Association in Toronto. He directs a workshop at the Palazzo Corsini in Florence, Italy.

1999

In June, he is an invited artist-in-residence at the Vermont Studio Center, which he has visited for the past fifteen consecutive years. In September, he gives a workshop in Damme, Belgium, which he will describe in an article published in *Travel + Leisure* magazine in 2009. He lectures on landscape-painting problems at the Museum of Fine Arts, Boston, and speaks on a panel entitled "Jackson Pollock" at the National Academy Museum.

2000

Kahn receives an honorary doctor of fine arts degree from Wheaton College in Norton, Massachusetts. In July, he travels with his daughter Melany to the African country of Namibia, where he is drawn to the dry, brushy landscape. He spends three weeks touring the country doing pastel studies that become a major influence on his painting style. *Wolf Kahn: 50 Years of Pastels* is organized by the Jerald Melberg Gallery in Charlotte, North Carolina, and then travels to the Virginia Museum of Contemporary Art in Virginia Beach; the Hickory Museum of Art in Hickory, North Carolina; and the Butler Institute of American Art in Youngstown, Ohio. *Wolf Kahn: Pastels* is published by Harry N. Abrams.

2001

Kahn is the honoree at a National Academy benefit. His daughter Melany marries Bo Foard in September, and they settle in New Hampshire with Bo's two children, Emily and Cooper. Kahn travels to New Orleans to begin work for a show featuring his depictions of the trees of New Orleans at the Ogden Museum of Southern Art. He has numerous solo shows, including a major exhibition of his work in Hamburg, Germany. The German show takes place at Galerie Brockstedt and the Museum für Kunst und Gewerbe, which has a reproduction of the music room from Kahn's great-aunt's mansion in its courtyard. This is Kahn's first time back in Germany since the war. It becomes a personal homecoming for him, generating much publicity.

2002

A new grandson, Mason Foard, is born three days before Kahn's seventy-fifth birthday. The Ogunquit Museum of American Art in Ogunquit, Maine, hosts an exhibition of Kahn's work. He is awarded an honorary doctor of fine arts degree from Union College in Schenectady, New York. Wheaton College in Norton, Massachusetts, hosts the exhibition *A Shared Passion for Color: Artists Wolf Kahn and Emily Mason*, as well as his lecture "Six Reasons Not to Paint a Landscape."

2003

Wolf Kahn's America: An Artist's Travels is published by Harry N. Abrams. The publication is the topic when Kahn is a participating artist in the *Artists Talk on Art* panel series in New York City. Kahn has his first show with Ameringer | McEnery | Yohe in New York (now Miles McEnery Gallery).

2004

The National Academy invites Kahn to curate a major exhibition entitled *The Artist's Eye: Wolf Kahn as Curator*. A special exhibition of his own work,

Wolf Kahn: Nature and Color, is presented in an adjacent gallery. Kahn appears on New Hampshire Public Radio's *The Front Porch* and Vermont PBS Television's *Profile.*

2005

A new granddaughter, Ally Foard, is born in October. Kahn travels to Niagara Falls, New York. There he creates many paintings and pastels, some of which are done from the vantage points of earlier American painters, including Frederic Edwin Church and George Inness. The filmmaker Alan Dater creates a short film of Kahn's time at Niagara Falls. Kahn delivers a lecture at the Hirshhorn Museum and Sculpture Garden in Washington, D.C., "Art and Immorality."

2006

The National Academy of Design presents Kahn with its Lifetime Achievement Award. Wolf Kahn Day is declared in Vermont by Governor Jim Douglas and the Brattleboro selectmen and is celebrated with a large party around his exhibition at the Brattleboro Museum and Art Center. Kahn gives a lecture at the Brattleboro Museum entitled "The Uses and Misuses of Painting," and gives a lecture entitled "Growing Up Privileged, and Jewish, in Nazi Germany" at the Cohen Center for Holocaust Studies at Keene State College in Keene, New Hampshire. He travels to New Orleans to do post–Hurricane Katrina pastel drawings of the same trees he drew in 2001. These new pastels are exhibited alongside the earlier drawings at the Ogden Museum of Southern Art. The Niagara Falls work and Dater's 2005 film are exhibited together at the Castellani Art Museum of Niagara University in Niagara Falls, New York. The Provincetown Art Association and Museum exhibits Kahn's early works, many of which were created during his years studying in Provincetown under Hans Hofmann. The Gibbes Museum of Art in Charleston, South Carolina, hosts the exhibition *Wolf Kahn's Barns.* Kahn appears on WICN Public Radio's *Inquiry.*

2007

Kahn celebrates his fiftieth wedding anniversary with Emily Mason in March and his eightieth birthday in October. *Art in America* publishes the journal of his 2006 visit to New Orleans.

2008

Kahn delivers a lecture at the Smithsonian Institution in Washington, D.C., "Subject Matters." A visit to Wyoming and Montana includes time in Yellowstone National Park.

2009

Kahn gives a lecture at the Brattleboro Museum and Art Center, "Are Artists Special?" He travels to Turkey and the Netherlands, and he does a series of barns based on the ones he sees in the Netherlands.

2010

Kahn delivers a lecture at the Brattleboro Museum and Art Center, "Can Art Be Taught?" He again travels to Turkey. *Wolf Kahn: Pastels* opens at the Morris Museum of Art in Augusta, Georgia.

2011

The main gallery of the Brattleboro Museum and Art Center is named the Wolf Kahn and Emily Mason Gallery in honor of their commitment to the institution over its forty-year existence. Additionally, the museum hosts an exhibition of Kahn's pastels. An expanded second edition of *Wolf Kahn* by Justin Spring is published by Harry N. Abrams, fifteen years after the original publication. It includes a new essay by Karen Wilkin.

2012

Kahn gives a lecture entitled "Planning and Spontaneity" at both the Vermont Studio Center and the Brattleboro Museum and Art Center. He celebrates his eighty-fifth birthday in Vermont among many friends. An interview from

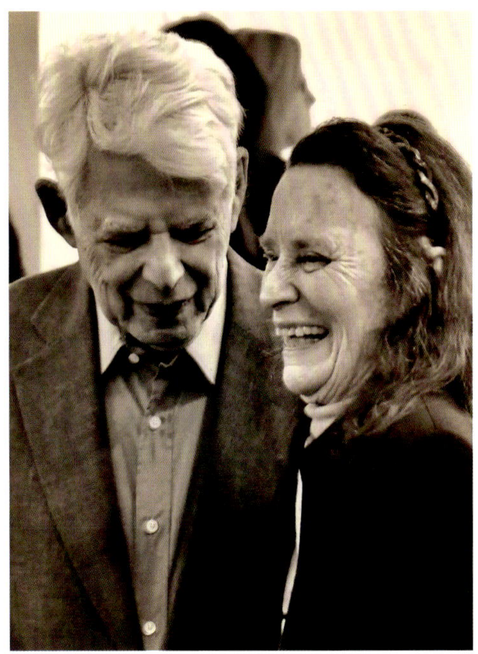

Wolf Kahn and Emily Mason at Kahn's 2015 NYC opening at Ameringer | McEnery | Yohe

Story Preservation Initiative is included in *Inspired Lives,* airs on New Hampshire Public Radio, and is posted online. Kahn is presented with an Alumni Professional Achievement Award by the University of Chicago.

2014

Kahn presents a lecture at the Brattleboro Museum and Art Center, "Control and Letting Go." A survey exhibition, *Six Decades,* is held at Ameringer | McEnery | Yohe (now Miles McEnery Gallery).

2017

Kahn receives the U.S. Department of State's International Medal of Arts. He celebrates his ninetieth birthday in Vermont.

2019

Kahn and his wife of sixty-two years, the artist Emily Mason, are each awarded the honorary degree of doctor of arts from Marlboro College in Vermont. Emily Mason dies on December 10th.

2020

Kahn dies on March 15th at the age of ninety-two.

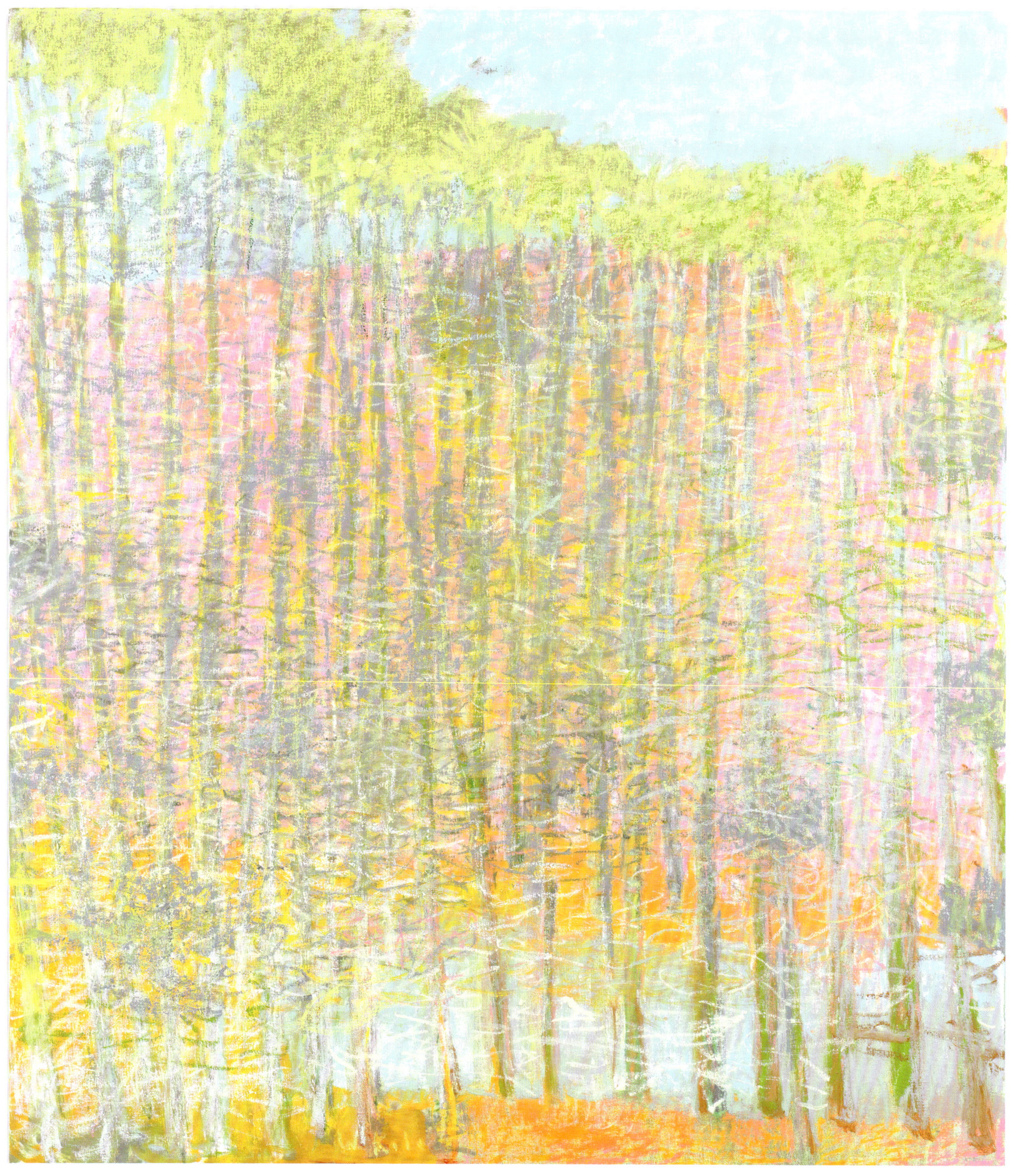

SELECTED PUBLIC COLLECTIONS

Ackland Art Museum, University of North Carolina, Chapel Hill, NC

Albrecht-Kemper Museum of Art, St. Joseph, MO

Albright-Knox Art Gallery, Buffalo, NY

American Academy of Arts and Letters, New York, NY

Archives of American Art, Smithsonian Institution, Washington, DC

Arkansas Art Center, Little Rock, AR

Art Institute of Chicago, Chicago IL

Asheville Art Museum, Asheville, NC

Baltimore Museum of Art, Baltimore, MD

Barry Art Museum, Norfolk, VA

Berkeley Art Museum & Pacific Film Archive, University of California, Berkeley, CA

Blanton Museum of Art, The University of Texas at Austin, Austin, TX

Boca Raton Museum of Art, Boca Raton, FL

Brooklyn Museum, Brooklyn, NY

The Butler Institute of American Art, Youngstown, OH

Canton Museum of Art, Canton, OH

Carnegie Mellon University, Pittsburgh, PA

Castellani Art Museum, Niagara University, NY

OPPOSITE
Dispersed and Concentrated
2014
oil on canvas
72 x 64 inches

Cheekwood Botanical Garden and Museum of Art, Nashville, TN

Chrysler Museum of Art, Norfolk, VA

Colby College Museum of Art, Waterville, ME

Cornell Fine Arts Museum, Winter Park, FL

Dallas Museum of Art, Dallas, TX

Daum Museum of Contemporary Art, Sedalia, MO

David Winton Bell Gallery, Brown University, Providence, RI

Davis Museum, Wellesley, MA

Dayton Art Institute, Dayton, OH

De Young Museum, San Francisco, CA

Dubuque Museum of Art, Dubuque, IA

Eli and Edythe Brode Art Museum, Michigan State University, East Lansing, MI

El Paso Museum of Art, El Paso, TX

Farnsworth Art Museum, Rockland, ME

Figge Art Museum, Davenport, IA

Fitchburg Art Museum, Fitchburg, MA

Fleming Museum of Art, University of Vermont, Burlington, VT

Fogg Museum, Harvard University, Cambridge, MA

Fort Worth Community Arts Center, Fort Worth, TX

Frances Lehman Loeb Art Center, Vassar College, Poughkeepsie, NY

Fred Jones Jr. Museum of Art, The University of Oklahoma, Norman, OK

George Segal Gallery, Montclair State University, Montclair, NJ

Gibbes Museum of Art, Charleston, SC

Heckscher Museum of Art, Huntington, NY

Hickory Museum of Art, Hickory, NC

Hirshhorn Museum and Sculpture Garden, Smithsonian Institution, Washington, DC

Hofstra University Museum, Hempstead, NY

Hood Museum of Art, Dartmouth College, Hanover, NH

Indianapolis Museum of Art, Indianapolis, IN

Iris & B. Gerald Cantor Center for Visual Arts at Stanford University, Stanford, CA

John and Mable Ringling Museum of Art, Sarasota, FL

Kemper Museum of Contemporary Art, Kansas City, MO

Krannert Art Museum and Kinkead Pavilion, University of Illinois at Urbana-Champaign, Champaign, IL

Lauren Rogers Museum of Art, Laurel, MS

List Visual Arts Center, Massachusetts Institute of Technology, Cambridge, MA

Los Angeles County Museum of Art, Los Angeles, CA

Marianne Kistler Beach Museum of Art, Kansas State University, Manhattan, KS

Massachusetts College of Art and Design, Boston, MA

Mead Art Museum, Amherst College, Amherst, MA

Memorial Art Gallery, University of Rochester, Rochester, NY

The Metropolitan Museum of Art, New York, NY

Michele and Donald D'Amour Museum of Fine Arts, Springfield, MA

Middlebury College Museum of Art, Middlebury, VT

Mildred Lane Kemper Art Museum, Washington University in St. Louis, St. Louis, MO

Milwaukee Art Museum, Milwaukee, WI

Minnesota Museum of American Art, St. Paul, MN

The Mint Museum, Charlotte, NC

Montgomery Museum of Fine Arts, Montgomery, AL

The Morgan Library & Museum, New York, NY

Morris Museum of Art, Augusta, GA

Mount Holyoke College Art Museum, South Hadley, MA

Museum of Fine Arts, Boston, MA

The Museum of Fine Arts, Houston, TX

The Museum of Modern Art, New York, NY

National Academy of Design, New York, NY

National Gallery of Art, Washington, DC

National Portrait Gallery, Smithsonian Institution, Washington, DC

The Nelson-Atkins Museum of Art, Kansas City, MO

Neuberger Museum of Art, Purchase College, State University of New York, Purchase, NY

Nevada Museum of Art, Reno, NV

New Orleans Museum of Art, New Orleans, LA

Newark Museum, Newark, NJ

North Dakota Museum of Art, Grand Forks, ND

Ogden Museum of Southern Art, New Orleans, LA

Ogunquit Museum of American Art, Ogunquit, ME

Palmer Museum of Art, Pennsylvania State University, University Park, PA

Parrish Art Museum, Water Mill, NY

Pennsylvania Academy of the Fine Arts, Philadelphia, PA

Philadelphia Museum of Art, Philadelphia, PA

Portland Museum of Art, Portland, ME

Princeton University Art Museum, Princeton, NJ

Provincetown Art Association and Museum, Provincetown, MA

Rahr-West Art Museum, Manitowoc, WI

The Raymond Jonson Collection, University of New Mexico Art Museum, Albuquerque, NM

Rhode Island School of Design Museum, Providence, RI

The Rose Art Museum, Brandeis University, Waltham, MA

Ruth and Elmer Wellin Museum of Art, Hamilton College, Clinton, NY

Saint Louis Art Museum, St. Louis, MO

The San Diego Museum of Art, San Diego, CA

Smith College Museum of Art, Northampton, MA

Smithsonian American Art Museum, Washington, DC

Southern Alleghenies Museum of Art at Loretto, Saint Francis University, Loretto, PA

Spencer Museum of Art, University of Kansas, Lawrence, KS

Syracuse University Art Galleries, Syracuse, NY

Tufts University Art Gallery, Medford, MA

Tulsa Performing Arts Center, Tulsa, OK

United States Embassy, Quito, Ecuador

University Art Museum, State University of New York, Albany, NY

University of Colorado Art Museum, Boulder, CO

University of South Florida Contemporary Art Museum, Tampa, FL

Utah Museum of Fine Arts, The University of Utah, Salt Lake City, UT

Vero Beach Museum of Art, Vero Beach, FL

Whitney Museum of American Art, New York, NY

Williams College Museum of Art, Williamstown, MA

Worcester Art Museum, Worcester, MA

Yale University Art Gallery, New Haven, CT

Yosemite Museum, Yosemite Valley, CA

AWARDS AND APPOINTMENTS

Marlboro College, Honorary Degree of Doctor of Arts, 2019

U.S. Department of State, International Medal of Arts, 2017

University of Chicago, Alumni Professional Achievement Award, 2012

National Academy of Design, Lifetime Achievement Award, 2006

Union College, Honorary Degree of Doctor of Fine Arts, 2004

Wheaton College, Honorary Degree of Doctor of Fine Arts, 2000

Vermont Arts Council Walter Cerf Medal for Outstanding Achievement in the Arts, 1998

New York City Art Commission, member, 1993–95

American Artist Achievement Award, 1993

National Board of College Art Association, elected to membership, 1980–85

American Academy and Institute of Arts and Letters, elected to membership, 1984; Vice President for Art, 1993–96; Art Award, 1979; Hassam Fund Purchase Award, 1979

National Academy of Design, elected to membership, 1980; board, 1982; treasurer, 1990–94; honoree, 2001 benefit; Lifetime Achievement Award, 2006

John Simon Guggenheim Fellowship, 1966–67

Fulbright Scholarship, 1962

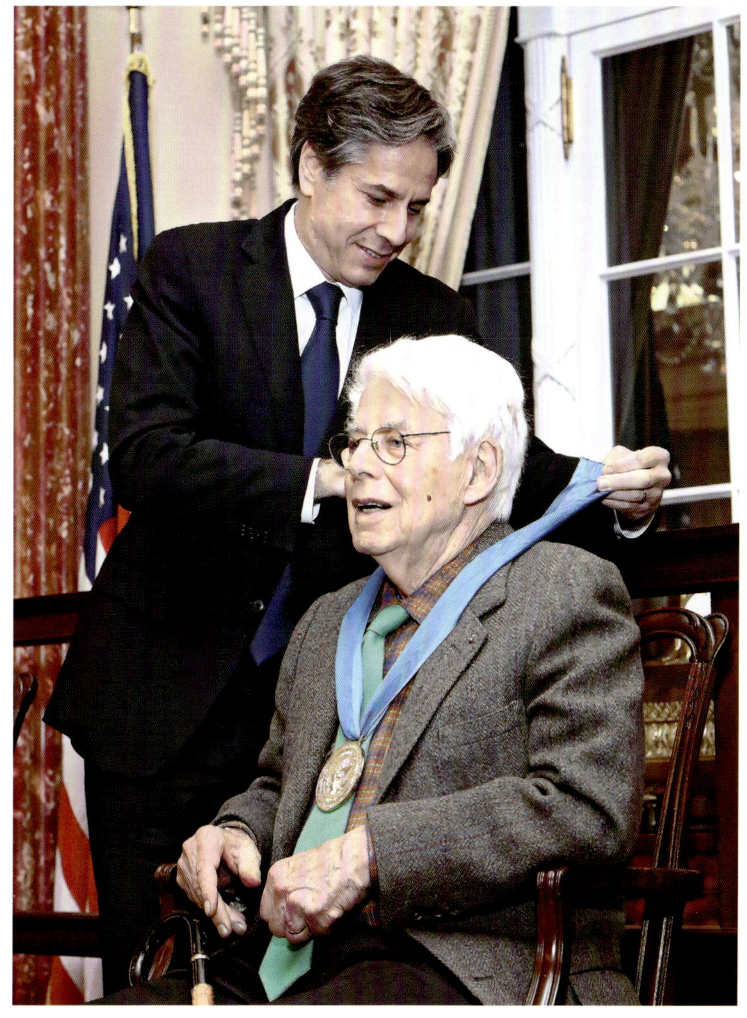

Wolf Kahn receives the U.S. Department of State's International Medal of Arts

INDEX

NOTE: Page numbers in *italic* type indicate illustrations. In addition to the General Index are the following indexes for works by Kahn: Essays and Lectures, Oil on Canvas, and Pastel on Paper.

GENERAL INDEX

ESSAYS AND LECTURES

OIL ON CANVAS

PASTEL ON PAPER

Authors: Sasha Nicholas and
William C. Agee

Publisher: Charles Miers
Associate Publisher:
Margaret Rennolds Chace
Editor: Ellen R. Cohen
Designer: Patricia Fabricant
Production Manager: Kaija Markoe
Managing Editor: Lynn Scrabis

Printed in China

2022 2023 2024 /
10 9 8 7 6 5 4 3

ISBN: 978-0-8478-6859-9
Library of Congress Control Number:
2020936673

PHOTO CREDITS

All images © 2020 Wolf Kahn / Licensed by VAGA at Artists Rights Society (ARS), NY

Courtesy Addison/Ripley Fine Art: pages 55, 139

Courtesy Jerald Melberg Gallery: pages 11, 31, 77, 93, 117, 121, 123, 138, 172, 192

Courtesy Miles McEnery Gallery: pages 4, 13 (fig. 1), 13 (fig. 2), 14 (fig. 3), 15 (fig. 4), 18 (fig. 9), 19 (fig. 10), 22, 26, 29, 33, 35, 36–37, 39, 41, 43, 45, 46, 47, 49, 51, 53, 57, 58, 59, 61, 62, 63, 65, 66, 67, 69, 70, 71, 72, 73, 74, 75, 79, 81, 83, 85, 87, 89, 91, 94–95, 97, 99, 101, 102–103, 105, 107, 109, 110, 111, 113, 114, 115, 119, 125, 127, 129, 131, 133, 135, 136–37, 140, 141, 143, 144–45, 147, 149, 151, 153, 155, 157, 159, 161, 163, 164, 167, 169, 171, 173, 175, 177, 179, 180–81, 183, 185, 187, 189, 191, 193, 195, 197, 198–99, 200, 203, 205, 207, 209, 211, 213, 215, 217, 219, 224, 234

Photos by Christopher Burke: pages 2–3, 6, 17 (fig. 7), 226, front endpaper, back endpaper

Photos by Diana Urbaska: pages 8, 24–25, 232

Photo by Jeff Burkett: page 233

Photo @ Tate: pages 17 (fig. 8), 19 (fig. 11)

Photo by Tony Powell: pages 237

Photographer unknown: pages 229, 230 (both), 231 (both)

PAGES 2–3: Wolf Kahn's New York studio, 2015
FRONT ENDPAPERS: Wolf Kahn's New York studio, 2017
BACK ENDPAPERS: Wolf Kahn's New York studio, 2019

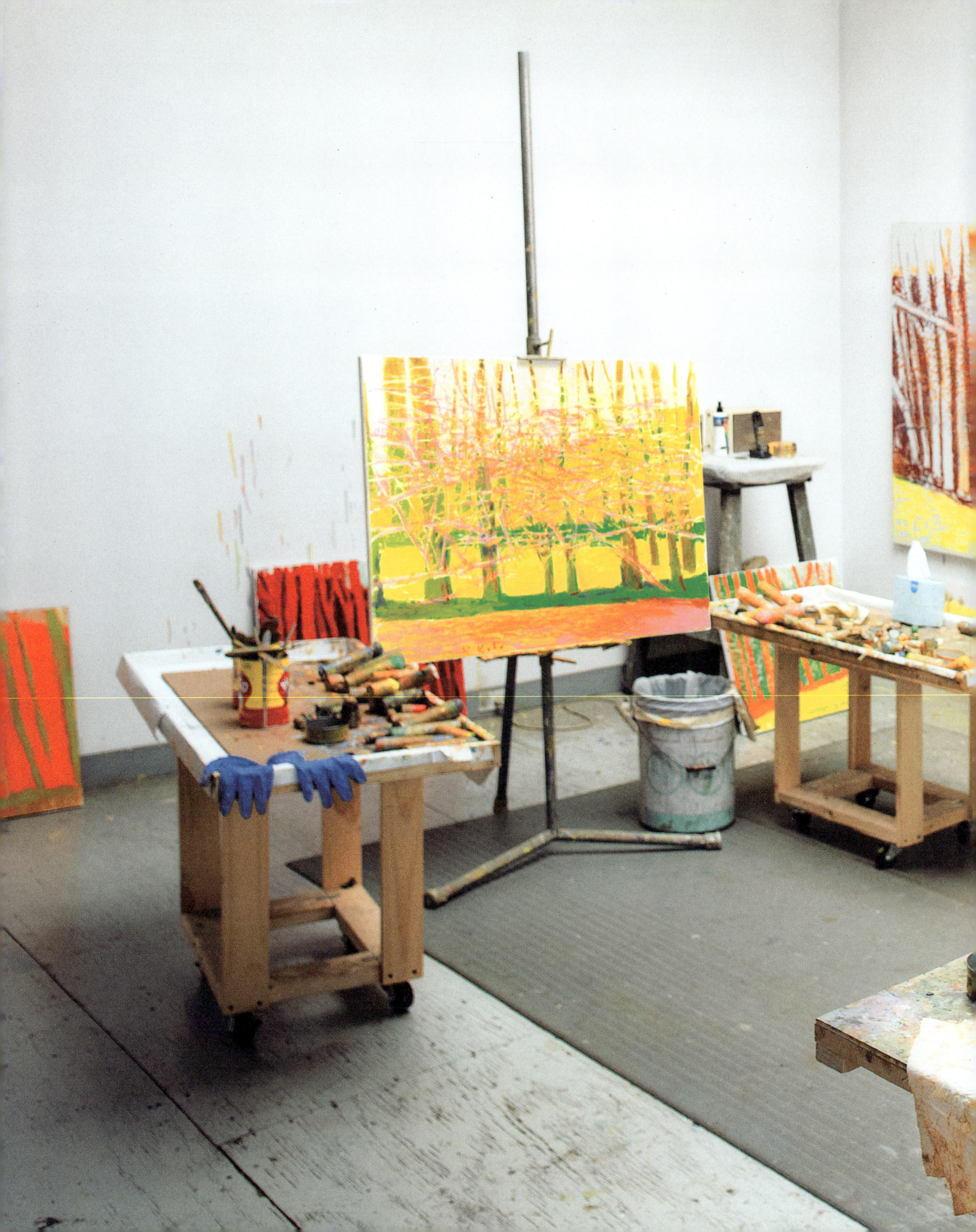